JOHN B. STEPHENSON
Appalachian Humanist

edited for publication by
William Jerome Crouch

JOHN B. STEPHENSON
—— *Appalachian Humanist* ——

An Anthology
compiled and edited by
Thomas R. Ford
with a biographical sketch by
J. Randolph Osborne

The Jesse Stuart Foundation
Ashland, Kentucky
2001

Library of Congress Cataloging-in-Publication Data

Stephenson, John B., 1937-
    John B. Stephenson, Appalachian humanist / edited by Thomas R. Ford.
        p. cm.
    Includes bibliographical references.
    ISBN 1-931672-03-2
        1. Stephenson, John B., 1937- 2. Berea College--Presidents--Biography.
    I. Ford, Thomas R., 1923- II. Title

LD392.7.S74 A3 2001
378'.0092--dc21
[B]   2001038976

Published by:
The Jesse Stuart Foundation
P.O. Box 669, Ashland, Kentucky 41105
2001

Contents

In a walk across campus in 1987, John pauses to be photographed in front of Draper Building by student Kara Beth Brunner on a labor assignment in the college's public relations office.

Acknowledgments

The individuals listed below contributed in various ways to the production of this book. Their assistance is gratefully acknowledged.

Bill Best
Harriet Ford
Janet Ford
Cara Gardner
Melissa Gardner
Charles Haywood
Loyal Jones
Wayne Kernodle
Ruth Kernodle
Marlene Pettit
Julia Stammer
David Stephenson
Jane Stephenson
Robert Stewart
Frank Winchester

*President John Stephenson officiating at one of the
College's commencement exercises.
(Photo by David Stephenson)*

PART 1
Why this Book?

Thomas R. Ford

John Stephenson and I were friends for nearly 30 years. It was a relationship that gave me considerable pleasure and a sort of avuncular pride. But being a friend of John Stephenson hardly conferred a unique status. His friends numbered in the hundreds, perhaps thousands, if students are counted, as they should be. Still, being not only a friend but also a professional colleague for such an extended period gave me a better opportunity than most to observe his transformation from an eager young scholar to a mature academic executive.

I first met John when he applied for a faculty position in the Department of Sociology at the University of Kentucky in 1965. At the time, he was completing his Ph.D. at the University of North Carolina, Chapel Hill. The following year, when he joined the faculty, I was serving as chairman of the department. By that time I had been in the academic ranks for about 15 years and had acquired enough professional and administrative experience to recognize scholarly talent when I saw it. Even then I had no doubt that John had the potential to become an outstanding scholar and teacher.

In later years John credited me with bringing him to the University of Kentucky, not because of my position as departmental chairman but because of our shared scholarly interests, particularly in Appalachia. In the early 1960s I had directed an extensive study of the region and had edited the published report based on the research findings. John had become familiar with the report while he was completing his graduate studies at the University of North Carolina, Chapel Hill, where he knew and was influenced by Rupert Vance, a distinguished sociologist and demographer at the university, who had served as one of the directors of the Appalachian survey.

John's decision to accept the position at the University of Kentucky was also influenced by the research of another member of our faculty, James S. Brown, whose doctoral thesis at Harvard University was a study of an Appalachian community, one of the earliest of its kind. John's dissertation at UNC was also a study of a mountain community, which in revised form was published in 1968 by the University of Kentucky Press. Many years later, while he was president of Berea College, John and I collaborated in editing and publishing the Brown dissertation under the title of *Beech Creek*.

Over the years John and I worked on a number of projects, including the founding of the University of Kentucky's Appalachian Center, which he directed for five years before becoming president of Berea College. Our relationship was a case of familiarity breeding increased respect. For me it produced a growing appreciation not only of his abilities but also of his application of them.

To those of us who worked closely with him, John was a remarkable person. Although his virtues far outweighed his faults, he was not a self-appointed candidate for sainthood. He was foremost a human being and, while fully cognizant of the limitations of that role, genuinely tried to make the most of it. No doubt other friends saw his essential character differently, not only because they viewed him from diverse perspectives but also because, in addition to being a complex and versatile individual to begin with, he was in a continuous state of transformation.

John was extraordinarily dedicated to understanding the society—indeed, the whole world—in which he lived, and his life was a premeditated response to that endeavor. Acquaintances familiar with his easy ability to establish warm relationships with strangers from diverse walks of life were often surprised to learn that as a child and youth John was considered something of a loner, a solitary individual who preferred his own company to that of others. Only when he entered college did he begin to lose this quality, and even then he was not a Mr. Congeniality. The reasons for his decision to attend college and to major in sociology are not self-evident. Based on his later behavior, it could be argued that his lifelong quest to understand society was for the purpose of bettering it. But in my judgment, that would be a misapprehension of his priorities. Certainly he sought to use his knowledge to correct social ills or, perhaps more accurately, to better social life, but he was not a naïve do-gooder hell-bent on implementing social reforms. Indeed, he was often critical of well-intended social actions undertaken without an adequate understanding of the problems they were meant to solve. In a sense, though, the objective of social betterment did provide John with an acceptable social rationale for his boundless exploration of society.

For John the peculiar characteristics of human behavior were reason enough to study society. He was fascinated—and often amused—by the ways people, including himself, behaved. He became a sociologist because the discipline offered rational methods for studying society. But for the guidance provided by a sociology professor, R. Wayne Kernodle, in his undergraduate studies at the College of William and Mary he might have become an anthropologist or some other type of behavioral scientist. The subject matter of anthropology, especially social anthropology, was of great interest to him, and the observational methods widely employed by that discipline were probably more compatible with his own inclinations than the quantitative techniques that have come to dominate current sociological research.

It is probably safe to say that John was not a "true believer" in any specific research technique or, for that matter, academic discipline, a view that accounted in part for his staunch support of liberal education. Perhaps the main influence on his choice of research methods was his enjoyment of people—all kinds of people. His favorite research technique was "participant observation," in which he was a member of the social group that he was studying, for that gave him an opportunity to learn not only about them but about himself as well. Given his interests and orientation, I think it more accurate to describe John as a humanist than a social scientist, although he would rightfully object to being pigeonholed in either— or any—category. Still, my judgment appears to be supported by one of his own poems, written in July of 1991, which he entitled "The Science of Humanity."

> The copious hours spent in studying
> The alleged patterns of human action and feeling
> Seem sometimes wasted
> The patterns cannot be doubted
> But the world is still filled with surprises
> Mostly unpleasant, it seems, but not always
>
> No rigid laws can comb the human experience smooth
> Cowlicks and rooster tails will not be tamed
> by mere science
> We will not be teased into perfection
>
> But control should not be our proper aim
> Wisdom and acceptance may have to suffice
> We will be what we will be, and
> Maybe even God knows not what whorls and sweeps
> Will next resist the order we impose.

As I noted earlier, John's self was not a static one. It grew as his knowledge of society grew, and as he gained in wisdom he became more of a social and educational activist. His role in bringing about change became more significant but not necessarily more pleasurable than observing change take place. It is difficult to say whether this assumption of greater social responsibility represented the emergence of some latent sense of social obligation or was simply the next rung on the professional ladder that led from college student to college president. I am inclined to think the former, at least partly because of his continuing concern for the people of Appalachia, especially for their educational needs—a concern that culminated in his appointment as president of Berea College.

I believe that John enjoyed the status, prestige, and especially the decision-making power of a high level academic administrator. In that role he could carry out, not simply recommend, social and educational policies. This is not to say that he exercised arbitrary authority or even wished to. Rather, he had moved into a position to get done those things that he thought needed doing. But with those positions of authority came obligations that were often burdensome and at times unpleasant. These included fund raising for Berea College, a task at which he proved remarkably successful even though it was far from being enjoyable. Those obligations were not unanticipated, but undoubtedly they created at times a longing to return to the simpler life of teaching and research. Significantly, John continued research even while serving as an administrator, and he looked forward to resuming it on a broader scale after his retirement.

John's more personal writings disclosed other qualities of his life and character that endeared him to his friends. Among these were the sermons periodically delivered in the Berea Chapel and other churches. Equally revealing were the reports (that he referred to as his "despatches") to the faculty on his trips to mostly Appalachian areas from which Berea drew most of its students. And it was to current students that he directed his playful "Messages to the Pres" that appeared irregularly in the campus newspaper, *The Pinnacle*. Finally, and most revealing of his personal attributes, were the stories written for his children and his poetry, written largely for himself. It was certainly a mark of his character that few of his friends knew he wrote poetry and fewer still had ever read any of his poems.

Many phases and facets of John's life are apparent in the pieces selected for this volume. Through them we can see the unfolding of his career from an earnest young student to a competent scholar and capable administrator. But, even more important, we see also the personal growth and change of an exceptional human being—intelligent, curious, considerate, warm, caring, humorous, and devoutly religious without being sanctimonious. Guided by the Book of Micah, which he frequently quoted, John truly sought to live up to the standards of the good Christian life. To the best of his ability he acted justly, loved mercy, and walked humbly with God. But John's life was remarkably similar to that of Job, another virtuous Old Testament character whose good deeds were rewarded with a variety of afflictions. Particular poignant in John's case was his decision to resign the presidency of his beloved Berea College when he felt that he could no longer administer it effectively. As Randy Osborne reveals in his brief biography that follows, John looked forward to resuming his research and writing, expanding on themes that he had earlier established. This was not to be and we are the worse for it. At best we can only identify those themes that he considered important and let his own writings address them, recognizing that even they cannot capture the full richness of his being. But they should suffice to reveal why his myriad friends, drawn from all walks of life, considered John a man truly deserving to be remembered, honored, and emulated.

And that is why this book.

PART 2
Measure of a Man:
A Biographical Sketch

J. Randolph Osborne

Let me ask you,
if I can
How do you measure
the worth of a man?

Is it by height,
stature or weight
things you can measure
or accurately state?

Is it possessions
or things that you wear
a stepping forward
at every date?

It must be more
than these passing scenes,
for they leave unnoticed
more significant themes.

A gracious smile
and a heart to care—
an outstretched hand
and courage to dare.

A meaningful word
that's lifted above
can we rather say
that the measure is love?

John Bell Stephenson's life was characterized by a number of passionate loves. Naming them is easy. Love of family—parents, wife, children. Love of education and the pursuit of knowledge. Love of the mountains—their culture, heritage, people, and religion. Love of Berea College—its history, its mission, its commitments, its young people. Love of God and the God-given calling to which he dedicated his life. Love of life with all of its promise and its problems, its foibles and its future, its hope and its hurts, its challenges and its comforts. Our task and our joy in the pages that follow will be to look at the life of John Stephenson and to hear him speak through that life.

John Stephenson's life began in Staunton, Virginia, on September 26, 1937. He was the second child and only son of Louis and Edna Stephenson. His sister Nancy Ann was born almost two and one-half years earlier. Louis Stephenson and Edna May Moles were married on August 10, 1931, at White Hall, Illinois. John's destiny eventually to become a Kentuckian might have already been etched into history, for his maternal great grandmother (Elizabeth Brady) was from Kentucky and had married there.

Louis Stephenson became a lieutenant in the United States Army and was assigned to the Pentagon, which was sufficient mandate for the family to move to Arlington, Virginia. In 1945, when he was discharged from the Army, the family moved back to Staunton where Louis worked in a bank, then in real estate. Later the family settled in Warrenton, Virginia, where Louis worked in another bank.

Those early years in Virginia were capsuled by John Stephenson himself and expressed in a letter to the Berea College Search Committee, as they were considering him for the presidency of the college. He wrote:

> My early years in Virginia were spent in Staunton, Arlington, and Warrenton, where my family attended Baptist churches. I joined the church at the age of eight in the First Baptist Church of Staunton. It was a wonderful religious event for me, representing my serious commitment to a Christian way of life. In the years of my adolescence I entered a period of questioning, but although I attended churches only episodically I maintained my fundamental commitment. Over a period of ten years I found that I was working out a new, deeper, and somewhat less Baptist personal theology.

In 1955 John enrolled at the College of William and Mary in Williamsburg, Virginia, where his "period of questioning" continued. His mother Edna Stephenson said about him: "Johnny was constantly striving, trying to find his place in the world. He never, never wanted to conform. He wanted to be different and he was."

In a letter to his parents, postmarked December 7, 1956, he provided a brief insight into some of his thinking, particularly regarding social functions, one of which he was expected to attend when he came home from college for the Christmas vacation.

I have no desire to attend social functions, whether given by me or anybody else, but, there being nothing else to do, and to avoid any pressure which may be brought to bear, I will paste on a smile and a tie and join the crowd. My view on parties, dances, and the other social gatherings grows dimmer with each season I labor through them. These things were not created for my benefit. The people who revel at these forms of entertainment are pedigreed drunkards who only want to flaunt their striped ties and mannerisms in each others faces. Each assumes his proper position and coldly surveys the rest, asserting himself because he fears his inferiority. There is no warmth here. There is only an air of forced cordiality until several rounds of drinks are served. Understand, I am not against moderate drinking. But I am not like them; I do not drink.

John successfully completed his work at the College of William and Mary, graduating in 1959 with a B.A. degree in sociology under the tutelage of Dr. Wayne Kernodle and Dr. Edwin H. Rhyne. For many years the life, advice, and wisdom of Professor Kernodle, for whom he had great admiration, would influence him.

Immediately after graduating from William and Mary, John entered the University of North Carolina at Chapel Hill, from which he received an M.A. degree in sociology in August 1961. His master's thesis was "On the Role of the Counselor in the Guidance of Negro Youth," which he completed under Dr. Ernest Campbell.

In the same month of the same year, John accepted his first teaching position as a member of the faculty at Lees-McRae College in Banner Elk, North Carolina, a position he held from 1961 to 1964. Upon arrival at Banner Elk, he wrote his parents a letter, dated August 31, 1961, and said: Arrived here about 6:30 EDT this afternoon. . . . About Banner Elk at night: in the words of John Wayne, it's quiet out there." In a follow-up letter dated September 3, he expanded on this characteristic of life in the mountains.

> I think I got more quietude than I bargained for in coming to Banner Elk. . . . The absence of sound is distracting. Time seems to inch along. Occasional crickets and playing children are all that break the silence.

> This removal from the humdrum of daily commerce and from the bustle and interruption of hurrying humanity is what I have dreamed of—but it seems to make me nervous, jumpy, and slow to sleep at night.

> I will be teaching only 12 hours this semester, but have been saddled with the housemothership of McAlister [a residence hall for men].

John's early impressions of Banner Elk and the college were always a part of his continuing communication with his parents. His letters contained subtle humor and candid statements of his impressions of places and people. Regarding the president of the college, he related the following observations in a letter dated September 14, 1962:

> Daddy, you would like to meet our glorious leader, the Colonel. He reminds me of you a great deal. He's so organized he probably goes to the bathroom by the numbers. He surely likes or-

> derly living. I got off to a good start the first day
> by forgetting a faculty meeting. He put me on
> KP for a week and took away my weekend pass.

John's dislike of certain organizational necessities within the college community was expressed in an October 4, 1962, letter. "I have never believed in committees; in fact, I hate committees. Name one great book, piece of music, painting, sculpture, or scientific theory originated by a committee. But there is life staring you in the face again."

However, Banner Elk and Lees-McRae College would provide the medium for one encounter that would change his life dramatically. One of his passionate loves came into his life. At the first faculty meeting which he attended, he met a colleague whose name was Jane Ellen Baucom. By Thanksgiving of the same year they were engaged and in March of the following year they were married.

One consequence of the experience of life at Banner Elk was that another of John's passionate loves was beginning to take root and grow in his life—a love of the mountains and their people. Listen to him talk about it in a letter to Wayne and Ed, dated January 9, 1963:

> I love the mountains and their people. I have felt
> a completeness, a sense of fulfillment here that I
> haven't known in other places. . . . There is a sense
> of doing something that needs doing. It needs
> doing worse here than in the flatlands. And it
> needs to be done by people who want to change
> things without changing them, if you know what
> I mean. Part of a way of life needs to be preserved
> and not sacrificed on the altar of progress. . . .
> Many of these mountain people are like losers
> in a nation-wide game of Monopoly, the rules of
> which they don't understand.

While maintaining a keen sensitivity to the present moment, John was also thinking about his future. In late 1962 and early 1963 he was in the midst of making a decision regarding his doctoral studies. By February 1963 he had decided to return to the university at Chapel Hill and pursue a doctorate. Upon completion of his doctorate, he wanted to return to Banner Elk. He said:

> Why Banner Elk? There just isn't another place like it, that's all. It's a great place to work, even under conditions where people supposedly in command buck you at every turn. . . . There's a feeling of doing something worth doing, and of doing it with people who are headed in the same direction you are. . . .

His vision for the future was totally inclusive of the people in the mountains. In a letter dated March 18, 1963, to John Ehle, a good friend from whom he rented a basement apartment while at UNC, he spoke of things he would like to get done for mountain people. "The first is a thing I have, without obvious success, been trying to get going here at the College: a series of workshop conferences on selected problems in the mountain region, especially Western North Carolina. . . . The second thing is maybe a pipe-dream, but a necessity: the establishment of mental health clinics in Western North Carolina. . . ."

By April 1963 he was experiencing the full thrust of the academic regimen at the college. In a letter to his sister Nancy Ann, he said:

> Sometime I'm going to figure out why spring is so hectic in academia. . . . Kids here are breaking out in rashes, headaches, and general anorexia nervosa all over the place. Everybody seems jittery, like they were waiting for the earth to crack open and Armageddon to arrive. I'd personally

rather spring came in the fall. It is too good a
time of the year to waste in coping with anxiety.

A new professional status and a new marital status were soon
to be joined by another of John's passionate loves. In January 1964
he wrote to his good friend and mentor, Wayne Kernodle: "Second
reason for writing is that I think I may acquire a new family title
(father) late this summer, and I wanted to share the good news."

While the good news was reason for elation, there was also a
developing cause for concern about the situation at Lees-McRae
College. In a letter to John Ehle (February 1964) he observed: "Things
are restless here in Banner Elk right now. If the College and the
Association of which it is a branch don't straighten out soon I will
probably be in Chapel Hill next fall grinding toward the PhD."

In the spring of 1964 the correspondence between John and some
of his friends and mentors was heavy. Nearly every letter contained
details about some aspect of the tension which existed at the college. In three separate letters to Wayne Kernodle from late February to late March, he made these observations:

> The Colonel is giving me static about (among
> other things) getting speakers back who have
> already been here. What it amounts to is that he
> doesn't trust my judgment about speakers.
> Which is understandable, I suppose.

> Right now we've got more snakes stirred up than
> the Board of Trustees . . . can kill in a month of
> meetings. If, when we settle the dust again, and
> I'm still here, and we don't get some intellectual
> excitement around here, then I'm gone. My pa-
> tience is wearin' plumb thin.

There is a bitterness to life that makes it rather unpleasant right now, and I feel most of the time like the sword of Damocles is inches over my head. But I am hoping (and betting a lot) that all this will pass away, and that soon we will get back to a reasonable state of brotherly love and good work. I still think this place could amount to something more than an escape hatch for scared underachievers and a playground for the offspring of the idle wealth, which seems to be what we are into at present.

By early April the developing tension had reached a breaking point, and he wrote in a letter to Harrison Taylor, a friend and colleague at Lees-McRae College, dated April 2: "I got canned yesterday, in a very unusual way. I was offered a choice between accepting a contract without tenure and getting no contract. I chose the latter. . . ." However, as things worked out, he was offered a contract with tenure. And the Colonel did put a letter in his file stating that the college would like for him to return after completing his doctoral work at Chapel Hill.

But John's professional future was not to be at Lees-McRae. His continuing intellectual growth and his own personal experiences with the college began to stimulate the discontent that would draw him in other directions. Consider his thinking, as expressed in a letter to B.H. on April 20, 1964:

I am not certain that things are a great deal better here now than they ever have been. Maybe it is just one of my fluctuating moods, but I am convinced at least for the moment that the Board, and that Presbyteries, aren't going to do a damn thing that would make Banner Elk what is could and should be. . . .

Put very simply, there are people who think and people who don't. In this day and society they are represented by the intellectual and the businessman, respectively. . . . The businessman comes into life feet first; the intellectual head first. The greatest distance between any two points on a man's body is between his foot and his head. They are hard to get together. They weren't made to. So with these two elements of society. Nonthinkers think thinkers are useless; thinkers think nonthinkers are missing the point of being alive. . . .

We have all made a mistake here in looking for the devil personified in one or several individuals. The devil is in the nature of man and therefore in the nature of the human social situation--the individuals are mere pawns (see *Lord of the Flies*?), 99% of the world is nonthinking. The nonthinkers are therefore the possessors of power. . . . That leaves the rest of us on the short end of a long seesaw.

At the end of the academic year in the spring of 1964 John Stephenson's professional relationship with Lees-McRae College concluded. He moved with his wife and baby daughter Jennifer and reentered the University of North Carolina at Chapel Hill to pursue doctoral studies, which he completed in 1966 with a Ph.D. in medical sociology. During his final year of doctoral work at UNC he wrote a letter to Dr. A. Lee Coleman, chairman of the Department of Sociology at the University of Kentucky, inquiring about the possibility of a job. In mid-December 1965 he visited the University of Kentucky. Before Christmas he had received a letter from

Dr. Coleman, offering him an appointment to the department beginning September 1, 1966. The salary range was $8,000 to $8,800 per academic year, with the higher figure contingent upon completion of his doctorate.

From 1966 until his untimely death in 1994 John Stephenson was a full-fledged Kentuckian. On this Kentucky soil he would live, raise his family, engage himself in the life of the church, address the pain and the problems of the mountain region, participate in the preparation of young people for service to their society, provide original leadership in the organization of people for educational purposes, serve as president of one of the foremost liberal arts colleges in America. The loves that dominated John's life found rich development here, though the blossom of his own life was not allowed to reach its fullness.

John's eighteen years at the University of Kentucky served as an incubation period for his single-minded and purposeful mission to the people and region of Appalachia. These would be years during which he achieved numerous special distinctions, honors which he tended to downplay, at least for personal benefit. He was comfortable standing in the shadows, while giving direction and motivation and inspiration to the action which was a part of the human drama in which he participated. A quick glance at the chronology of his life will bear witness to these achievements, while those who knew him well recognized the humility that was characteristic of him. Titles and special honors often seemed to cause him a sense of discomfort and even embarrassment. John was most impressed and fulfilled by those things which brought meaning and purpose, hope and promise to all of God's people.

John Stephenson was a man of moderate physical stature but of tremendous spirit. It was his spirit that guided his life's activities. The last twenty-eight years of his life were consumed in pursuit of his educational goals, his family's welfare and future, his mission to the mountain region, and a search for the faith which would give purpose, direction, and meaning to all of the elements of his life.

As an educator, John's career was characterized by steady and progressive increments in position and responsibilities. Whether as classroom teacher, administrator, counselor, or innovator of new ideas and directions, he seemed to be unrestrained by the conventionalities which could hinder "the plowing of new ground." From his position at the University of Kentucky he would be able to ask new questions, to restate old questions and launch new initiatives.

As co-founder in 1975 of the Shakertown Conversations on General Education, he helped set in motion continuing discussions among academics from various parts of Appalachia regarding the problems of and prospects for education in the region. As a founder and planning staff member of the first Kentucky Governor's Scholars Program, he helped initiate a statewide summer program for gifted high school juniors from Kentucky.

John's knowledge of the Appalachian region and its people derived from his own inquiring mind and first-hand experience. At Lees-McRae College his compassion for the people of Appalachia surfaced in a manner that directed the rest of his professional and personal goals. Publication of his doctoral dissertation—*Shiloh: A Mountain Community*—in 1968 raised his visibility as one of the emerging young scholars on Appalachian family, work, and community life. Other publications brought him to the attention of prominent national scholars in the field of sociology. As an important voice on general education, he sought ways of preserving or reviving liberal education while providing students with opportunities to gain experience in applied activities that were more directly related to their vocational interests. In pursuit of his goals in this area, he became active in a number of organizations such as the Education Program Division of the National Endowment for the

Humanities, the Campus Compact's Institute on Integrating Service with Academic Study, and the Association for General and Liberal Studies. In addition, John was the author or co-author of various articles concerned with the importance of general studies. In these he made clear his view that he was not opposed to vocation-oriented study at the college level, but considered such programs to be supplements to rather than substitutes for general education.

John's early role as a leader in the area of Appalachian studies became more prominent when the University of Kentucky was awarded a grant by the Rockefeller Foundation to establish a center for Appalachian studies. As dean of undergraduate studies, he participated in the planning of the center and then relinquished his position as dean to become director of the Appalachian Center in 1979. In keeping with his usual mode of operation, he quickly became involved in a variety of activities pertinent to this new position. These included the organization of a program of Appalachian studies at the University of Kentucky and major roles in the establishment of the Appalachian Studies Conference, as well as service on the editorial boards of *Appalachian Journal* and *Appalachian Heritage Magazine*.

In 1981 John was awarded a Fulbright Senior Research Scholarship to work in Scotland while on sabbatical leave from the university. His stated goal was to compare the development of regional consciousness in Scotland with the sense of regional loyalty in Appalachia. That research culminated in his book *Ford: A Village in the West Highlands of Scotland*, published in 1984.

While in Scotland doing research, John kept up correspondence with some of his close friends in Kentucky. To James Still, in a letter dated November 15, 1981, he wrote:

> This country has such regard for the country-
> side that it has passed laws and local regulations

which protect rural areas from housing pollution. . . . The local authorities are biased heavily
in favor of building in existing towns and villages and against scattering the population. A
dispersed population costs more in the delivery
of services, and it is the surest way to uglifica-
tion of the countryside.

To Dr. Thomas Ford at the University of Kentucky dated November 6, 1981, he wrote:

Maybe we are over-organized, or at least organized along the wrong lines. We do too much
feeding and never allow students in the kitchen.
And I also have those dark moments still when I
think we are trying to educate the non-educable.

In a speech "Appalachia Today" to the Bridge of Allan Rotary
Club on October 22 regarding life in America's highlands, he commented:

There is a rich Appalachia and a poor Appalachia. Rich Appalachia lives much of the time outside the mountains. Poor Appalachia either stays
in the mountains (in the "hollers") or migrates to
the cities to look for work, much as your Highland people have done for many generations.

These mountaineers are stubborn people and
they are willing to put up with hardship in order
to remain in the region, which is their home. . . .
These good folks have learned to get by with very
little and they are good neighbors to each other,
always helpful in times of need. . . . There is a

certain suspicion of outsiders, but I think they
are only waiting to learn whether a stranger can
be trusted or not. Like your Highland culture,
there is a fervent religious spirit which exists side
by side with a very secular culture involving
much drinking and displays of masculine prow-
ess. The religion is often old-fashioned and strict;
it divides the world into the saved and sinners.

The Highlands of both your country and mine
have much to offer a busy, jaded old society that
has traded part of its soul in order to advance
our industrial civilization. I hope we can learn to
neither totally exploit nor totally ignore these
peripheral areas, but to learn from them some
decent human values and to help them restore
their birthrights.

In another reflection at an Appalachian Conference held at the
University of Rome in May 1984, John noted:

An American Indian friend, Vine Deloria . . . has
pointed out that Appalachians share more of the
fate of the American Indians than they realize.
The way he puts it is that the only difference
between Indians and Appalachians is that they
both live on reservations but Appalachians don't
know it yet. Interestingly, Harry Caudill has referred to Appalachia as a paleface reservation.

The signal professional achievement in John Stephenson's life was
his appointment in 1984 as the seventh president of Berea College.

He was chosen from a pool of 175 applicants. Regarding this new opportunity and challenge in his life, John was interviewed in the April 14 issue of the *Kernel*, the University of Kentucky newspaper:

> "At first I could not imagine John Stephenson being president of anything," he said about his nomination to the Berea post. "I had to be persuaded by a lot of people to take it seriously. It was a match between what things I'm interested in and concerned about and what that college stands for." Stephenson said he strongly believes in the "marriage" between learning and work. "It introduces a kind of democratic flavor to the campus . . . a strong sense of community and shared purpose. When you're fortunate enough to get into a work situation where everyone is pulling together and moving in the same direction, it's irresistible," he said.

The *Lexington Herald-Leader* reported on his appointment as the next president of Berea College in an article written by Cheryl Truman dated January 19, 1984:

> Stephenson, 46, told an audience of students, trustees and the press yesterday that the various experiences of his life "have led to this point . . . to Berea College." He called the college "a marvel of tradition and innovation." Kroger Pettengill, Chairman of the Board of Trustees of Berea College, said: "To find someone like John Stephenson, who was born in Appalachia, and got his education in Appalachia . . . and is a leading scholar on Appalachia, is extremely fortunate."

In response to a request from the Presidential Search Committee for a statement about his religious life and values, John provided this comment:

> I think of myself as a religious person because of my inner commitment and values. I think of myself as a Christian because of vows made years ago to try to follow in His footsteps. But I do not wear my religion on my sleeve. I do not evangelize or proselytize. I try to live my religion, demonstrating my beliefs through the examples of my life and work. Some ministers have explained that this is a form of witnessing. To me, this is a means of making life coherent and purposeful. I'd rather do something in the name of love than talk about it.

In his first address to Berea students as president in September 1984, he said, "What we want to give you here cannot be bought at the college supermarket. We want to give you what you need and what the world needs right now: an education for character and an education for commitment as well as an education for the mind and hands." Later, in an interview with the *Richmond Register* before the spring commencement in 1990, he said his special wish for graduating seniors was for them to call to mind the joys and obligations of servanthood.

One of John's earliest personal initiatives as president of Berea College was to acquaint himself firsthand with conditions in the region from which the college accepted most of its students. He initially envisioned a "Month in the Mountains," but time constraints did not allow him to carry out his original plan. Thus, a series of visits to the mountains was spread over several months, beginning in September 1987 and ending in July 1988. The places visited included Buchanan County, Virginia; the North Carolina counties of Avery, Mitchell, Yancey, and Buncombe; the Virginia counties of Lee and Wise; Raleigh and Greenbrier counties in West Virginia; and Hancock County, Tennessee. For each of these visits he wrote "A Despatch from Appalachia" in which he reflected on the excursion, offering his observations and conclusions.

As special assistant to the president during John's first four years (1984–88) at Berea College, I helped him plan and prepare for these visits and, when possible, accompanied him. One of the memorable visits was to Lee and Wise counties in Virginia and to Hancock County in Tennessee. We visited with common folks in their private homes, met professional people in their offices, and worshipped with people in their churches.

One Sunday night he was scheduled for a speaking engagement at the Admant Baptist Church in Stone Creek, Virginia. Upon arriving at the church and after having a brief conversation outside with some of the men who were having their last "smoke" before the speech, we went inside. Getting a bulletin with the order of worship from one of the deacons, I noticed that the sermon was being given by "Brother" John Stephenson. John asked if this meant what he thought it meant, and I assured him it did. John said he needed a few minutes alone, which were graciously granted him by our hosts. A few minutes later he emerged from his temporary and self-imposed isolation to declare that his sermon was prepared. Its title: "Brother, Are You Ready?"

On the same visit he met with many people in Sneedville, Tennessee, who spoke of their "melungeon" heritage, especially those in the county courthouse. During this entire visit, he "walked their walk and talked their talk," returning to the college campus enriched and inspired.

Fund raising is an ongoing necessity for an undergraduate institution renowned for affording young people of Appalachia and

John has a traditional school picture taken during the third grade.

elsewhere a high quality and tuition-free education. When John was inaugurated, Berea College had just completed its seven-year Second Century campaign and had raised $45 million. Subsequently, he guided a "Best Vision" capital campaign which ran from 1987 to 1992. Two months before the target date of June 30, 1992, over $65 million had been raised and the contributions ultimately totaled more than $70 million. Of the total raised, more than $9 million was contributed by 63 percent of Berea's alumni. The monies were used for the renovation of the Hutchins Library, a new computer center, the all-new Seabury Center for Wellness and Physical Education, faculty and staff salary increases, for the establishment of the Goode Endowed Professorship in Appalachian and Black Studies, and for the Education Ventures Fund.

The Stephenson years at Berea were also years of outreach initiatives. The Brushy Fork Institute for Appalachian leadership development, the Black Mountain Youth Leadership program, and the New Opportunity School for Women are three sterling examples. In May 1992 President George Bush awarded Berea College a "Point of Light" for Students for Appalachia, a tutorial program for the young and the old. A consortium of colleges in the Appalachian region, the Appalachian College Association, came into existence in 1990 as a result of his interests, concerns, and leadership. John was president and member of the Executive Committee of this association, still active and headquartered in Berea.

As president of Berea College, John was instrumental in two significant international initiatives, both of which continue as programs of strength and promise today. The most important of these was his pioneering effort to make provision for educational opportunities in the United States for Tibetans living in exile in India, a project culminating in the visit of the Dalai Lama to Berea College in 1994. The stimulus for this initiative was provided by a visit of the niece of the Dalai Lama to Berea College.

In order to coordinate this program, John made two visits to India, meeting with the Dalai Lama on both occasions. On his first visit, in April of 1990, he was accompanied by Dr. Al Perkins, academic vice president and dean of the college, and by two other persons. The purpose of this visit was to have face-to-face meetings with officials of the Tibetan government-in-exile, to establish the procedures and requirements pertaining to the acceptance of students, and to interview the first candidates for admission to Berea College. Upon returning to the United States, John continued his efforts on behalf of those prospective students. In an article in the *Tibetan Review* of February 1994, he stated: "In addition to the nine students enrolled at Berea, I was able to place two students at Bellarmine College in Louisville, Kentucky, and they have since been joined by a third. Another of the students I interviewed in Dharamsala was enrolled at Alice Lloyd College in Kentucky. . . ."

On his second visit to India, October 27–November 10, 1991, John's son David, an accomplished photographer, accompanied him. In addition to having a second audience with the Dalai Lama, John was able to provide pictorial documentation of the visit and of the conditions of the Tibetans-in-exile. The primary purpose of the visit, however, as stated in the *Tibetan Review* article, was:

> to learn more about the current state of second-ary education for Tibetan exile students, the ex-pectations of prospective students regarding higher education, the level of English Language fluency among students, and the needs for fur-ther education of these students in America in the views of Tibetan education officials. Detailed selection procedures were elaborated, and the blessing of His Holiness the Dalai Lama was sought and received.

A visit of the Dalai Lama to Berea College was scheduled for October 1992 but had to be postponed because of health consider-ations. It was rescheduled for April of 1994. This official visit of His Holiness the 14th Dalai Lama was viewed as significant achieve-ment of Berea College under John's leadership. As reported in the *Richmond Register* of April 25, 1994, John regarded the visit as "one of the most important events in the life of the commonwealth in recent years." A reporter for the *Lexington Herald-Leader*, Paul Prather, made a more definitive statement in an article dated April 24, 1994: "To gauge the significance of the visit, think of it this way: Essen-tially the Dalai Lama is to Buddhism, particularly Tibetan Bud-dhism, what Pope John Paul II is to Roman Catholicism."

Two public appearances of the Dalai Lama on the Berea College campus were held in Phelps Stokes Chapel, with standing-room-only audiences. A line formed around the chapel several hours before he spoke. His first lecture, on April 24, 1994, was on "World Peace and the Kinship of All People." Attending this lecture was Kentucky Governor Brereton Jones, who presented the Buddhist world leader with a rather large wedding-ring quilt tucked in a wood basket. In his speech on world peace, the Dalai Lama said:

> World peace—I think everybody wants genu-ine, lasting world peace. War makes disaster and destruction; so therefore our desire for world peace is important. . . . If education is balanced with a good heart, all the knowledge becomes constructive and there is no danger of destruc-tion to people.

His second public appearance was on April 25 at a convocation for the college's students, faculty, and staff. Berea College conferred upon him the honorary degree of Doctor of Humane Letters. The presentation statement conferring the degree upon this 1989 Nobel Peace Prize winner included these comments:

> The 14th Dalai Lama, Tenzin Gyaltso, has con-tributed greatly to the furtherance of many of the Great Commitments of Berea College. He has, understandably, taken a keen interest in the progress of Berea's Tibetan students. Quite be-yond Berea, however, he has contributed inesti-mably to the cause of world harmony. It is in rec-ognition of these extraordinary contributions that the Dalai Lama of Tibet is recommended for the honorary degree of Doctor of Humane Letters.

John's own reflections on this world famous religious leader were expressed in an article written in early January 1992 for the *Lexington Herald-Leader*: "Meanwhile, he is teaching the world to smile more ('It makes life much more pleasant, and it does not cost anything.'), and encouraging us to love our enemies, from whom we learn patience . . . the simple advice the Dalai Lama offered in my first audience with him in April, 1990, is worth sharing: 'Keep a warm heart and serve your community.'"

The second international initiative in which John played a crucial role was the Sister City-Sister Region between Berea-Madison County, Kentucky, and the Yatsugatake Region in Yamanashi Prefecture, Japan. In 1987 initial discussions about such an international relationship were proposed by the Japanese. The town of Takane wanted a sister city in Kentucky and the Berea City Council was approached by them. At that time I was, in addition to being a special sssistant to the president, a member of the Berea City Council. John gave his full support to the relationship and asked me to represent him and the college in following through with the Japanese. In October 1988 John and his wife Jane visited the Yatsugatake Region in Japan, along with a sizable delegation from Madison County. The Sister City agreement, which had been signed in Berea in May 1988 was signed in Takane in October 1988.

Subsequent to that initial agreement, a Sister Region relationship was established with Madison County in 1990. As a result, delegates from Japan come to Madison County and delegates from Madison County go to Japan each year. Berea students have been primary beneficiaries of this new international relationship. Since 1990 a Berea College student broommaker has gone to Japan each year to demonstrate that art and craft. For several summers two or more Berea students have spent their summer months working and studying in the Yatsugatake Region of Japan.

The mayors of the towns in Japan have expressed continuing interest in having a "college like Berea" established in their region, an idea first expressed to John in 1988. The Yatsugatake Region in Japan is mountainous and populated by farmers and small town businessmen. The continued growth and strength of this program is a tribute to John's protracted vision of Berea College's mission to people in need, wherever in the world they might be, as well as a far-reaching commitment to providing international cultural elements to the Berea College educational experience.

John was among thirty-three distinguished leaders appointed to Kentucky's Task Force on Education Reform in 1989. The same year saw him elected to the board of directors of the National Association of Independent Colleges and Universities. In recognition of his leadership in and knowledge of the region, Governor Brereton C. Jones appointed him chairman of the Kentucky Appalachian Task Force. The mission of this task force was to "review the current status of the Appalachian Regional Commission and make recommendations regarding strategies for maximizing funding for Kentucky, the potential and viability of an expanded Appalachian Development Program, and assess the programs which provide services in the Appalachian Region." Seven meetings of the Task Force were held from February through July of 1994. One of the key recommendations was that "the state universities should establish a Kentucky Appalachian Institute, a think tank that would invigorate the process with criticism and new ideas."

The years 1992–94 were the most difficult ones for John's presidency of Berea College. Five years after his appointment, he learned that he suffered from chronic lymphocytic leukemia or CLL, not to be confused with acute leukemia, a fast-acting and usually fatal disease. He compared his illness to diabetes, which can be controlled. The formula for controlling CLL included medication, rest, exercise, and diet. Of course, the last three were virtually impossible to regulate properly, considering the schedule of a college president. John made an effort to keep a proper balance in those areas, but the demands of the office always came first. As a result, he often suffered excruciating pain, which could not be alleviated fully even with the expertise of the University of Kentucky Medical Center's Pain Clinic. During those difficult periods of pain and confinement, his thoughts and hopes and questions were poured out in poetry and other musings.

On May 26, 1992, he wrote:

> It occurred to me that I was observing myself
> Finding faces hidden in the patterns of wallpaper
> Linoleum patterns, tree leaves, clouds.
> Here's a bear's face
> Here's a little boy, a woman, an angry man
>
> Who has time to look for faces?
> Only little children, old people, the sick
> The idle generally.
> And now that I dwell on it, it's fun again
> To go back and find the people and the animal friends
> In their familiar places on
> the water-stained ceiling
> And on the knotty floor,
> And amongst the tremoring green leaves outside my
>   window

And on June 16 of the same year:

> And so it goes. Long talk with Patrick [Kelleher, John's personal physician] about depression yesterday. Today—up at 8:00, exercises, meditation, then prepare for chores in town—bank, hardware, garage, video store, Judy Stammer's office, etc. Then to Davis's. With Ken's help,

> brought Skye to the barn, groomed and saddled, rode her in the barn and then outside to the 'new ground' and back. It was good workout. Dismounting was the hardest because I land with a good deal of weight on my left foot. Still, I felt invigorated at least momentarily. Will I pay for it in foot pain tonight and over the next days? No matter; I'd rather be hurting there than in my psyche.

During these months, John spent much time at his rural cabin at Disputanta, about 12 miles from Berea. On some of those occasions I was able to take him to the cabin and spend several hours with him there. We especially cherished the cold wintry days, when we could build a roaring fire in the wood stove, smoke our pipes, drink Earl Grey tea, and talk about the meaning or seeming meaninglessness of it all. But it was in the quiet solitude of this rustic homesite nestled in the woods that he could reflect and write—inspired by the sights and sounds of nature, the simple and graceful surroundings which are so often overlooked. With the enforced slow pace needed for recuperation, he could see again and anew things which had been speedily passing him by, and from this new perspective he wrote many poems reflecting the natural world.

One of the most excruciating dilemmas that John had to face during his illness was related to his responsibilites as president of Berea College. He had envisioned for himself an extended relationship with the college, a relationship which was being threatened by his illness. The demands of the presidency and the requirements for keeping his illness under control were simply not compatible. Exercising a realism that was a major part of his practical approach to life, John resigned the presidency of Berea College in early 1993. The resignation was to be effective June 1994. The personal agony of that decision is impossible for anyone to understand, including those closest to him. He did not allow himself to consider seriously his resignation for a long time, retaining an optimism about his health that was not sustained. His reluctance to step down as president of the college more than likely contributed to his untimely death. The last fifteen months of his presidency were filled with the activities, planning, and projections entailed by his retirement. Such a demanding schedule could only aggravate his condition, though the emotional high points were unforgettable and gave a boost to his saddened spirit.

John dons cap and gown for graduation from
Warrenton (Virginia) High School in June 1955.

On August 1, 1994, John presented to his successor Dr. Larry Shinn the keys to the president's office, Lincoln Hall Room 200. Within days he was on his way to Scotland with members of his family. The reunion with old friends of the past, a special time with family members, and a time for spiritual reflection were elements of this longed-for and long-awaited return visit.

As was his custom, John had not left his future to the whims of chance. He had planned! During the months of October and November 1994 after the visit to Scotland, he would teach a course at Harvard University's Graduate School of Education entitled "Inside/Out: Presidential Roles in Higher Education."

For the even more distant future, John had drafted a proposal for a fellowship from the Faculty Scholars Program of the University of Kentucky and the Appalachian Colleges Association that would permit him to resume his research in the Appalachian community Shiloh and the Scottish community Ford. In addition, he proposed to conduct an assessment of the state of science instruction in Appalachian colleges. Written in September 1994 the proposal was for the calendar year 1995. Unfortunately, his plans were never to be realized.

Upon returning from Scotland, John and his wife Jane moved to the Boston area, their spirits uplifted by the excitement of this new opportunity in such a highly charged intellectual environment. Soon, however, the excitement would turn to dismay and the dismay would turn to despair. His body's defenses weakened by the chronic leukemia, John became a victim of a rare virus, which attacked the brain. Even the medical specialists in Boston's hospitals had difficulty identifying the cause of a debilitating illness that rendered him unable to teach his class. With John growing weaker, Jane decided to bring him back to Kentucky by medical air ambulance. He spent the remaining weeks of his life at the Berea Hospital—attended by his close personal friend and physician Dr. Patrick Kelleher and surrounded by family members and close personal friends.

The life of John B. Stephenson ended quietly and with dignity in the early morning hours of December 6, 1994. He was only slightly past "the somewhat young age of 56," as he stated the previous year in his proposal to the Faculty Scholars Program. Yet he had achieved so much in those years!

The legacy of John B. Stephenson will continue in ways known and unknown, simple and profound, physical and spiritual. Personally, he was a sensitive and private man. Professionally, the public was his focus and he engaged it with verve. His students will remember a zeal for learning which he shared with them. Colleagues will remember a man of firm resolution and quickening intellect. Close friends will remember his compassion, unfettered love of nature, and utter devotion to his family. When his daughter Jennifer was married in 1989, John wrote the following statement for her wedding program:

> Marriage is the high aspirations of humans to realize the eternal in a relationship. It is the hope and the belief that there is truly a forever together. The eternal and the forever are things of God only; therefore, any promise of loving and living together forever may be asked by us but must be given by God. Be grateful for God's gift of marriage.

During his years as president of Berea College, John's spiritual perspectives were both challenged and changed. He became seriously interested in deep study of the Bible. He preached sermons in area churches and would have done so regularly if his schedule had permitted. He performed wedding ceremonies for select couples. He even contemplated taking some Bible courses at a seminary during his retirement years. Old Testament prophets and their calls for social justice were among his favorite persons and themes of the Bible.

John Stephenson was a multi-faceted man with multi-talents to match. A person's person who rarely forgot the names of those whom he encountered. A visionary, never quite satisfied with things as they are, when he could envision things as they should be. A keen cross-examiner of your assumptions and presumptions. An observer of and a participant in the Christian faith, who was strong enough in that faith to ask the difficult questions, which rarely satisfy us with the specific answers desired by late twentieth-century minds. For John, however, the satisfaction was in the search for answers, in asking the questions. Faith remained a prerequisite.

This aspect of John's faith was a featured part of the funeral sermon that I delivered on December 9, 1994, at the Union Church in Berea. With particular reference to his inquiring faith, his insatiable quest for new knowledge, and his unbending belief in and anticipation of the future, I commended the spirit of a dear friend to a gracious and all-comprehending God:

> This IS the day, John—the day of new beginnings for you and for all who knew you, the day when life's ultimate mystery is yours to know and ours yet to ponder, the day when "the substance of things hoped for" produces for you "the evidence of things not seen."
>
> THIS is the day, John—the day the Lord has made, the day when WE say the race has been run, the day when FAITH says life has only begun, the day of victory for the faithful visionary, your day because it is ultimately God's day—and you are God's.

Part 3
Sociological Studies

Most of John's early research was focused on community change and was guided by his concern for the Appalachian region and the changes taking place in its communities. He had ambivalent feelings about many of these changes. On the one hand, he saw the necessity of improving deplorable social and economic conditions in much of the region. On the other, he was disturbed by the nature of the transformation that was occurring—changes that in the name of development "modernized" communities at the expense of destroying local cultures.

Social Change in an Appalachian Community

John's first community research was part of a larger study of a North Carolina mountain community conducted by the Institute for Research in Social Science of the University of North Carolina, Chapel Hill. John used his part of the study for his doctoral dissertation in sociology. It was later modified and published in 1968 by the University of Kentucky Press as *Shiloh: A Mountain Community*. In the preface to the book John wrote:

> This study has its origin in my interest in mountain people and the changing society in which they live. That there are problems in the moun-

tain region calling for understanding is testified
to by the recent organization of regional, state,
and federal agencies charged with the specific
mission of combating such problems. Appalachia in general, and the Southern Appalachian
Region specifically, has been recognized officially as a multiproblem area. Depressing statistics on unemployment, dependency, low income, lack of education, infant mortality, and
other indicators of social malaise abound. But
before these statistics can take on full meaning,
I think we must understand what they reflect in
the local societies within the region. What is the
nature of the local social order? How is it changing from what it was in the last generation? How
are the mountain people affected by these
changes? Are the regional statistics an outgrowth
of the inability of old social structures and old
personal adaptive styles to cope with the new
order? I hope that the study reported here will
help in some way to answer these questions.

My interest in the mountains has not always
been so problem-centered. In fact, I, like many
people raised in and near the Appalachians, was
not so aware that we had such problems until
someone informed me. I had always thought of
the mountains as a fine place to visit and an even
better place to take up residence, except that I
couldn't afford to live there. Only later did I realize that I wasn't the only person who could
not afford to live there—many of the people liv-

ing there couldn't afford it either. But they were sticking it out anyway, taking it rather than leaving it, in Rupert Vance's words. Only gradually did I come to realize that the people referred to by Michael Harrington—and Harry Caudill and John F. Kennedy and Vance and the *Saturday Evening Post*—were the same ones I had as neighbors and school friends when I was a child. In truth, I still think of the mountains as a corner of heaven first and a national disgrace second. And I think of the mountain people as good, kind, rough, gentle friends before I think of them as poverty cases, social problems, or flies on the nation's face.

Data for the study were collected primarily through participant observation as John lived in the community for four months (June–September 1965). His first-hand observations, conducted in homes, work places, churches, stores, bootlegger's business sites, and wherever residents carried out their daily lives, were supplemented by interviews with a number of local residents as well as by analyses of official statistics. In reading the excerpts from *Shiloh* that follow, one must remember that this was essentially an academic work. As a consequence it incorporates the disciplinary terminology and literary style of the scholarly establishment. Nevertheless, it is neither a stodgy nor esoteric treatise, and frequently conveys John's irrepressible sense of humor.

In conducting his research, John focused primarily on the mountain family and its adjustment to the momentous, but not necessarily rapid, changes taking place in the community. To organize his analysis, he devised a classification of family types based largely on the occupation of the chief breadwinner that corresponds roughly to a social class system. A brief sketch of these types, given in the table below, is important for understanding the excerpts from chapter five that follow.

Occupational Type and Social Level in Shiloh

Family Type	Solution to Economic Problems	Social Level
I	Full-time employment: managerial, white-collar, own business, etc.	Top
II	Full-time employment: blue-collar, semi-skilled, wage-worker, etc.	Middle
III	Fairly steady employment	Middle
IV	Sometime or no employment	Bottom

ADAPTING TO MODERNITY

By this point a fairly clear picture should emerge, a picture of a community rapidly opening into a larger social system, a community whose economic base is shifting from subsistence agriculture, mining and timbering to mill and factory wage work, a community made up of different social levels, subcultures, and families. The picture, however, will not be complete until the major problems and stresses as they are felt and dealt with by different families in the community have been described, and until some relationships among the phenomena of change and adaptive modes can be formulated.

When one reviews existing theories or studies of social change he is likely to come away with the impression that sociologists concern themselves almost exclusively with large-scale, global, or macrosocial change phenomena. Much social research consists of the marking of historical trends of one sort or another. Much social theory is on the same high level, the most abstract example being the varieties of evolutionary theory. There is, of course, a wide range of abstractness in theories and studies of social change: from the evolution of whole societies to the process of institutionalization of relatively small groups, from the study of cultural trends or societal demographic trends to the study of the life cycle of a family. But for the most part the macrosocial approach to social change concentrates on indexing change and explaining it at a relatively high level of abstraction. Opposed to change as experienced by the demographer looking at census data, there is another approach which concentrates on change as it is experienced by participants in particular situations. The more microsocial approach empirically involves the study of individuals and groups acting and interacting in situations, and it requires frequently that the student understand the meanings and definitions of situations in the minds of participants, where the macrosocial level of study usually abstracts out global "variables" to manipulate at a distance thrice removed from social reality as it is known to interacting participants.

It is probably not necessary to point out that these two levels of study are not incompatible; they are different levels of abstraction from the same reality, and, in fact, they complement each other nicely. Trends such as those regarding communication and the economy in Shiloh act as the stage set or backdrop against which the citizens of the community act out their parts from day to day. The backdrop, the situational conditions, must be known before the performance of the actors makes much sense. But, likewise, some actors must be on the stage or the setting itself has no function or significance.[1]

In short, social change can be studied on at least two levels, which can be categorized as macrosocial and microsocial. What appear as social trends on the macrosocial level—trends such as those taking place in Shiloh—appear on the microsocial level as modifications of situation, as gradual or sudden, problematic or benign situational "crises" (in Thomas' sense)[2] which must be adapted to.

Two general areas of change emerge as the dominating trends in Shiloh since 1940. One is the changing economy: the closing of some occupations and the opening of others, the increasing need for cash and the decreasing ability of families to sustain themselves through subsistence farming and home manufacture. The second lies in the relatively rapid opening up of the community to the outside world, exposing its members to alternative life styles and values through increased travel, communication, and use of mass media. These two areas of change are not unrelated but are mutually interactive: changes in occupation have brought about changes in life style, and exposure to new values—especially consumer desires—has led in many instances to change of job.[3] Furthermore, concomitant with changes in these two areas have been others: an increase in "scale" (as defined by the Wilsons); an increasing plurality and complexity in the social system as roles (especially occupational) have become more differentiated[4] and as greater vertical differentiation has taken place; and a greater involvement of outside agencies in making decisions that affect the local area—the "Springdale" phenomenon.[5]

These global systemic changes might be characterized in a number of ways, and no single statement will take into consideration all important aspects of change. Nevertheless, there is a striking design in this fabric of change which always seems to move to the foreground of our perception. This design is not the changing economy or occupational structure as such, nor the increasing number of television sets and cars as such, though it is intimately bound up with these and other systemic alternations. The dominating trend, rather, seems to be a kind of *transformation of culture*, a change in total way of life. Yet this is still not an accurate statement, because it implies that all families in the community are simultaneously undergoing this cultural transformation and that all segments of the community are marching in lockstep toward urban industrial "progress." Implications of this kind appear to be the consequence of taking whole communities as units of analysis instead of analyzing them as subunits that are affected differently by global changes and therefore respond differently to them.[6] It is not correct to say "The community is moving from a folk to an urban way of life" (or whatever terms one wishes to use), except at a certain level of analysis. It would be more accurate to say "Both folk and urban (or whatever) ways of life exist in this community, and an increasing number of individuals and families are moving from the former to the latter." Such a statement reflects differences in subcultural orientations: families may be located more or less completely in one of the subcultures or they may be somewhere between; they may be either moving or stationary. The most prominent design in this complex woven fabric, then, is the emergence of individuals and families from one subculture into another.

Conceptualizing changes in the social system of Shiloh in this way allows the analyst to place any given family on a line connecting two spheres of existence representing two subcultures. The two spheres represent relatively deep commitment to either the traditional or the modern way of life, and the line represents all the possible points of transition between the two. Although movement along this line is almost uniformly in the direction of the modern, it must nevertheless be allowed that the traditional exerts a gravitational pull of its own, even while families move away from it. These forces exerted by two ways of life represent the loyalties, personal influences, group membership, and exposures to contrasting values that make up the situational conditions of particular families.

In describing the kinds of situations in which families and family members find themselves, I am, in a way, characterizing both the situation itself and the adaptive responses that have been made to the situation or to similar previous situations. That is, one's present situation is in part determined by his responses to past situations. This important point was brought forward in an earlier discussion of subcultures, although the terms of the argument were slightly different. The conclusion reached then was that cultures can be regarded, in part, as adaptive responses to situations, as in the case of the shortened-time perspectives of the lower class. But subcultures are not only responses invented for the adaptive purposes of the moment; they are relatively stable over time, are capable of being transmitted more or less intact over generations, and have the power to influence definitions of new situations. If the lower class subculture, for example (there is, of course, no such single entity), were only a response to situation, if it were only a contraculture, then it would change as the situation changes. Instead, there is usually a lag of some kind, as the stability of the subculture acts as inertia: people define new situations in old terms and value old things that may not be viable for survival under new conditions. Thus, only conceptually and never empirically can situations be separated from responses, especially on the level of culture as response.

Nevertheless it will be instructive at times if we proceed as though the situation and the response to it were empirically distinct phenomena. The situation problems of the four types of families can then be described.

Type I. There are certain discrepancies among reference groups in Type I families. It appears that members of these families must frequently ask, "Do I accept and judge myself by local standards or by those I know or think to exist on the outside?" There are immediate pressures from family and friends for a member of a Type I family to define himself in local terms. Likewise, there are contacts with the outside through what is learned in school, through travel, through the mass media, which by their very contrast with local society, might enhance local identification. One is tempted from many sides to remain a "big fish in a little pond." On the other hand, many of these same sources also pull one's identification in the opposite direction. This fact is especially true of schools, mass media, and personal contacts on the outside, as well as any other agent of influence that tends to define individuals in the context of larger social circles.

Thus, for example, storekeepers are faced with the dilemma of meeting the expectations of personal services on the part of his tradition oriented customers and running an efficient business as it might be run on the outside. The ambiguity toward tourists and the tourist industry is also related to this discrepancy between local and outside standards. Another symptom of the identification problem is the sensitivity to outsiders' criticisms and stereotypes.

Another example of this kind of discrepancy in reference groups is offered by the case of Craig Bowman, who is uncertain how he should define success for himself. By local standards he is already successful in business, occupies a position of leadership in his church, lives in one of Shiloh's newer homes, and is personally liked and respected by everyone. But occasionally he will see a fraternity brother from college, especially one who has a five-figure annual income as a salesman, and he wonders if he could not have made it that big on the outside himself. He is sure he could have, but, as he says, he will never know: "The worst part about it is not knowing whether I could have done it."

. . . .

Because of the discrepancy in standards, Craig is uncertain where he fits in the local scheme of things. "The other night I said there were four social classes: the low, the middle, the high, and then me, but I've decided I don't fit anywhere here—Craig, the fat, atheistic storekeeper!"

This man has found a solution in staying in the community, being the big fish, and segmenting his life into two spheres. An alternative that others in his situation have found viable is that of migrating to the outside, where presumably they can live by one set of standards. But costs are incurred by this adaptive maneuver, too, because one leaves behind him the safety and security of the little pond, especially his family of orientation. When he returns home, he must attempt again to leave the outside behind him and live by local standards. Thus he segments his life, playing to the local reference groups at home and trying to be his more worldly self on the outside.

. . . .

An interview with a Type I 30-year-old migrant to the outside who had returned home for his vacation revealed that he was cognizant of some of the costs of migration.

> *Interviewer:* Have you ever thought of coming back here?
>
> *Informant:* I think about it a lot. The cost of living in Knoxville or any big city is awfully high. But it's more than just the cost of living. I guess once a person is raised up here it's harder to get it out of you. The people are a lot friendlier. People live at a slower pace; there's not all the hustle and bustle of the city.
>
> *Interviewer:* How do you feel about your present work in Knoxville?
>
> *Informant:* It's a good job and it pays well. I get awfully tense at work, though. It's all the minor details that eat on you. I do exercises every morning and they help the tenseness. This week at home I've been running up and down the road and soaking up the sun to get back in shape.

There appear to be three positions one can take with regard to the reference group dilemma, regardless of whether he is a migrant or stays in the community. The first is that he can take his cues

entirely from the local group, as sometimes happens even when people move out—some of these outmigrants apparently do not even attempt to adapt to their new situations, but continue to define themselves in terms of past situations at home. Second, he can take his cues from outside reference group. If he does this and chooses also to remain in his home community, he must turn his back on local reference standards and groups either flagrantly or covertly. It appears a little easier to choose this alternative if he moves out of the community and immerses himself in contemporary society. Even in these new situations, he may feel marginal and show the signs of overconformity that often accompany marginal membership in a highly desired group; he may become highly competitive and achievement-oriented, or he may adopt conspicuous consumer patterns: several cars, a boat, a new house, expensive clothes. The third position consists of taking cues from both local and outside groups, the position most likely to be taken insofar as an individual is probably in contact with representatives of both worlds, no matter whether he has stayed home or has migrated to the outside. This position amounts to remaining in the dilemma, which is probably resolved from situation to situation through the individual's segmenting his personality and behavior rather than being permanently solved through commitment to one side or the other. The member of any given Type I family, of course, will probably adopt all three positions over a long period of time, but like the pendulum that swings between the extremes, it seems likely that they will naturally come to rest in the middle of the dilemma.
. . . .

Related to this dilemma of reference groups, but analytically separable from it, is the problem in intergenerational differences that sometimes occurs between parents and grandparents. The problem that Kaplan referred to as "the changing role of the aged" is created partly by the underlying phenomenon of generational differences, for if the younger generation had not changed its outlook and way of life the older persons in the family probably would not feel so strongly that they had been "put on the shelf."[7] A lack of meshing of generational gears creates problems on both sides. For the younger generation, the older family members represent a substantial pull toward an older way of life and thus may constitute part of the reference bind. For the older generation, the younger family members may represent the same kind of pull in the opposite direction, which puts them in a bind between wanting to be progressive yet wanting to hold onto the cherished ways of a lifetime.

In the situation of one Type I family the differences between parental and grandparental generations are played down by means of a sort of compromise between them. The widowed grandfather, who in fact lives in his son's household along with his daughter-in-law and four grandchildren, seldom gives advice and does not make his presence felt in an authoritative way. He spends his days visiting his son's store and chatting with friends who stop there. At home at night, he reads the paper in his own chair, sits back and watches whatever television program the rest have chosen, and retires at his own discretion. He lives his own life, but in a most unobtrusive way. Likewise, the son and his family do not seem to intrude into his father's life. Any differences existing between the son and his family orient themselves more toward local than outside reference groups and individuals, so that the older man's expectations of himself are not as inconsistent as they might otherwise be.

In another Type I family situation a clearer gap exists between the same two generations, where the grandmother seems less willing to compromise some of her ways and her daughter is more oriented toward outside groups than the son just discussed. The daughter married into a Type I situation, and she and her husband live alone, their only child having died some years ago. The grandmother lives in another part of the community. The adaptive technique used to keep down intergenerational tensions in this case is segregation, where each person more or less keeps out of the other's way. Even here, however, there is an element of compromise, for the daughter conforms behaviorally to her mother's expectations when she is around her.

> *Interviewer:* I wonder if maybe there are differences of outlook and differences of opinion between generations—differences between father and son or mother and daughter.

> *Informant:* Yes, that happens, I know from myself. The older people are a lot stricter—I guess they are what you would call "better" people than we are. There are differences between the way my mother and me sees things. This is just one little example, but maybe it will show you what I mean.

> My mother don't think it's right to wear Bermuda shorts. When she raised us up we were always full dressed, and if she caught us wearing short shorts, like some girls do now, she'd have killed us. I don't wear short shorts now, of course, but I do wear Bermudas—and she still says things to me when she sees me wearing them. She'll say, "Well, I raised you to be a lady," or something like that.

> *Interviewer:* What do you do when you have differences like that? Go ahead anyway?

> *Informant:* Yes, just go ahead. But I don't purposely do things around her I know she don't

> like. I don't wear shorts when I go visit her. Some-
> times she'll catch me here with them, but I won't
> go to her house wearing them. You have to—I
> guess the word is "respect"—people like that. Of
> course a lot of the new younger generation is more
> callous, it seems like. I think you have to respect
> these older people my mother's age.

. . . .

There are other kinds of situational problems and dilemmas facing members of Type I families which should also be mentioned,
though most of them appear to be related in some way or other to
the basic reference group dilemma. For example, certain modulated
anxieties naturally attend the playing of new roles. Persons living
in Shiloh spend a great deal of time playing to local audiences, and
most are well-practiced in playing roles (such as "good old boy" or
"pillar of the church"). They are not (and this includes most Type
I's) so well rehearsed in playing nonlocal roles to audiences from
outside. There is some self-consciousness about speech habits, educational deficits, and other elements of the Snuffy Smith stereotype.
There is sometimes almost too great an effort to let the outsider
know that they have kept up with the latest news and the latest
controversies on the outside, and that Shiloh, or at least some elements there, are not as isolated as the outsider might think.

. . . .

Type II. There is, in one sense, only a shade of difference between the situations of Type I and Type II family members; in this
sense it is only a matter of the degree to which families have committed themselves to a certain way of life, the degree to which they
can effectively muster resources in pursuit of these goals, and have
emerged into the modern subculture. Type II's are generally newer
to the scene than Type I's and are more unfamiliar with the scripts.
In fact, in some respects they have not always recognized that they

In his dormitory room, College of William and Mary
freshman Stephenson interrupts his studies to have his picture taken.

are undergoing a cultural transformation. The Type I's are therefore at an advantage, since they more or less openly repudiate the
old-fashioned and the local ways of life; this leaves only one subcultural avenue clearly open to them. The Type II's are not as certain of the direction they want to take, though they are committed
at least to certain elements of the modern way. Their occupations
are evidence of great involvement in nontraditional patterns, for
their jobs require a kind of punctuality, self-discipline, and subor-
dination of personal freedoms from restraint characteristic of modern industrial life. Like the typical situations of Type I families, many
Type II wives work outside the home for wages or salaries. The
houses, clothes, and cars belonging to Type II families look very

much like what one would expect to find among middle-middle and lower-middle class families on the outside, evidence that there is considerable commitment to the value of acquiring material goods and conveniences, rather than a commitment to doing without, which we found characteristic of the traditional way of life. Furthermore, Type II families often attend the modernist churches in Shiloh, just as Type I's invariably do.

It is easy, however, to be carried away by the points of similarity and be tempted to dismiss this whole segment of the community as merely a less affluent copy of Type I's. A closer inspection will reveal that the situation of the typical family Type II is considerably at variance from that of Type I, that the situation of the former present more adaptive problems to its members, and that the former has fewer resources with which to deal with its problems.

. . . .

In the area of the family itself, on the surface there appears little difference between the pattern of working wives in Type I and Type II families: many wives in each type work outside the home. Yet there is usually a difference in the formal authority structure and in the attitudes of Type II's about the phenomenon of working wives. The husband is somewhat more the boss of the Type II household, whereas Type I's seem more equalitarian. Equally significant, he is quite sensitive in many cases about this business of changing sex roles. In one unusual case there is a man who takes it all placidly, but this may be because he commutes to work for most of the week in a city thirty-five miles away—he is not home much even on weekends, when he likes to fish or exercise his coon dogs or join his buddies—and authority problems have little meaning when the potential antagonists do not interact. In the more typical case, the Type II man condones his wife's working as an economic necessity, but he still feels that his word should carry final authority. One man whose wife does not work, and who can perhaps therefore afford to express his more traditional sex-role attitudes, shows his keen sensitivity to female domination. His explanation of the phenomenon is also interesting in that it places blame on the men. He is referring to another family in the community in which the wife is seen as too dominating:

> I wouldn't put up with a woman like that. Almost every time they go somewhere, you'll hear her start in on "Henry, let's go home," "Henry, it's getting late," and so on like that. It kind of ruins the whole thing for everybody, like when you're all trying to sing. Now my wife ain't like that—if *she* acted like that, I'd tell her the next time she'd just have to stay home. One thing with these bossy wives, now, I'll have to say a lot of men have brought it on theirselves by not working and making their women work to pay the bills. I don't mean that, all the cases are like that but some of them are.

It appears that whereas in the Type I family situation the adaptive problems of working wives and changing sex roles have already been worked out fairly satisfactorily in favor of a relatively equalitarian arrangement (only one exception comes to mind of a husband who is hypersensitive on this matter), Type II families have not yet come completely to terms with them. Again, this would appear to be because they have one foot in each subculture, one of which prescribes the more modern arrangement, the other of which prescribes a formal patriarchal system of authority. A man in this situation probably sees neither and both as completely right, and so he allows his wife to work and to exert some authority in the home, but still tends defensively to claim patriarchal rights when playing to nonfamily audiences, or else avoids the issue by spending most of his time away from home. The issue is also sometimes avoided by the fact that marital partners are scheduled for different shifts and thus seldom interact with each other. Both partners are involved in external economic functions and internal housekeeping duties to some extent. These are in the nature of makeshift adaptational solutions to a problem which takes time to work out under any circumstances, but which is made doubly difficult because the family situation involves two inconsistent and competing definitions of the proper marital relationship.

Type II family members, like those of Type I, have the three basic alternatives of being completely modern, completely traditional, or resting in the middle of the dilemma. None has chosen the traditional altogether, even though it may hold some attraction, and yet none has all the skills, background, or knowledge totally to take on the modern. The Type II seems sometimes resentful that others are more fully enmeshed in outside ways than he is, and this resentment, combined with the traditional emphasis on "being as good as anybody," leads to a kind of defensiveness and competitiveness, directed at higher status groups. At the same time, there is sometimes a partial repudiation of those parts of one's past or of one's relatives and friends which smack of backwardness. The competitiveness, a trait that has doubtless helped to move families and individuals up the social ladder, runs against the traditional grain and tends to alienate tradition-oriented friends and relatives.

. . . .

Type III. At first glance, Type III family situations seem merely to shade off from those of Type II, just as the latter seemed to be the same basic situation as found among Type I's. But again, there appear to be enough differences between the two family types to warrant distinguishing their situational problems. There are similarities in reference group problems and sometimes in the areas of changing sex roles and religion, but on the whole there is a different flavor of life in the Type III situation, a different approach to the solution of problems; in short, a different type of family. Underlying both the problems and the responses to them are the twin facts that Type III families live between two cultural worlds and that they have not yet made up their minds whether to hold to the old or change to the new.

Not as many Type III wives work outside the home as do Types I and II, although an increasing number hold jobs at factories, work part time as store clerks, and a very few have their own income from picking evergreens. Those who do help with home finances usually do not overstep their traditional bounds and attempt to dictate how it should be spent. This is generally left to the man, as part of his role as patriarch. The significant exception to this pattern is the number of women who keep back part or all their earnings and run their own accounts at the store separately from that of their husbands. Type III men, like many Type II's, are quite ambivalent about women working and are very sensitive about the women's "taking over." These men may have grounds for concern.

Women appear to have great influence—albeit an informal, submerged influence—in setting family goals and in keeping families on the march toward them. This pattern is true even among type III families, in spite of the fact that superficial observation reveals a picture of straight-forward patriarchalism. There appears to be, in fact, a battle of the sexes going on in many Type III families, in which the women are attempting to lead their families toward a more modern way of life and the men try to maintain their families in that relatively effortless state of traditional life which seems natural and adequate. John Henry Sommers said one day: "I guess maybe the women are more dissatisfied than the men. They want to have more. I tell you, that's ruint more around here—women going to work and making money, helping with the payments and such as that. They get to wanting more say in things." The situation is prevented from becoming a true battle because the women usually take pains to avoid totally alienating their men, primarily by acting the traditional submissive role. For example, one couple is considered by many local people (mainly Types II and III men in the neighborhood or in the family) to be the most outstanding case of female dominance in the community, and it cannot be denied that the wife, Lois, does exert a great deal of control over the family. In fact, for her efforts in raising her family to a higher level of living than her friends, neighbors, and relatives (through suggesting to and nagging her husband, Henry), she has won the contempt of many people. She would deny her bossiness, however, and would choose the traditional role of the female if asked which role was more appropriate. The following are notes made after an informal gospel sing at Henry's house.

> Between songs at Henry's tonight I asked what they all thought the woman's place in the family ought to be. Lois spoke up first and said, "According to the Bible they ain't supposed to leave the home, and they're supposed to obey their man. I don't guess they ought to vote, either, but I did this time." Hope said she voted for the first time this last time, but that she didn't think she would any more. John Henry said he thought it was a good thing for women to vote, but that they ought to vote the same way their men did. Henry said he didn't think the Bible meant for men to boss their wives around like it might sound.
>
> Lois offered her interpretation concerning the Biblical injunction: "I think it means a man and woman should love one another and come to agreements on things and not just tell one an-

other what to do. The man shouldn't just decide
something and then tell his wife and expect her
to go along all the time."

. . . .

In this *sub rosa* battle of the sexes the women have built up a
kind of ideological justification for their subversive (from most
males' points of view) activities: they blame the men themselves.
Thus, the argument goes, if the men would get out and make something of themselves and take care of their families as they ought to
instead of loafing around and hunting and fishing and drinking,
the women wouldn't have to go to work.[8] Some of the men accept
this argument; others counter it with the claim that the extra money
from women working wouldn't be necessary if women didn't want
so many things that weren't really necessary—things the men think
people could well do without. . . .

The real complaint of the women seems to be not that the men
don't provide, but that they do not share the same sense of values
as their wives. What the women see as inadequate provision is only
part of this larger complaint. Thus, Type III wives for the main part
are trying to domesticate their husbands, i.e., convert them to a
more modern set of aspirations. This domestication take many
forms, only one of which is nagging. The women generally take
aim at the activities and people they see as dragging their husbands
in the wrong (traditional) direction: "That Hope is not entirely satisfied with John Henry's way of life was made clear this evening
when she asked if I had seen a newspaper article about a woman
suing her husband for divorce because he was spending more time
with his dogs than with his family. She laughed and said she thought
she'd try that." Worse than hunting or fishing or loafing is the drinking enjoyed by many Type III men. Few go on wild sprees, but many
enjoy having "a little sociable drink" whenever they can. The women

do not drink (with rare exceptions), and they don't like their men to drink.

. . . .

Outside the nagging, the wife's greatest instrument for domestication of the male is the church. It could not be maintained that a man's "getting right with the Lord" and his "living right" is the same as his being converted to the modern way of life; there are many inconsistencies between the fundamentalist gospel and the demands of middle-class success-seeking. Rather, if a man becomes a Christian (by the local fundamentalist definition), he has become at least stripped of certain loyalties and habits that presumably can be replaced by ones more relevant to success-seeking. In short, becoming a Christian is a good step toward making a man over into what a woman thinks he ought to be.

. . . .

John Henry's case is a good example of what happens in many Type III family situations, where the wife strives toward emergence into the modern while the husband, at best, tags along reluctantly. In this situation there is a constant tug of war between John Henry and the forces of progress represented by Hope, the church, the children to some extent, and his creditors. There may well be a tug of war within John Henry himself, for he is not so totally committed to the traditional that he sees no value in certain creature comforts and other advantages of progress. Still, he hangs back, unsure. And lined up on his side against the forces for progress are most of his peers, with whom he can daily or weekly escape into the woods and live the uncomplicated life. These are his compatriots in tradition.

The following excerpts from field notes may show the kind of dilemma a Type III man can find himself in when caught between these forces:

Two preachers are helping with the revival. The two of them have been taking turns about eating with various members of the congregation. Tonight they eat at Hope's.

John Henry is almost frantic. He feels very uncomfortable with one preacher in his home, and two is two too many. He begged me to stay for supper tonight of all nights, saying, "I ain't too good at this sort of thing. Come on in here and set down. You can't let me down now." [In this situation I was lined up on the side of tradition.] For one thing, he is afraid they might go to work on him to get right with the Lord, and while he hates not to go along with what somebody else wants of him, he just isn't having any right now. For another thing, he is afraid he will have to go to church tonight, and going to church would knock him out of a coon-hunting date. But Hope is happy.

And again, four nights later:

Tonight the preacher came by and applied a little more pressure. He asked John Henry if he didn't think it was time to change his ways. In fact, he told him it was time. These are the most dangerous ("parlous") times that's ever been. You don't know what might happen to you. So many people are getting killed in cars these days, etc. You don't know which day might be your last, so you'd better get right while you can. John Henry told him he knew he was a sinner and he ought to do better, but he felt he couldn't claim to be a Christian knowing that he really wasn't. . . . He and the preacher agreed it was better to be an honest sinner than a hypocritical Christian. John Henry adroitly steered the conversation to other matters.

Afterwards, when the preacher and Hope had gone to the revival, he reflected: "You know, it does make a man feel kindly bad, something like that. But I still think being an honest sinner is better than being a hypocrite, don't you?"

It is obvious that the Type III situation is not only awkward for the males but for the females as well. In some ways, in fact, they have a more difficult set of scripts to balance than the men do, since they must play, to some extent, the modern mother, the traditional wife, and the fundamentalist churchwoman. How does a woman spur the ambitions of her children and at the same time play the submissive, traditional female role to her husband? How can she be a good churchgoer and at the same time strive for emancipation from the past to emerge into the wider world? How does she act toward her husband's friends? They are, after all, his friends, even if they do drag him off to go drinking and spend time away from home when he should be putting water in the house. The problems of the wife and mother in Type III situation thus can be seen as reciprocals of many of those of the husband and father.

. . . .

Family roles are also played out against the background of increasing occupational involvement of women in this and other, higher levels in the community. As the assessment of the situation by John Henry given below indicates, greater involvement of women in this external, instrumental function naturally leads to their more direct involvement in decisionmaking processes. It also indicates that this changing pattern affects not only those women and men directly associated with the change through the wife's employment but also a number of nonemployed wives and their husbands.

> I guess there has always been some women that sort of run the family, but I believe this thing of women going to work has had something to do with this that you're talking about, don't you? I mean, when a woman goes out and makes money, and maybe the man gets down and can't work for a while and she has to meet payments and stuff like that. I'd think she'd want some say about more things. That'd be natural, don't you think?

> Tell you something else about this woman business. I think some of these women that do work has some influence on the ones that don't. Like they might get to talking to one another: "Why don't you do this or that?" or "Why don't you make him quit laying out?" or things like that. You know how they'll do sometimes.

. . . .

The responses of the women to the problems inherent in their situations have this . . . twofold quality: they can go either way, toward the traditional or toward the modern, depending on the demands of the situation. It is clearer in their cases, however, that beneath it all they have decided that they and their children are going to find a place under a larger sun than their menfolk are. One might say that whereas the men compromise in order to gain time to live the traditional way a little longer, the women compromise in order more effectively to reach their long-term aspirations for a higher level of living and a fuller participation in a larger social system.

If change "upward" or "downward" occurs, it seems likely that what will determine from which direction the push comes is the economic situation of these families. Largely because of the wife's influence, most Type III families buy on credit, paying monthly for stoves, refrigerators, television sets, pianos, cars, and housing improvements such as running water and indoor sanitary facilities. As Type III families attracted to the new comfort and status of shiny modern gadgetry, they are becoming enmeshed in an economic system that requires a fairly dependable source of cash income and, thus, steady work habits and other attributes more suited to life in industrialized society. As long as this process of increasing involvement in the economy remains stable, these families will probably move into modernism at a gradual and steady pace. Sudden economic reverses, on the other hand, or other major crises would probably set in motion the more basic traditional response patterns learned early in life, so that the movement of Type III families under these circumstances would be "downward."

The discussion of adaptive problems on the level of Type III families has concentrated on those aspects of the situation which demand inconsistency in the role performances of members. It is realized that other kinds of adaptive problems exist, both for Type III and for the other family types, but it is felt that this reference bind is the problem which is at the same time most central to most family members and most directly related to the change processes occurring in Shiloh. There are other kinds of adaptive problems, among them the problems presented by temporary migration of the husband and the resulting role gap in the family, the problem of deciding whether to remain in the community or gamble on making it better on the outside at the cost of weakening home ties, and the special problems of the very young who daily are faced at school with a way of life that must be reconciled with life outside the classroom. There are also doubtless special problems for the older family member, although it appeared to me that families on the Type III level had not yet begun to nuclearize to the extent of segregating older persons, who were included in households and in family interactions to a much greater extent than in higher level families. . . .

Type IV. Once again the Type IV families present a somewhat different order of situational problem from those found among other types of families. Unlike Type I families, they are for the most part not committed to the modern way of life; unlike Type II and Type III families, they are not even very undecided; they are committed to the ways of tradition. These are people who have by and large lived the farthest back in the coves and away from the main roads. Their geographic situation is, perhaps not coincidentally, indicative of their social and cultural situation, in that they have lived out of the mainstream of American society and out of the currents of change that have swept through the local community. Their geographic situation is symbolic in another way, too, because change has brought roads, power lines, and people past many of these once-isolated cabins and shacks, and it has become more difficult for these people to ignore the new ways of life. Thus, the problems of the type IV family can be characterized as problems of retreat rather than problems of assault or indecision; problems of simultaneously insulating oneself from the demands of this larger system which increasingly intrudes itself on one's affairs, while managing to survive within it.

The situation can legitimately be called one of intrusion because, in distinction to Type III's who to some extent go to meet outsiders naturally in the course of their daily round of life and work, the members of Type IV families seldom take the initiative in interacting with people who are oriented toward outside ways. Rather, except for occasional trips to the store, the doctor, or the evergreen wholesaler (or perhaps occasional jobs), they stay to themselves by and large, visiting among themselves and going to church and picking galax together as their major forms of social activity.

The intrusion can be illustrated in a number of ways. For example, Type IV families live closer now to roads and highways, not because they have moved toward them, but because the roads have grown out to reach them. They are nearer to telephones for the same reason. And for the same reason they are nearer to neighbors who live on a somewhat higher level and are more involved in the modern subculture, so that the visibility of alternative ways of thinking and living is higher. Likewise, when outlanders from Florida and other areas come to the mountains to search out summer havens, they look for the remote, Waldenesque settings such as Type IV families now inhabit, and more times than not they settle within shouting distance from some such family, so that, again, the visibility of outside ways is increased and the insulation of the purely traditional is broken. The expressed attitude of these summer residents might be called one of peaceful coexistence, but it is hardly one of respect. One man who plans to live in Shiloh about five months out of the year said: "There's one thing you can say about these local people: they just aren't interesting people. You have exhausted all possible conversation in about twenty minutes. They are mostly honest, sometimes hardworking, but they are living a vegetable existence." This man wants to find somebody in Shiloh who is conversant in his field of international relations. Another summer resident from Florida says he wants to preserve the backwardness of the area, because that is what attracted him to it.

. . . .

It is true that tourists and summer residents have some influence on *all* types of families in Shiloh. They have contact with the local entrepreneurs, who are mostly from Type I families, in their initial entry into the community and in church and social activities after they have settled there. Their influence on that level is in providing role models from outside the region for persons who wish to become assimilated into middle-class American society. On the other hand, they have considerable contact with Type IV families, who are their neighbors, and whom they hire to work for them at odd jobs. For some Type IV's these outsiders may be role models, but for the majority they are only reminders of what they themselves are not and do not especially want to be—in short, negative reference figures. As the last informant noted: "These local people are perceptive, very perceptive. People who come up here and 'put on a show' are not accepted. I guess you could say there is a resentment of what they think is an unnecessary display of money and education." He feels that outsiders provide positive role models for the young and better educated: "The young, the educated people see us and see that the outside is different from what they have known. They see that the old people just don't have it. Outsiders are coming in and changing the philosophy." But, he should have added, this is not so in the cases of most Type IV's, where even he noticed resentment.

. . . .

It is not only tourists and summer residents who are bringing elements of contemporary outside society to the doorsteps of Type IV families, though they provide a clear example. Also noteworthy in this connection are the agents of programs conceived outside the region which are aimed in one way or another at upgrading living conditions and changing attitudes. In addition to the county department of public welfare, agencies of both the federal and state wars on poverty were active in Shiloh during the summer the fieldwork was conducted, and their activities were directed at many of the families classified here as Type IV. It was too soon to tell what the impacts of these skirmishes were, but attitudes toward the war on poverty in general were mixed, regardless of level of the community.

. . . .

Certainly it could not be claimed that the traditional subculture is the perfect solution to the life situation of Type IV families and that problems only occur because of the interference of middle-class people from outside it. Even if the participants were completely isolated from modernity, there still would be the problems that seem to accompany poverty everywhere. Chief among these is finding a way to make a living or a way to supply the necessities for physical survival. There are problems of illness, family crises of various sorts, problems of unplanned parenthood (including illegitimacy), housing, diet, and transportation, to name but a few. Furthermore, it is plausible that shortened-time perspectives and the devaluation of the success motive, as well as other aspects of the traditional subculture have played a positive role in that this negative outlook has prevented disappointments and has allowed for adaptations that a less relaxed set of standards would not have permitted. It has also presented a kind of cushion in its stress on familism and the importance of personal relationships, for persons who could not find social supports in any other system (people who would have failed for one reason or another to achieve success as defined in another system).

. . . .

Certain problems would have remained, even if the modern way of life had not intruded upon these people. But since the intrusion has happened and is happening, it is changing the requirements and definition of successful survival and therefore has raised the problem of adaptation to an entirely different plane. For if one takes seriously the messages sent by the ambassadors from modernism, not only must he cope more vigorously with the problems he has been coping with for generations, but he must also give up the adaptive tools he has used to cope with them, since those tools—elements of the traditional—are themselves seen as part of the objectionable problem. Not only has the terrain changed, but the guide map is being taken away. It seems to me, then, that the major adaptive problem confronting most Type IV families is not illegitimacy or personal pathology or joblessness by themselves, but that of preserving a culture and a mode of adaptation being withdrawn slowly from them. The response to this threat could naturally be expected to be in a traditional vein; it amounts to a withdrawal, a retreat, an attempt to insulate oneself from an alternate way of life clamoring for attention on all sides.

. . . .

The school is another aspect of the Type IV situation, for the school is a great window to the outside and the contemporary. For Type I's, the educational system is a means to consolidating status gains and moving on to greater accomplishments, and for Type II's and many Type III's (especially the women) it is a place to send your children so that they can have something better than you have. For Type I's a college education usually is assumed. For Type II's a high school education is hoped for, and for Type III's a high school education is not so likely as completion of the eighth or ninth grade. But for most Type IV's, education is something for other people; Type IV's usually have few hopes for their children getting as far as high school. The children of these families may not do as well in school as other children (this is one of the premises of Project Headstart, at any rate). It is almost a certainty that they feel self-conscious about their appearances, especially in consolidated schools where there are enough pupils from different levels of the community to form a miniature copy of the community stratification system. One young lady frankly admitted that she did not like school after she started attending the ninth grade at the consolidated high school. People there were different, she said, and she just never could get used to it.

But mainly, the parents do not seem to see the relevance of a formal education for the probably future circumstances of their children (if they see the future at all). They have heard that it is important and they sense the truth and meaning of the advertised correlation between education and income, and in fact many are able to pronounce the value of education in glowing terms just like everyone else; or not quite like everyone else, because one wonders if they really believe what they are saying. . . .

> Carl Patrick wants to see his children get through high school and would like for them to go on to college, although he is very doubtful that the family can afford the latter and he was not . . . insistent on the former in view of the increasing costs of sending them to school. He himself went to the seventh grade, as did his brothers. He recognizes the need for a high school education in order to get good employment. He expressed no regret that he did not have such a background, though he did seem pre-occupied with fancied ways of making money and getting jobs. He is somewhat ambivalent about education, as he states that he "learned more in the Army about getting along—just common sense—than I learned all the time I was going to school," and that "experience is the best teacher."

Some parents reject "too much education" outright because it is "misused," "and "brings harm." The schools and education are rejected on religious grounds because "There's too much science taught," "It leads people away from the Lord," and "There's too much worldly foolishness." (Some also object to the Boy Scouts because it is a "worldly" organization.)

Nevertheless, the children are under the jurisdiction of the school for at least several years, so that the school does constitute part of the total family situation. The children's response to the school varies between apathy and acceptance, the difference apparently hinging on how well they are doing at the moment and what alternative are available to them. Different from pure apathy is an expression of hatred or resentment of school which is sometimes shown. Recent dropouts particularly seemed to center their reasons for quitting school around the resentment of certain teachers. The alternative to apathetic or resentful withdrawal from the school and what

John and Jane Baucom, a fellow teacher at Lees-McRae College,
cut their wedding cake after their marriage in 1962 in Banner Elk, North Carolina.

it represents is willful involvement in it, and some Type IV children do take the school's messages seriously. What happens when these children return home after school then becomes a problem, both for the children, who must compare what should be with what is and will be, and for the parents, whose own children are now lining up with the other representatives from the outside world, thereby becoming intruders in their own homes. This problem of intergenerational differences can be expected to become a greater one if programs like Project Headstart succeed in their aims, although at the present it does not seem to be serious.

The Type IV situation, then, is one of attempted withdrawal from a social system in which such families are increasingly becoming enmeshed. Some of the avenues of withdrawal are retreat into the family and the neighborhood. For the men there is also the traditional retreat into the woods. Last, one may retreat into one's self or into alcohol. None of these solutions is completely satisfactory, for all of them provide semipermeable membranes through which the outside way of life can seep. Some of them incur even higher costs than the original problems themselves; at best, most are temporary coping devices and not long-term adaptive solutions.

Measuring Modernism

In the same year (1968) that *Shiloh* was published John had an article accepted by the *American Journal of Sociology,* one of the leading professional journals in the field. The article, entitled "Is Everyone Going Modern? A Critique and a Suggestion for Measuring Modernism," was based on the Shiloh study. Within the broader context of social change, the article focused on some of John's concerns with the nature of such change and how its direction could be measured. How, for example, could one tell if a community like Shiloh was becoming more modern and, if so, whether it was proceeding at a faster or slower pace than other communities?

In this article he distinguished between the concepts of *modernization* and *modernism*. The former referred to a sociocultural change from a more traditional state to a more modern set of beliefs and values. *Modernism* was a measure of the degree to which individuals subscribed to the beliefs and values considered to be modern. A basic assumption of the measurement of modernization was that within a society or community such as Shiloh the greater the proportion of its members who subscribed to modernistic beliefs and values, the greater the extent to which modernization had taken place.

John was disturbed by the assumption that the cultural traits considered modern or traditional by social investigators were viewed the same way by the members of the society being studied. For example, to use one of his own measurement items, was the belief that "The old, small neighborhood school was better than the new consolidated school" indicative of a traditional viewpoint? Most outside "experts" on the subject of social change would probably agree that it was. But if the residents themselves did not identify the belief as related to traditionalism and modernism, should it still be considered a valid indicator?

John also questioned the assumption of many investigators engaged in cross-cultural studies of modernization that measures of modernism in one society were equally applicable to other societies. "It would appear," he wrote, "that the search for change-universals (so that one can emerge from his studies with the conclusion that 'everything is changing in the direction of X') has biased measures in favor of this discovery."

In raising the issues about the validity of assumptions concerning the universality of modernization indicators, John cited a well-known study by David Horton Smith and Alex Inkeles that had compared modernity in six different countries ("The O-M Scale: A Comparative Socio-Psychological Measure of Individual Modernity," *Sociometry* 29 [December 1966]: 353–77). Inkeles, at that time a professor at Harvard University and director of an international project on social and cultural aspects of economic development, was apparently upset by some of the issues raised in the article. Consequently he prepared a lengthy commentary that appeared in the *American Journal of Sociology* the following July ("A Commentary on 'Is Everyone Going Modern?'" *American Journal of Sociology* 75 [July 1969]: 146–50).

Inkeles was particularly annoyed by John's statement that "If no differentiation is made in the culture between traditionalism and modernism, then movement along the dimension cannot be recognized by the participants, and study of modernization in this cultural setting is meaningless." In his comments Inkeles strongly defended the validity of the modernism indicators developed by social scientists and based on theoretical considerations. He conceded, however, that "The theoretically derived measure of modernity is not, in any absolute sense, better than one based on the views of social informants" (p. 151).

John was both shaken and somewhat flattered by Inkeles' commentary. He had certainly not expected that a Harvard professor of some considerable standing in the field would bother to respond to his article, which was the first he had ever published as sole author. At the same time, Inkeles' comments could hardly be considered laudatory, despite the perfunctory introductory statement that "In my estimation John P. [*sic*] Stephenson has made a contribution to the measurement of attitudinal modernity in his paper 'Is Everyone Going Modern?'

Invited by the journal to respond to Inkeles' criticisms, John prepared a rejoinder whose temperate tone masked the inner agitation of a young assistant professor being challenged by a leading scholar in his field. John's response, which is reprinted in this collection, was published in the same issue as Inkeles' commentary. In it, John clarified the term "meaningless" that had roused Inkeles' ire, pointing out that it referred to participants in a culture, not to those who were studying it. That is, if the members of a culture did not perceive change in terms of a movement from traditional to modern, then the concept of modernization was meaningless to them. While agreeing that his modernism scale, based on the perceptions of the members of the changing culture, served a different purpose from Inkeles' scale constructed by expert observers, John still questioned why the correlation between the two types of scales was so low when both were used. It is a question that has still not been adequately answered.

IS EVERYONE GOING MODERN? A CRITIQUE AND A SUGGESTION FOR MEASURING MODERNISM[1]

The Problem

A. Current Interest in Social Change

The attention of social scientists has turned back again to the subject of change. Within the past fifteen years, neglect of the study of social dynamics has changed to active interest, as indicated by the increased number of articles in professional journals on the nature and consequences of change at various levels and in a variety of institutional areas—politics, economics, religions, for example—and of change in culture as well as social organization. In this growing body of literature different types of changes are given somewhat confusing and like-sounding labels, such as democratization, development, industrialization, urbanization, secularization, and modernization.[2] Agreement is not perfect, but it probably would be generally accepted that, whereas the terms "development" and "industrialization" are used to describe mainly economic growth, and urbanization is used to describe shifts in population dispersion and concentration, the concept of modernization has to do with a transformation of culture and of personality insofar as it is influenced by culture, rather than of some aspect of social organization or of human ecology.[3] This paper is concerned with modernization in the cultural and personality sense, and more particularly with *measurements* of modernism.

B. Measures of Modernism

It should be made clear that moder*nization* is not the same as moder*nism*. The idea of moder*nization* is that there is an alteration or a movement of something from a more traditional state to a more modern state from one point in time to another. The set of doctrines, values, or beliefs which makes up the "traditional" state is traditio*nism*, while the comparable state at the other end of the continuum—the set of "modern" beliefs and values—is moder*nism*. It is necessary to make this distinction because in discussing certain measures which purport to be indicators of "modernization," we shall find that it is not modernization itself that is measured, but the extent of modernism, or the extent to which individuals hold what are claimed to be modernist values. Changes in the proportion of people holding modern values, or changes in the extent to which individuals have "gone modern," constitute modernization. Thus, measuring modernism should be viewed as a means of assessing modernization. The latter, unlike the former, involves a temporal dimension.

The need for reliable and accurate indicators of modernism is thus obvious. Several such measures may be found in the literature, two of which will be reviewed briefly here.

In a recent article on culture change and stress in Peru, Kellert, Williams, Whyte, and Alberti look at the effects of "modernization" on symptoms of stress among a large sample of rural Peruvians.[4] We are here interested only in the three measures of modernism used by these investigators. In the first instance, "modernization" (Kellert's term for our "modernism") is measured by the degree to which individuals take sides with groups in the village representing "old custom" or "modern ideas."[5] A shortcoming of this indicator is that it does not specify the content of the old and the new ways. More serious problems in validity arise, however, with the other two indicators. One of these measures "modernization" by the amount of change in optimism or pessimism regarding the economic progress of the village.[6] The unstated assumption seems to be that the modern individual has the power of positive thinking and believes that everything is always getting better. The third indicator asks respondents whether they think the village is progressing slowly, not progressing, or going backward (no dimension of progress is specified).[7] Frankly, I need some assurance that the population under study adequately shared with the investigators the meaning of such a *yanqui* term as "progress." There is also a question regarding the relationship between perceived progress of local villages and modernism: Is this modernism to the researchers or to the respondents, or to both, or to neither?[8]

Another article, which outlines one of the most ambitious attempts yet to measure modernity, is one in which Smith and Inkeles report the cross-national application of 119–plus items which they conceptualize as relevant to individual modernity.[9] Their definition of "modern" and "modernity," with which this writer would basically agree, must be understood before describing the scales themselves.[10]

> . . . "modern" generally means a national state characterized by a complex of traits including urbanization, high levels of education, industrialization, extensive mechanization, high rates of social mobility, and the like. When applied to individuals, it refers to a set of attitudes, values and ways of feeling and acting, presumably of the sort either generated by or required for effective participation in a modern society. In this report we deal only with *individual* modernity.[11]

They proceed to describe the development of the scale:

> After reviewing the literature and defining our own theoretical position we identified some thirty topics, themes, areas, or issues which seemed relevant to a definition of modernity. . . . In this paper, unfortunately, we lack space either to define the content of any of these attitude and behavior realms or to indicate the reasons why we considered them relevant.[12]

This is indeed unfortunate, for even though the authors promise that explanations will be given in a forthcoming book, one must read the remainder of the article having faith that the areas selected either have some logical connection with the definition of modernity offered or that these areas were found to be meaningfully associated with modernism in the minds of the people to whom the scale was applied.

Application of the scale and the resulting findings lead to the conclusion that "there is an underlying dimension of psychological modernity pervading our set of 119 attitude items."[13] Reliability appears quite high. The question of validity gnaws at me throughout, however. Perhaps it is not the validity of the scale in the minds of the investigators which is open to question so much as the validity of the scale for the various populations and subpopulations studied. Smith and Inkeles are indeed convinced that they have measured what they set out to measure: "We do not see how one could do better within the limits we imposed."[14] What is open to question is whether they set out to measure the right thing.[15]

Such studies as Smith and Inkeles' appear to share another assumption which this investigator feels is open to question: namely, that all modern cultures are basically similar in content and that all persons who can be said to be "going modern" share the same traits, regardless of what culture they are part of or out of what past they have moved. What is defined as modern for one population is assumed to be indicative of modernity for any other. It would appear that the search for change-universals (so that one can emerge from his studies with the conclusion that "Everything is changing in the direction of X") has biased measures in favor of this discovery. Whether all peoples in the world are indeed moving from one particular set of values toward another particular set should be left open for empirical proof or disconfirmation.[16]

We might pause to reconsider this position in the light of Lerner's argument, based on research evidence, that "the Western model of modernization exhibits certain components and sequences whose relevance is global."[17] He observes that "the same basic model reappears in virtually all modernizing societies on all continents of the world, regardless of variations in race, color, creed."[18] Lerner's conclusion seems to provide ample justification for the assumption that traits of the modern and the traditional must be shared worldwide. Yet he notes that not every society has accepted the message of modernity in the same way. Of the Middle East he says, "Wanted are modern institutions but not modern ideologies, modern power but not modern purposes, modern wealth but not modern wisdom, modern commodities but not modern cant."[19] While pointing out basic similarities, even Lerner recognizes that the nature of modernism varies according to the specific context.[20]

Hoselitz makes a similar point regarding variations in traditionism and modernism when he says that "culture change is not unilinear, but multilinear." He points out that "different varieties of belief and attitude systems, all of which may be lumped together under the general designation 'traditional,' do exist. Hence the processes of change in these contrasting situations begin from quite different starting points, would show considerable variation, and ... the outcomes of these processes of change may vary considerably."[21]

C. An Alternative Definition of Modernism

A definition of modernization is needed which avoids the assumption that it is a universal process of unilinear change, and which avoids the assumption that the particular value contents of traditionism and modernism are everywhere the same, so that measures which follow from the definitions will not also be based on the same unfortunate assumptions. In this connection, the following definitions are suggested: *Modernization is the movement of persons or groups along a cultural dimension from what is defined by the cultural norms as traditional toward what is defined by the same culture as modern. Those values defined in the local culture as traditional comprise what may be called traditionalism; those defined as modern constitute modernism.* If no differentiation is made in the culture between traditionism and modernism, then movement along the dimension cannot be recognized by the participants, and study of modernization in this cultural setting is meaningless. If modernism and traditionism are seen by the population as different cultural entities, then measurement of change between the two becomes feasible through the measurement of changes in the extent of adherence to the particular value content of traditionism and modernism for that population.

An Illustration: the Shiloh Study

A case illustration may help demonstrate how such a definition can be put to use in actual measurement. It will be reasoned that although comparability across populations is lost, assertions about changes taking place in the population are given some empirical credibility, and assumptions about the universality of modernism and modernization need not be made. The illustration will revolve around the construction of an actual Guttman scale of modernism-traditionism for a particular population.

A. The Setting

The population under study is a small community (more precisely, a cluster of neighborhoods served in common by a school, churches, and stores) in the southern Appalachian mountains. Approximately 200–250 households are located there. The community had been relatively (but never completely) isolated until the 1940's and 1950's, when roads, schools, and mass media effectively raised the "pine curtain" between it and the rest of the country. New occupations in industry have become available to members of the community, while at the same time older forms of work in agriculture, mining, and timber have grown less economically viable. As in most other parts of the Appalachians, the population of Shiloh is almost entirely white and native-born.[22]

B. The Instrument

1. *Field survey.*——A four-month field study was conducted in Shiloh in the summer of 1965. Extensive notes were made of conversations, interviews, and observation. Among the varied statements made by the inhabitants of the community were many which indicated in local terms what it meant to be traditional and what it meant to be modern. Some informants referred, for example, to certain "oldtimey ways" or commented that to believe so-and-so was "old-fashioned." Others made reference to things that were "newfangled," "new," or "outside" (a term used synonymously with "modern"—for instance, it was once noted that a certain individual had become "minded to outside ways," that is, he had become oriented to values from beyond the mountains). Thus it was possible later to catalogue over fifty statements taken directly from field notes in which the community itself defined traditionism and modernism.

Information from the field study also made it possible to conclude that it was meaningful to study modern*ization* as a process occurring in Shiloh, since this kind of change was observed by many respondents. For example, one man noted that whereas some people stayed like their parents, others seemed to learn new ideas. More-over, some informants marked with regret the fact that many young people were leaving the old ways; others ridiculed people who were old-fashioned and wouldn't, like themselves, become more up to date. Such statements are testimony to the existence of movement from traditionism to modernism in the community; it is a kind of change meaningful to the population under study.

2. *Use of judges.*——In the winter of 1967 the fifty-odd statements referred to above were subjected to judgment by a panel of seven persons who were asked to sort them on the basis of their "tradi-tional" or "modern" content. All the judges could be considered "expert" in the sense that they had had first-hand experience with Appalachian populations and were familiar with the notions of modernism and traditionism. Three of the judges were professors of sociology who can safely be said to be recognized authorities on the Appalachian region. Two judges were Ph.D. candidates in soci-ology who have lived and worked in southern Appalachia and who can claim personal as well as academic knowledge of the people of that area. The two remaining judges were not sociologists but were individuals who had been exposed at length to the concepts of modernism and traditionism through me. They were called on for judgment primarily because of their lifelong residence among mountain people and their untrained natural capacity for analysis of those people.

The judges were required to sort statements into three piles: one which indicated a clearly "modern" attitude, one which clearly showed a "traditional" attitude, and one which showed neither and was therefore ambiguous. While systematic inquiries were not made into the criteria of classification held by the judges, comments oc-casionally were recorded which offer some insight into these stan-dards. For example, one judge observed that the task of classifying statements was clouded by mental reference to particular individu-

als who had made such statements. Another noted that it was difficult to separate the traditional-modern dimension from a dimension of social class. One judge raised the possibility that there were
several types of modernism rather than just one, a fact which raises
doubts about the unidimensionality of the items in his mind. One
of the non-sociologist judges admitted that he had been influenced
by me in his conception of modernism and traditionism, but said
also that his decisions were guided by "particular stereotypes" built
from his own experience. Again, another of the sociologists said he
was "confused because many items are multidimensional (indeed,
modernism is multidimensional)." He also encountered frustration
in attempting to keep modernism-traditionism distinct from social-
class differences. By inference from these observations, it appears
that among the criteria used for classification by these judges were
reference to particular known individuals, value differences related
to social class,[23] and conceptions obtained from me. (It appears, furthermore, that there was some discomfort among the judges when
they were required to assume unidimensionality of modernism
among an Appalachian population.)

Prior to the judging, each statement was coded to indicate which
of seven "value areas" it represented: time, achievement, work,
education, person-versus-object orientation, religion, sex role orientation. After the judging was complete, the two statements on
which there was highest agreement were chosen from each value
area to be placed in the final instrument.[24] With the addition of another last-minute insertion, the total battery of value statements
included was fifteen[25] (see Table 1). [Tables 1 and 2 that appeared in
the original article, pp. 271 and 272, have been omitted from the
discussion of scale construction here on the assumption that most
readers would not understand them.—Ed.]

3. *The larger instrument.*——The interview schedule of which the
fifteen-item modernism-traditionism battery was a part was con-

structed for the primary purpose of collecting data in order to test hypotheses about modernism, marginality, and mental health. Interviews lasted between thirty and forty-five minutes on the average and were conducted for the most part in the homes of respondents.

4. *The sample.*——The sample consists of 130 respondents who are members of "whole" families with children living at home. The sample is almost coterminous with the number of people in this category who live in Shiloh, the remainder of the population being made up of older residents and couples who have retired here from "outside." The rate of refusals, most of them by females, was around 20 per cent. Where men and their wives were both interviewed, they were questioned simultaneously in different rooms by an interviewing assistant and myself. In only a few instances were the couples interviewed sequentially by the same interviewer.

The sample includes seventy-one males and fifty-nine females. Occupations of heads of households ranged from professional, managerial, and white collar (20 respondents), through full-time blue collar, such as factory work (40 respondents), and seasonal blue collar, semiskilled and unskilled work, such as farming, mining, and timber (59 respondents), to no significant gainful employment or dependence on agency support (11 respondents). Sixty respondents could be classified as upwardly mobile, in that their jobs were higher on the above fourfold occupational scale than the jobs of their fathers. Fifty-three could be labeled non-mobile by the same criterion, and twelve were downwardly mobile.[26] These figures reflect a change in the occupational structure affecting the people of Shiloh as the community becomes "industrialized."

. . . .

Conclusions

The traditionism-modernism scale from Shiloh illustrates the kind of measurement procedure which must be followed if we are not to assume what we set out to prove. Data from an earlier field survey indicated that modernization, as we have suggested that it be defined, is occurring in the community, and that study also provided a source from which to draw a pool of value statements comprising a single "universe of content." The use of judges gave even more assurance that the items used were valid indicators of traditionism and modernism. The fact that six of the fifteen original items form a Guttman scale makes more credible the contention that we are measuring something real "out there," and that that something is what we thought it was. We have not merely imposed a measure of modernism on the population under study, but have allowed the population to tell us whether modernism exists and what form it takes.[30]

To anticipate criticism, the heaviest argument against following this kind of procedure may also turn out to be an argument in favor of it. The greatest weakness of the present scale, it will probably be maintained, is that it obtains only for the population under study. Following the same procedure with any other population would probably yield a different set of value statements and hence a different scale. Therefore, with this type of measure of modernism, it becomes impossible to compare stages of modernization across cultural groups, something which would appear highly desirable. But is it realistic to expect that modernization *could* be comparable from one culture or society to another, or is it not at the very least an empirical question? For if we assume that modernism measures are comparable and valid cross-culturally, are we not forced to assume (1) that traditionism consists of the same set of values and beliefs wherever it is found,[31] (2) that the same path is followed from traditionism to modernism, via the same value "steps," and (3) that modernism consists of the same set of values and beliefs wherever it is found? How many would be willing to make those assumptions?

Therefore, it may not be proper, even if it appears possible, to compare the traditional-modern standing of one group with that of another. The technique illustrated here will permit such comparison when it is justified.

ALEX INKELES' COMMENTS ON JOHN STEPHENSON'S "IS EVERYONE GOING MODERN?"

In my estimation John P. [*sic*] Stephenson has made a contribution to the measurement of attitudinal modernity in his paper "Is Everyone Going Modern?" (Stephenson 1968). In the course of doing so, however, he enunciates some *principles* for guiding research on this topic which should be more critically examined, and he makes some judgments of the efforts of others—including my own[1]—which I must challenge.

Stephenson urges that in selecting the criteria for measuring modern attitudes in individuals (modernism) we should use dimensions which the community being studied defines for itself as establishing a continuum from modern to traditional. If he were content to advocate this as but one approach to measurement among others also acknowledged to be legitimate, there would be little to quarrel about. But he evidently feels the need to establish a monopoly for this particular approach. He says: "If no differentiation is made in the local culture between traditionalism and modernism, then movement along the dimension cannot be recognized by the participants, and the study of modernization in this cultural setting is meaningless" (Stephenson 1968, p. 268).

Stephenson's statement itself is not meaningless, but it is scientific nonsense. It is tantamount to asserting that only the patient can decide on the proper criteria for the physician to use in deciding whether he does or does not have a particular disease. It is to say, in effect, that unless a culture accepts heightened temperature as an index of illness, and acknowledges the thermometer as an appropriate measure of temperature, it is "meaningless" to use that instrument to diagnose illness in the given culture. Impressed as I am by the wisdom of much folk medicine, I cannot see the necessity of substituting its criteria for those of medical science. Indeed, Stephenson is himself not ready to follow his own prescription. If it is really to be left to the culture to decide which are the relevant dimensions of modernism, why then did he bring in a panel of seven expert judges, five of them sociologists, to screen the statements of the local people? Such caution is probably wise. But should Stephenson not then bring his announced convictions into line with his practice?

Tests to ascertain what the people think, feel, or perceive to be the changes most relevant to judging individual modernization could certainly be a valuable component of a complete set of measures of this particular process of social change. But there will inevitably be other dimensions which the local citizens never thought of, or which are not salient to them, which a social scientist will, nevertheless, want to consider either on theoretical grounds or because he has empirical evidence from other studies to indicate they are important. Since the modernization of society is generally measured by a series of structural changes, one obvious theoretical interest is to ascertain how far attitudes and values are changing in response to the social structural transformations. An alternative sociological model would emphasize certain individual orientations as necessary elements for the functioning of a modern industrial system and would seek to establish how far a particular population was able to provide sufficient numbers of individuals with the requisite personal attributes. In either case, the attitude changes important to the sociologist might be taking place along dimensions which the local population did not conceive of as relevant to an assessment of individual modernization; which they might acknowledge to be important if questioned about them, but which are not ordinarily salient to them; or which might be salient, but could not accurately be assessed by the local citizens.

John as a member of the Department of Sociology at the
University of Kentucky, circa 1968.

To make the point concrete, let us consider joining voluntary organizations or taking an interest in world affairs. No questions touching on these themes were included in Stephenson's set of scale items, presumably because his interviewees did not identify them as salient to the local community. To include such items would, if I read Stephenson correctly, be defined by him as "meaningless." How can we know they would be "meaningless?"

I think we can easily see how they might be quite meaningful. For one thing, Stephenson is probably confusing what is *salient* to the local population with what is *relevant* to them. The people in

Shiloh did not seem spontaneously to use joining trade unions or following world news closely as ways of judging an individual's modernity. But we do not know what they would have said if Stephenson had asked them directly: "Would such attitudes and behaviors be useful in efforts to distinguish a man with 'new ways' from those who follow the 'old ways'?" In many other researches on modernization, including our own, those judged modern on other attitudinal and behavioral criteria did more often join organizations and take a strong interest in foreign as against local news. I strongly suspect that if Stephenson had put the question he would have discovered that the people in Shiloh also consider such behavior relevant in judging whether or not a man is modern.

Whatever the local people *thought* about it, the true correlation between interest in foreign news and other components of modernism can actually be known only by including such questions in the initial set tested. Since Stephenson did not include them in his questionnaire, he cannot make his assertion on the basis of fact. We did include such items in our scales of individual modernization (OM) in six developing countries, and they are in fact strongly associated with items of the type which found their way into Stephenson's own scale of modernism in Shiloh[2]. There is every reason to assume that these questions would play the same role as good indicators of individual modernity if they had been included in the test of his community.[3]

We are clearly moving over from the question of how legitimate it is to use the social scientist's criteria of modernism to the question of what difference it makes in empirical relationships. In other words, we are moving from an evaluation of validity based on theoretical grounds to a judgment of it on empirical grounds. It follows from Stephenson's position that, if we used a scale founded not on the criteria of the local community, but rather based on the allegedly "meaningless" criteria of an outside social scientist, then the indigenous scale would "work" and the scale of the social science outsider would not. That is, only the indigenous scale scores would vary significantly in relation to relevant social indicators.

What should these social indicators be? Stephenson says "one would logically expect respondents of the more traditional scale type to be older, less educated, living farther from main roads, and in more traditional occupations" (p. 273, n. 29). These are precisely the sorts of determinants of modernism which other studies have cited, both on theoretical grounds and on the basis of empirical evidence, to validate their scales of modernity. While recognizing the high reliability of our scales, Stephenson goes on to report "the question of validity 'gnaws' at me throughout." But relief for his distress was in his very hands. The same *Sociometry* article which he quotes presents one form of our modernity scale (Short Form 3) derived by the criterion method, a method which is basically a test of validity.[4] The criteria we used—education, occupation, and residence—are much the same as those used by Stephenson (p. 273, n. 29) to validate his own scale. Furthermore, we quite explicitly describe (Smith and Inkeles 1966, p. 360) as a "test of adequacy," that is, of validity, the relation of our scales "to social indices which are generally acknowledged to be associated with modernity," and report (in n. 12) five-country average correlations of .434 with education, .179 with factory experience, and .142 with rural/urban origin. It is puzzling that Stephenson's use of such criteria of validity should be sauce for his goose which apparently will be denied to our gander.

If Stephenson really meant to show that measurement based on criteria external to the community is "meaningless," he should have constructed, or borrowed from elsewhere, a scale of the type he believes to be meaningless and then tested its relation to the same structural variables—such as age, education, residence, and occupation—used to validate his scale. Since he did not do so, he has no basis of fact for making his assertions. We do have the facts, and the evidence shows Stephenson to have produced a scientific red herring.

In the Indian phase of the Harvard Project on Social and Cultural Aspects of Economic Development we explicitly addressed ourselves to the theoretical and empirical issue which Stephenson raised and then promptly settled without reference to any evidence.[5] The following quotation from our report should make it immediately obvious that we were concerned with precisely the issue raised by Stephenson: "Can there be," we asked, "an entirely local, native, culture-based measure of modernity," and if it exists, what relation does it have to the transcultural measure of modernity which the project applied indiscriminately in six developing countries? To see if there was a distinctive local concept of modernity, Singh, my Indian collaborator, constituted a group of students as a local informant panel in Ranchi, much as Stephenson conducted his interviews in Shiloh. The students did indeed suggest a set of special qualities they felt distinguished between the modern and traditional man in Bihar. The traditional man, according to these local informants, would, for example, prefer well water to tap water, a twig (*datwan*) to a toothbrush for cleaning his teeth, and a wife who automatically gave the best portions of food to her husband. Translating these ideas into questions yielded a strictly local Indian set of ten items to measure modernity, none of which did we include in our transcultural measure.[6] These special questions were then combined in a distinctive Indian, or indigenous, scale of modernity.

The correlation of this indigenous scale and the transnational scale applied to the same population was .560.[7] This result is significant far beyond the .01 level. Indeed, it compares very favorably with the best results obtained when we related the summary modernity scale (OM) to other subscales of the transnational variety.[8] Thus, while the indigenous scale is far from being identical to the transnational, the two are clearly tapping the same underlying psycho-social attributes of the individual. If the indigenous Indian scale is taken as the criterion, therefore, we can firmly assert that the scale produced by the social science outsiders, who had not consulted the local population, is nevertheless decidedly "meaningful."

An alternative to assessing the meaningfulness of the social science outsiders' scale in competition with the indigenous version is to test the relation of both to some third, preferably objective, criterion of modernization. The most appropriate test is the association between the scales and social stsructure variables. When we submitted the two scales to such a parallel test with our Indian sample, the outcome was relatively unambiguous. The transnational scale was at least equally strongly related to independent variables of the sort Stephenson identified as logical tests of the relevance of a scale of modern attitudes. For example, the correlations with education are .658 for the transcultural and .451 for the indigenous scale; in the case of residence, the Pearsonian r is, respectively, .189 and .277; and for the ethnic membership, that is, for tribal and nontribal, the coefficients are respectively, .369 and .129. On balance, the transcultural measure derived from sociological theory predicts "modern" social characteristics more accurately than does the indigenous measure constructed on the basis of advice from local informants!

Clearly the transnational scale is not a "meaningless" measure, unless the indigenous scale, constructed by exactly the same procedure as was Stephenson's, is also "meaningless." In other words, to measure individual modernity, it is not necessary to restrict oneself to themes designated by community members as relevant dimensions. Relevant dimensions can also be derived, as ours were, from sociological theory.

In affirming the meaningfulness of scales derived from theory, however, we must be careful not to commit the very error into which Stephenson fell. The theoretically derived measure of modernity is not, in any *absolute* sense, better than one based on the views of local informants. It is meant to serve a different purpose. If your purpose is to identify the way in which local people see that process of change so often called modernization, then Stephenson's method of scale construction is clearly the one you should use, although you should stick more consistently to principle than he did. If, on the other hand, your purpose is to measure attitude change on dimensions which sociological theory identifies as important because of their relation to social structure, the method we used is probably more relevant. And if your purpose is merely to discriminate most accurately attitudinal differences among a set of men, still a third method might be, by that standard, the best. However, all three approaches would, within the terms of reference stated, be quite decidedly meaningful.

Alex Inkeles
Harvard University

THE AUTHOR REPLIES

I find Professor Inkeles' comments helpful in several respects. First, his remarks very effectively make the point that there is room in the world for more than one procedure for scaling the same attribute, a point which I seem to have obscured in trying to make. A valid and reliable transcultural measure of individual modernism certainly has its uses, as does a scale of modernism derived from a specific culture, and I would agree that the type of scale one chooses depends on the purposes one has in mind. Second, a major source of misunderstanding about my critique lies in the interpretation of the term "meaningless," and Inkele's commentary offers an opportunity to clarify the intent of that term. The sentence in which that term was used most strongly was the one that Inkeles quotes in his "Comments": "If no differentiation is made in the [local] culture between traditionalism and modernism, then movement along the dimension cannot be recognized by the participants, and the study of modernization in this cultural setting is meaningless." I should have added, "to those participants," but I felt that this redundancy was unnecessary since it was implied by the context. In short, I would agree that it may be possible to derive measures of modernism and modernization which are meaningless and unrecognized by a local populace but meaningful to someone outside the culture. Of course, there are dangers inherent in devising such measures, and I hope Inkeles would agree that among them are the possibilities of ethnocentric and even professional biases.

The likelihood of introducing this kind of influence is enhanced, it seems to me, when one takes too seriously the analogy drawn between the measurement of personal and cultural traits and the diagnosis of organic disease. The more proper analogy may be between modernism and mental health. Pneumonia, I expect, is pretty much the same wherever one finds it, and cases of equal severity probably incapacitate the afflicted individuals physically to about the same extent, no matter where they are located. Diagnosis by the physician is at least equally useful and probably superior to "folk medical" diagnosis in determining extent of impairment. Indeed, it would matter little (though it might matter some) whether the doctor and patient were from the same culture or whether one of them was from Park Avenue and the other from the Peruvian highlands.

The case is different with mental health and illness. Assuming that a transcultural nosology were available (and there may be some significance in the fact that there is not), would it not be true that the same professionally diagnosed illness may take somewhat different forms in different localities, and, furthermore, that the same professionally diagnosed illness may be incapacitating to different degrees in different localities? How "maladjusted" a given mental illness renders a person—and therefore how "healthy"—depends on the requirements of the system in which he is stationed and on the perceptions of the "illness" by other members of that system. Judgments of the extent of impairment might vary greatly depending on the social system and culture of the "patient" and the doctor, respectively.

Still, I will grant that it may be possible to devise a universally applicable scale of mental health. I would only suggest that such a scale runs the danger of taking on the properties of the persons who make it up. If it does, and if it is useful to know how much like oneself other people are, then it is a useful scale. It may not tell how "healthy" those people are, except to an egotistical operationist. To the extent that the scale is grounded in something besides personal conjecture, it takes on meaning in terms of these other grounds, and these grounds, be they theoretical, empirical, or whatever, must be known before one can know the meaning of the measure.

To return to the subject of modernism, when I wrote the original article, I was precisely at this point. For, granting that meaningful measures of modernism can be constructed which do not take into account criteria of modernism recognized by local participants—measures which measure the same thing universally— there is still the question whether the OM scale is such a measure. I never meant to say it was meaningless, but I did mean to raise the question of what it meant. Is everyone going modern? I was simply uncertain from the information presented in the article by Smith and Inkeles[1] whether we could answer that question. It is one thing to find a sorting device which separates populations into different piles; it is another to determine the basis on which the device does the sorting.[2]

A third contribution made by Inkeles's comments is his useful distinction between "salience" and "relevance." As I interpret it, this distinction implies that a given criterion of modernity may be meaningful to a group without being recognized by that group. Using that distinction, the criteria in the Shiloh scale are salient, but they do not represent all possible criteria which are relevant. (Does any scale?) Inkeles speculates that there are a number of (at least two) other criteria which would have been relevant in Shiloh (the test for relevance apparently being item-to-scale correlation coefficients). His reasons for this speculation are (1) the finding that "they are in fact strongly associated with items of the type which found their way into Stephenson's own scale of modernism in Shiloh," and (2) the fact that the same kinds of correlations were found in Hazard, Kentucky.

I am not prepared to make this leap of faith with Inkeles. First, we do not know the extent to which particular items in the Shiloh scale operate like their supposed counterparts in the OM scale. (For example, the OM item on "old ways" is set in the context of an intergenerational discussion of corn raising, whereas the Shiloh item on "old ways" simply says, "I think the old ways are mostly best for me.") Second, even assuming the items are identical, one would like to know exactly what the "strong associations" were, especially in view of some of the relatively low item-to-scale correlation coefficients found in table 1 of the Smith and Inkeles article. An item-to-scale correlation of .294 means that one of these variable explains only 8.6 percent of the variance in the other. Some of the correlations in table 1 are lower than .10, meaning that less than 1 percent of the variance is explained by those items. If these low correlations are acceptable,[3] then one wonders what constitutes a strong association.

Third, there is the matter of the finding for Hazard, Kentucky. I hesitated and am still reluctant to comment on the Hazard footnote to which Inkeles pointedly calls my attention because, again I would like to have more information than that brief reference makes available. (I have, incidentally, attempted without success to pry a copy of this paper loose from the undergraduate librarian at Harvard.) The case for the universality of the OM scale would certainly be strengthened if it were found that the same set of items yielded the same results in Hazard as in six other societies (i.e., the same item-to-scale correlations, the same relationships between scale scores and external criteria, and the same relationships to local expressions of modernity and traditionism insofar as they differ from the OM dimensions). Whether the OM scale would yield the same results in Shiloh as in Hazard is an open question--one which I would be interested in having answered--since there are considerable differences between the two communities in population size, economic history and present economic structure, centrality of location, and political dominance (Hazard, unlike Shiloh, is a county-seat town). Whether such differences would affect the operation of the scale is unknown. With regard to the two specific criteria of "interest in foreign news" and "joining organization," my guess is that Hazard and Shiloh might show internal differentiation on the former, but only Hazard on the latter.

In short, I do not believe we have quite "every" reason to assume that the OM scale items would be good (relevant) indicators of modernity in Shiloh, even using Inkeles's methods of determining relevance.

Inkeles's comments are helpful in a fourth way because they bring up the question of the relationship between modernism scales and external indicators. Certainly I would permit the makers of the OM scale to sauce their gander. I confess to being very much impressed by Short Form 3, derived by the criterion group method, which correlates highly (around .80) with other "theoretically derived" forms, although I wonder if one should not expect fairly high correlations among scales which contain many of the same items.[4] But my distress is not greatly relieved by the "test of adequacy" referred to by Inkeles (p. 360 of the Smith and Inkeles article), which yields correlations of .434 with education, .179 with factory experience, and .142 with rural/urban origin. Tests of significance may have shown that the odds against such correlations occurring by chance are great, as one would expect with a sample of about 4,770, but the sizes of the coefficients themselves indicate that the strength of the relationships between the social indices and the OM scale leaves something to be desired (and explained). The coefficient of .434, for example, means that education accounts for about 19 percent of the variance in scale scores. Factory experience accounts for little over 3 percent, and rural/urban origin about 2 percent, according to my slide rule. Thus, knowledge of a person's education, factory experience, or origin would not permit accurate prediction of OM scale scores in a very large number of cases.

Incidentally, I would not like to think that the validity of the Shiloh scale stands or falls on the evidence presented in footnote 29 of my article. Indeed, the fact that this sparse information on relationships of the scale to external factors was not granted the dignity of space in the main text may show that I did not wish to use much of this sauce on my goose!

The fifth and most useful contribution made by Inkeles's comments is his presentation of information on relationships between an indigenously derived scale and the social scientist-derived OM scale. It seems to me that the case for the validity of the OM scale is strengthened enormously if it is shown to be highly correlated with indigenous scales such as that constructed for India. Indeed, if we were to view the external criterion method and the "indigenous scale" method as two independent ways of assessing scale validity, and if a scale passed muster on both counts, then the greatest skeptic should be silenced. I have pointed out my reasons for hesitation in claiming complete validity for the OM scale on the basis of external criteria. The moderately high correlations between the Indian "toothbrush" scale and the OM Long Form is more impressive. Of course, two things remain to be shown. How well does the OM scale correlate with indigenous scales derived in other cultures than India? (I would be interested in knowing how well it correlates with the Shiloh scale as well.) Second, if such correlations are high, it would still have to be shown that the universes of content being measured were the same.

It is not immediately apparent how preferring tap water and toothbrushes is related to, say, feeling about whether a man can be good without religion. These are questions which can be answered with more research and better theory construction.

To summarize, Inkeles's comments require me to acknowledge that the case for the indigenous scale of modernism, such as that derived in Shiloh, may have been overstated. I can see that it is ambiguous and subject to misinterpretation. But Inkeles's response also provides an opportunity to point out that the case for the transcultural social scientist-derived scale, such as the OM scale, is not completely airtight either. Both of us have some homework to do. I would agree with Inkeles's concluding sentiment that one's purpose should dictate the type of measurement used.[5] To understand how these various measures are related to each other, both empirically and in theory, is also important. Finally, I fear that the set of attributes to which we refer as modernism or modernity are not related to each other or to "structural" variable in nearly so simple a fashion as either Inkeles or I imagine and that we would both do well to reread Gusfield's (1967) essay on "misplaced polarities in the study of social change"[6] before returning either to the sociometric laboratory or to the field.

Reassessing Change in Appalachia

Although the time he could spend on Appalachian community studies was increasingly restricted by growing administrative duties, John's interest in the field never flagged. In 1972 he and a colleague David Walls published a collection of articles under the title *Appalachia in the Sixties: Decade of Reawakening.* John did not contribute any articles to the book, but his continued concern with the region and its social and economic problems was evident in the preface. Based on their assessment of Appalachian conditions, Stephenson and Walls found "few if any grounds for optimism" regarding the solution of the region's problems. Earlier problem definitions, they pointed out, were inadequate guides for dealing with current problems, which required more than ameliorative efforts. They required fundamental social reconstruction.

PREFACE TO APPALACHIA IN THE SIXTIES

More than ten years have passed since John F. Kennedy's visit to West Virginia during the campaign for the 1960 presidential primary, the visit which precipitated a declaration of war against the social, economic, and human problems of the Appalachian Region. Ten years have passed since the research was carried out which led to the publication of *The Southern Appalachian Region: A Survey*.

In that volume, and in a later article . . ., Rupert Vance suggested a decennial follow-up on the problems and progress of the region. How far have we come in ten years? There is no study comparable to the survey on which to rely for an assessment. Despite the absence of quantitative data, despite the lack of scholarly research on the matter, information is available which could lead us to a tentative answer. This information is found in the observations, impressions, and evaluations of journalists, field workers, local residents, politicians, and social scientists who have lived with, worked with, watched, and written about the problems they have seen and the programs established to cope with them. These mostly front-line reports come in a variety of published forms, from national literary magazines to action group house organs, from articles in famous dailies to letters to the editors of county weeklies. . . .

The Appalachian Region is itself an elusive entity, as can be seen from the number of conflicting definitions given it by scholars, reporters, natives, and politicians over the years. How many counties in which states are included? For the most part, we are concerned here only with the southern portion of the region, and within that portion we have concentrated mainly on the coalfields of West

Virginia, eastern Kentucky, southwestern Virginia and north-central Tennessee. These are the areas that first attracted the attention of the nation in the early sixties; they seem to have been the places where there was the greatest depression, the greatest concentration of antipoverty efforts, the most heightened response to local, state, and federal programs, and the greatest degree of organization around common interests by the end of the decade. What has been written about central southern Appalachia applies in varying degrees to mountainous areas which are further north or south, lower in altitude or more "Piedmont" in nature, based more on agricultural economies, or which have not had the complicating factor of coal added to their otherwise broadly comparable histories. It should certainly not be thought that places like western North Carolina and much of eastern Tennessee are not truly Appalachian in their culture, character, and problems; it is only that less is known about them, and that what is known suggests that settlement patterns, economic history, and current prospects are different enough for other Appalachian subregions to require a separate accounting. Something registers when you tell many Americans about places called Hazard and Bluefield, but who knows of Spruce Pine or Erwin? The presence of coal seems to be an important common denominator of central southern Appalachia, and perhaps it is coal that has made this area unique, both in its history and in its uncertain future.

Mass unemployment caused by mechanization in the coal industry forced Appalachia to the attention of the nation at the beginning of the sixties. Theorists of the automation revolution prophesied that Appalachia foreshadowed a national employment crisis. Hazard became a symbol for the New Left of the sixties as Harlan had been for the old Left of the thirties. The violence associated with the roving picket movement in eastern Kentucky dramatized the need for intervention by the federal government. By the end of the decade it became clear that coal had been one of the most labor-intensive, technologically backward sectors of the economy, and the Appalachian crisis had not been as representative of the national economy as some had imagined. The roving picket movement thus turned out to be the last gasp of the old era of labor struggles in the mountains. The movements of the later sixties, in contrast, were premised on the existence of a mechanized mining industry and a permanent welfare state designed to care for the industry's casualties.

The Area Redevelopment Administration, established in 1961 with a program for stimulating private industrial development, quickly proved inadequate to the problems of depressed areas in America. The Economic Opportunity Act of 1964 packaged a patchwork of liberal proposals, including a public employment program disguised as "work experience and training," and the dramatic Community Action Program with its call for "maximum feasible participation" of the poor. The much criticized work experience program, concentrated disproportionately in eastern Kentucky, managed—together with the food stamp program—to defuse the violence that had haunted the coalfields in the early sixties.

A few far-sighted individuals called for an Appalachian version of the Tennessee Valley Authority as a solution to the chronic problems of the southern mountain region. This idea had little widespread support at the beginning of the sixties, however, and proposals for public ownership and development of the region's resources were quickly scuttled by the coal industry and private utilities. Instead of a new TVA, the Appalachian Regional Development Act of 1965 created the Appalachian Regional Commission as a funnel for federal money into the mountains. Overshadowed by the more controversial Office of Economic Opportunity programs in the middle sixties, the ARC by the end of the decade had firmly established its network of local development districts as the focus

John, who loved horses, introduces his daughter Rebecca to a
friendly horse at a Lexington farm in 1968. (photo by Jane Stephenson)

of developmental activities for the early seventies. Perhaps as many as half of OEO's community action agencies had maintained some independence of local courthouse and schoolboard political machines for three or four years, until amendments to the Economic Opportunity Act whittled back the scope of the program and returned control to local public officials. The ARC's development districts never presented any such embarrassments, as they were dominated by their respective local establishments from the start. Up for renewal in 1971, the ARC won an overwhelming endorsement from Congress, despite opposition from the Nixon administration, which wished to substitute its own revenue sharing proposals for the regional development plans.

At the end of the sixties, some of the focus of grassroots activities had shifted from Kentucky to West Virginia. The Association of Disabled Miners and Widows began legal action to obtain benefits they claimed were due them from the United Mine Workers of America. The Black Lung Association led a wildcat strike that took 40,000 men out of the mines, shutting down the coal industry in West Virginia until the state legislature passed a measure providing adequate compensation for coal miner's pneumoconiosis. The Miners for Democracy movement attempted to restore self-government to the districts of the UMWA. Sparked by Kentucky's Appalachian Group to Save the Land and People, the opposition to strip-mining spread to West Virginia and was the subject of major legislative battles. In the mountain areas of both states welfare rights organizations were concerned with a wide range of issues from free school lunches to disability criteria. Many of these activities had been stimulated by Office of Economic Opportunity's community action and VISTA programs. A small number of the organizers and lawyers who were attracted to Appalachia by the War on Poverty stayed on past the demise of these programs as forces for change and made their homes in the region, continuing to give support to grassroots social movements.

We draw two generalizations from our survey of the Appalachian scene as of this writing in 1971. First, there are few if any grounds for optimism regarding "victory" (or even moderate success) in the "war" on the region's problems. Second, to measure progress in 1971 by reference to problems defined in 1960 is misleading, because neither the manner in which problems are currently defined nor the yardsticks by which change is gauged are the same as a decade earlier. Our impression is that the quantity of human suffering, privation, degradation, and confusion, and the extent of environmental rape and devastation in Appalachia have not decreased significantly. These problems represent a kind of absolute standard by which to judge the well-being of a region. Beyond them, and the very minimal kinds of expectations which they connote (for example, that people should have decent housing and should not be victims of malnutrition), there are significant dissimilarities in the ways problems, solutions, and progress were viewed at the beginning and at the end of the decade.

This change may simply reflect changes occurring in the rest of society during that ten years, especially among people concerned with programs of social action—civil rights and minority protest, the antiwar movement, and the youth, consumer, women's, and ecology movements. The major aspect of this change has been that what were initially brought to consciousness as problems-in-themselves are now seen as symptoms of more fundamental, underlying conditions. These problems are now viewed as incomprehensible when not taken in their relationships with other problems and conditions. Thus what once might have been praised as progressive, forward-looking, and humanitarian programs of social and economic amelioration are derogated as "bandaids" and "aspirins." Individuals and families in suffering are looked upon as casualties of an unjust social and economic system which is itself the real problem.

Thus, solutions to the problem of Appalachia today are cast in terms of reconstruction, not amelioration, and the signposts to progress are marked in political and organizational mileage instead of numbers of new privies, schoolhouse repairs, or even increased median incomes. If there is to be a movement for progressive change in Appalachia, the evidence of this volume suggests it would result from a diverse coalition: poor people's grassroots groups, conservationists, a revitalized UMWA, teachers and parents concerned for better education, dedicated students willing to work for constructive change, and church bodies committed to social action.

In our view, what signs of optimism and hope there exist for the future of the Appalachian region grow out of this very redefinition of the problem. The sixties witnessed the awakening of a spirit of self-determination within the mountain region; whether this "Appalachian nationalism" will find wider acceptance will be seen in the seventies. We see the possibility that the people of the mountains may come together in new social forms which will permit and encourage them to have a real say in the directing of their futures. Without such consequential collective participation in their own fates, a large portion of the people of the region can be expected to remain as powerless and resigned as they have been since before the days of Campbell and Kephart, and we can expect to continue to roll bandages and nurse wounds instead of reducing injuries through democratic, preventive social engineering.

Appalachia and Development

Among John's constant concerns for Appalachia was the destruction of its culture in the name of economic development. Like most, he viewed development of the region as a relatively recent process, largely of the twentieth century. Consequently, he was more than a little surprised to find in an 1889 issue of *Harper's New Monthly Magazine* an essay entitled "Comments on Kentucky" by one Charles Dudley Warner, calling for the salvation of the region through industrialization. Indeed, it was Warner's firm belief that Eastern Kentucky was "on the eve of an astonishing development . . . that will revolutionize eastern Kentucky and powerfully affect the iron and coal markets of the country." Perhaps what struck John most was the similarity of Warner's concept of "progress" to contemporary "economic development," expressions of the same perspective and spirit almost a century apart. "One questions, indeed," John wrote, "whether the passage of time has aided our perception, whether history makes us in fact wiser, whether we are not still trapped in some foggy valley searching for the way out."

John's observations on Warner's essay were published in *Appalachian Journal* and are reproduced here. While he denied that his views expressed either despair or cynicism, the title of his article,

"Appalachia and the Third Century in America: On the Eve of an Astonishing Development—Again," manifests a black humor deriving from a pessimism earlier evident in the preface to *Appalachia in the Sixties.*

APPLACHIA AND THE THIRD CENTURY IN AMERICA: ON THE EVE OF AN ASTONISHING DEVELOPMENT—AGAIN

I discovered recently that in 1889 Charles Dudley Warner, co-author with Mark Twain of *The Gilded Age*, wrote an essay for *Harper's New Monthly Magazine* called "Comments on Kentucky." While it was partly a travelogue of the sort fashionable in that day, Warner also offered an assessment of the past, the present state, and the future prospects of the Commonwealth, concentrating especially on the Appalachian portion of the state. In its own way that piece was itself a review of roughly the first 100 years of Appalachian Kentucky as a part of the Great American Experiment, Warner noting in an early paragraph, for example, that Boone's trail through the wilderness at Cumberland Gap was marked in 1775.

Warner's is not an unbiased report, of course. Even if it were, the truth about Eastern Kentucky won't stretch to cover all of Appalachia. Nevertheless, this article provides a sense of history and lends us some perspective as we attempt to visualize the third century of this region as part of America. Therefore, I have found it useful to pore over Warner's Victorian phrases, to use them as a Time Machine, to bend myself back in time to a place I know in a time I don't. The more I reflect on his thoughts, the more I believe they capture some of the spirit of his time, and therefore that of our own.

In 1889 the Civil War had been over for only 24 years, and its effects could still be seen. (It was fresh enough in his mind that Warner attributed some of the lawlessness of which he heard to "the disorganization during the war.") In the late 19th Century the North was industrializing rapidly, while the South was still exhausted and crawling back up to agricultural peonage. Everything was going crazy out West. The first great run for homesteading land in Oklahoma was in 1889. Geronimo surrendered only in 1886; Wounded Knee did not occur until 1890. The transcontinental railroad had been completed for only twenty years. At the same time people were pouring out into the West, new people were pouring into the East. Immigrants were seeking refuge and opportunity, *en masse*, in America—over five million in the decade preceding 1890 alone. And at this time the rate of technological invention was gathering an incredible momentum. The Bessemer converter was scarcely twenty years old. The compressed air rock drill was 18 years old. Dynamite had been invented 13 years before, in 1866. The incandescent lamp and the electric railway were invented 10 years before, in 1879. The list is incredible: the telephone, 1876; the four-cycle internal combustion engine, 1887, and the gasoline automobile, the same year; barbed wire, 1874; the transatlantic cable, 1866; and the cash register, 1879.

What a time! There was nothing we Americans could not do. It was working—the Great Experiment was working. Even in Appalachia.

At least that was what Charles Dudley Warner thought. Oh, it is true that when he meandered through the Clover Fork area he saw depressing scenes of poverty, lawlessness, and bare feet among the splendors of natural beauty. He said at one point, in fact, that "the inhabitants of the region are primitive and to a considerable extent illiterate." He found Harlan Court House "an old shabby hamlet." He was plainly dismayed by the lawlessness, which he attributed not only to the war but also to the "abominable cookery" characteristic of the region. He concludes that "the race of American mountaineers occupying the country from western North Carolina to eastern Kentucky is a curious study. Their origin is in doubt. They have developed their peculiarities in isolation."

But not to worry. Shabby, wanton, peculiar, unlettered victims of foul cookery though they be, Warner finds he is not so despondent for their future as to call them "worthless, good-for-nothing, irreclaimable." This is because, to quote from the same paragraph, "railroads, trade, the sight of enterprise and industry, will do much with this material."

Now that the world needs coal in abundance for its Bessemer converters, incandescent lamps, and stock tickers (invented in 1870), commercial interests will beat a path to Eastern Kentucky, and the old civilization will be replaced with the new. Because of the importance of coal and iron ores, Eastern Kentucky "becomes one of the most important and interesting regions in the Union." It is "on the eve of an astonishing development—one that will revolutionize eastern Kentucky, and powerfully affect the iron and coal markets of the country." That is "why the gigantic railway corporations are straining every nerve to penetrate the mineral and forest heart of the region. A dozen roads, projected and in progress, are pointed toward this center. It is a race for the prize."

This prescription for the ills of that same barbarism of which Toynbee spoke in his famous example of backsliding civilization is written unequivocally in a passage where Warner has just finished his comments on undesirable and lawless elements of the population: "This state of things in eastern Kentucky will not be radically changed until the railways enter it, and business and enterprise bring in law and order. . . . I think no permanent gain can be expected till a new civilization comes in. . . ."

And it will come in, because that is where, as he says, the prize is, referring to the "fuel which has been so long stored for the new civilization." He concludes: "It is my belief that this central and hitherto neglected portion of the United States will soon become the theatre of vast and controlling industries." (Surely no one today will dispute this particular conclusion.)

Well, we must be charitable; we must understand the times. Perhaps it comes as no surprise that Warner's travel through Eastern Kentucky leads him to describe hope, promise, and salvation through industrialization, in the same breath as he expresses revulsion and indignation at the savagery he describes. We would not see Appalachia that way. Appalachia is different now; the problems and the solutions are not the same. And our theories are better.

As the reader will have suspected by now, I wish to challenge that notion. One must read Warner in the original, of course, to benefit from the rich detail and the aura. I have read it through many times now, in different moods, settings, and states of need. The closer my relationship to it grows, the more I am able to see that one does not need to bend himself back in time to understand its points of view. They are all here, now. It is ourselves, our generation, our way of life.

One questions, indeed, whether the passage of time has aided our perception, whether history makes us in fact wiser, whether we are not still trapped in some foggy valley searching for the way out. Inescapably, one concludes it is highly likely that some such piece of writing will appear near the end of the next one hundred years. This is not despair, nor cynicism, but rather the acknowledgment that the core ideas of a civilization do not disappear quickly, especially not because a few people with different ones are born and die.

Progress, as the poet e.e. cummings cleverly observed, is a comfortable disease. It is also an obstinate one because it has made some people extremely wealthy and most of the rest of us at least unwilling to complain.

The roots of progress—the idea—are unreachably deep in history and our psyches. We may know they are there but we cannot dig them up even if we should want. Not that we want to very badly, for even when in anxious moments we suspect those roots are eating the ground from under our very feet, we encourage their fructification with every device available.

And so the spirit of Progress, with her handmaiden, Commerce, thrives in our time, too. Responsibly, of course. We do not speak of robber barons today; ours are all honorable corporations with records which clearly favor mine safety and economic benefits for all. (Events which appear to contradict such recorded statements are acts of God.) And with commerce there still survives a kind of hardnosed realism for which Western economists are well-known. This realism encompasses the view that a higher economic calculus exists which defines out certain human traits, such as sentiment and irrationality, by means of which the future of a people can be ciphered and the cost of achieving any desired end estimated. The commercial ethos is also still characterized by the belief that ordinary people prosper only if General Bullmoose profits.

So we believe yet, do we not, that there is hope for Appalachia. (The more clearly we see the grounds of despair, the more we must hope, dear God.) And we do still believe that realizing such hope depends on bringing to Appalachia the same devices and machines of progress that have worked so well in the rest of the nation. We do agree that Eastern Kentucky and places like it are rich in resources and that in this era of concern with energy we are about to witness the awakening of the sleeping giant. And do we not still hear that the less desirable peculiarities of these poor mountain people will fade with the end of isolation and the coming of economic sufficiency?

We still believe in the same comfortable disease: Progress. And with it, optimism, commercialism, "practicality." We believe these things because they are in fact our civilization. In our generation we call progress "economic development." In Warner's mind there was no great question who would take charge of progress. Frost's name-calling ten years later didn't stop "the jackals of civilization," nor has anyone else. The irony is that Appalachia is part of the working out of an entire civilization, and it cannot be "cured" in isolation from the rest any more than it was created in isolation from the rest.

It is our civilization that has led to a hundred years of extraction from this great quarry of resources. The trunk and branches and fruit of that way of life are in a thousand towns and cities in America; the roots are eating out the ground in Appalachia.

Nihil sub sol nova. In 1775 the Wilderness Trail was marked. By 1880 the railroads were piercing Kentucky so that the Taking Away could commence. Approximately one hundred years later we can mark the completion of many miles of superhighways in Eastern Kentucky under the auspices of the Appalachian Regional Commission. There have been increasingly numerous travelers down the Clover Fork and to Harlan Court House over those two hundred years. But what they see, what they feel may not have changed so much as one might at first think. Nor have our thoughts improved much about what to do.

Social Change in a Village of the Scottish Highlands

In 1981 John was awarded a Fulbright Senior Research Fellowship to conduct a community study in Scotland, later published as *Ford: A Village in the West Highlands of Scotland*. His Scottish host institution was the University of Stirling, which appointed him a Visiting Research Fellow. John's interest in Scotland stemmed in part from its being the native land of some of his forebears, including one William Stephenson, who immigrated to the United States in 1732 via the Irish county of Donegal. *Ford* is partly dedicated to his memory. But John's interest in the West Highlands of Scotland, as he notes in his introductory chapter, was more than "idle curiosity." As he expressed it, "There is much to be learned about the life and death of small communities through the study of their histories, their rounds of daily life, and what is happening to their populations. . . . Perhaps with the accumulated knowledge from such studies from around the world we can determine what forms of adaptation lead to vitality in peripheral human communities."

. . . .

John's study of the small village of Ford focused on two related issues: (1) Would the community die, as numerous other small Highland villages already had, as a consequence of its residents moving to larger towns and cities? (2) And, after John's discovery that, contrary to local conventional wisdom, Ford's population was actually increasing, who were the newcomers and what were their effects on the social life and culture of the community?

The latter question was one he had raised in his 1980 revisit to the Appalachian community of Shiloh. On that visit he had become acutely aware that the town was being repopulated by inmigrants whose life styles differed sharply from those of most of the residents whom he had studied only 15 years earlier.* The invasions of both the newcomers to Shiloh and the incomers to Ford had met with some resistance, but there was little doubt that they were introducing major changes in the traditional social organization and culture of the two communities.

The question of whether Shiloh would continue to exist as a community was never seriously raised except in the sense that it would never again be the Shiloh that John had studied in 1965. The survival of Ford, though, was an authentic issue, and John's perception of local feeling was that "Ford is dying, like a lot of other places that have gone before it." (p. 17) Although his initial reaction was to accept this dismal prognosis, John found in the course of his investigation that Ford exhibited enough signs of vitality to raise doubts about its apparent moribund condition.

In the final chapter of *Ford*, which is reproduced here, John returned to the question of the community's future survival. After a careful analysis of the available evidence, he concluded that "Ford is not dying; it is, however, going through another watershed change in its long life" (p. 194). But his conclusion was not completely sanguine, for he realistically recognized that Ford's future would depend ". . . as much on events far removed from this locality as on anything the people of the village do to save it, as vitally important as those efforts are." And that loss of local control, he maintained, ". . . is anything but a sign of community vitality" (p. 143).

FORD TOMORROW: SURVIVAL, CONTINUITY, AND CHANGE

> I believe in the beloved community and in the spirit which makes it beloved, and in the communion of all who are, in will and deed, its members. I see no such community as yet, but nonetheless my rule of life is: Act so as to hasten its coming.
>
> Josiah Royce, quoted in Roland L. Warren,
> "The Good Community—What Would It Be?"

To ponder the future of the village of Ford is to consider the lives of all such communities everywhere. The issues upon which its life or death turn are at one level the same issues which confront and transform small places in many nations.

'Life' and 'death' are, of course, metaphoric terms, taken from a biological context (where their meanings are obscure enough already) and applied, sometimes uncritically, by sociologists, anthropologists, journalists, and other observers of the human scene to forms of human association whose organic qualities have led thinkers to confuse communities with living organisms. Communities do not live as organisms live, and they do not die as organisms die, but it is nonetheless true that some localities seem to thrive while others wither—and sometimes disappear altogether. The metaphors of life and death have their uses as well as their limits.

To 'die' can mean something quite different in the case of a community in contrast with dying organisms. For example, dying, according to some writers, can become a permanent state of being, a form of association in its own right.[1] Thus, only to exist may not be sufficient to qualify a community for the term 'living.'

To what signs should we look, then, in determining whether places such as Ford are living or dying? Without intending to stretch the metaphor beyond its limits, we can ask what should be examined as signs of life in small communities, and by implication, we shall be asking what, in the absence of these signs, constitutes death. With answers to these questions, however tentative, the specific question of the future of Ford (and places like it) can be addressed more systematically and concretely.

At the very minimum, the living community requires, as a necessary pre-condition, humans inhabiting a locality. But people living in a bounded space do not necessarily constitute a communal form of association; that is, people living in proximity do not by virtue of this make a place a community. People in propinquity can be almost completely atomized, separated from each other by social space, living their lives, as in certain bedroom 'communities,' almost totally in social orbits which pull them into patterns of work, friendship, and affiliation dominated by centers outside the locality of their households. Thus, the fact of people occupying a delimited space is only a minimal requirement for community.

In common parlance, those communities said to be thriving are those growing in size, while those that are 'dying' are the ones declining in population. (Those which witness little or no change in size are presumably in 'stable condition.') While it is unarguable that a shrinking population will ultimately disappear if the decline is unchecked, it is not necessarily true that increase equals life. Growth may breed business expansion, cause new buildings to be built, multiply roads, swell the schools, and increase the town bud-

get. Growth may bring the social amenities and all those attributes
we like to associate with modern town living. But by itself, growth
may not increase community life: it may not (probably will not) increase the coherence of neighborhoods, make it more likely to solve
shared problems collectively, or reduce the perception of social separation from other members of the community. It is, therefore, misleading to associate population increase closely with community
vitality. It may be enough simply to say that the absence of continued decline is a necessary pre-condition of good community health.

Aside from such pre-conditions, at what kinds of evidence should
we look to find signs of health and vitality—the 'vital signs' of community? From experience and from an examination of the ideas of
others who have concerned themselves with this question,[2] I suggest the following five community life signs should be considered:

1. The presence of shared, purposeful activity related to the collective interest of those inhabiting the locality.
2. The presence of locality-based institutions, or organized patterns of living.
3. The presence of shared identity rooted in a sense of place.
4. The presence of at least some minimal degree of authority
   over part of the decision-making which affects the locality.
5. The presence of shared overall goals and values regarding
   the community.

Each of these items deserves a brief word of explanation.

Vitality would seem to require a degree of shared, purposeful
activity, the goals of which are related in some fashion to the locality. In plainer English, there is life in the community whose members get together to work on something which has to do with the
community itself. There is less vitality in the community whose
members are highly active solely on their own behalves, but where
there is no shared work toward a 'common good.' Where there is

evidence of apathy, fatalism, or cynicism about communal good and the work required to achieve it, there are signs of dying. The emphasis in this criterion of vitality is on the sharing of action, the working out of problems together, the working toward realized definitions of the good of the community among those who live there.

Another related expression of community vitality is the presence of locality-based institutions and organized living patterns. When people associate with each other in patterned and repetitive ways, are the sources and objects of the association relevant to the locality, or are they oriented to some other, non-local centre? The *origin* of a patterned association can, of course, be outside the community while the *object* can be internal, as would be the case with churches and schools. But the fundamental issue has to do with the bringing of people together in some patterned and regular relationship, the intended or unintended object of which relates to the locality.

A third sign of life in a community would seem to have to do with shared identity rooted in a sense of place. The sense of *belonging* is not, of course, exclusive: humans typically express belonging in a large number of social contexts simultaneously. We can belong to many groups concurrently and draw our identities from all of them. *Place* is one of these potential sources of attachment, belonging, and identity (indeed, it is possible to feel strong attachments to more than one place at a time, or to concentric places).

The sense of place is a complex and unexplored area of study, about which more will be said below. I do not think we understand much about how identification with place happens; indeed, it does not always happen. Somehow the felt uniqueness of a locality will become translated into a shared perception of specialness which is the source of group identity in that community. Where this occurs, there is another sign of life. Where it is weak or absent, there is less, or no vitality. Shared, purposeful activity will certainly have some effect on the level of shared sense of place and vice-versa, and both will be a cause and an expression of institutional patterns which are locality-relevant, so that none of the three life signs discussed so far is really independent of the others.

An issue discussed by some as the key to the life or death of small communities is that of the extent of local authority over decision-making.[3] It is difficult in this rudimentary stage of development of theories of life and death in communities to discern which are causes and which are symptoms of dying, but I am inclined to believe that a reduction in local control over the affairs of the community may be both. At the least, it constitutes an insidious, long-term trend which undermines other vital signs. While it may not operate as the sole cause of the decline of locality-based associations, it is unquestionably a powerful and pervasive one. Local control erodes to the extent that communications and transportation networks have grown more efficient, facilitating the control of peripheral areas from centralized (usually urban) localities. Whether cause or symptom or both, the relative absence of control by localities over the making of decisions which affect them as collective associations is anything but a sign of community vitality. But few communities have ever enjoyed complete autonomy. On a scale which reaches from the one extreme of total control to the other of absolutely no control over local affairs, there are none in the contemporary world which comes close to achieving the maximum. Any actual community today must be measured against what is probable rather than against what is theoretically possible.

Shared core values would seem to be another vital sign in a living community. I do not mean by this that there need be consensus on each and every matter which comes before the residents of a locality; uniformity of opinion in fact has a deadening aspect, and the extreme desire to achieve it leads to totalitarianism. Opposition and argumentation are healthy signs—if the argument is contained within agreed-upon boundaries and if it does not become an end in

*John as newly appointed dean of undergraduate
studies at the University of Kentucky, 1970.*

itself. It is the agreement upon over-reaching goals and values (domain assumptions) which is important to the life of a community. Where conflict is unbounded, we may be certain that community vitality has, at least for the duration, ebbed.

I am purposefully vague about the *degree* to which a community would have to register positively on each of these criteria in order to qualify as a 'good community.' I agree with Roland Warren that we have not thought sufficiently about the consequences of some of our idealized sentiments regarding community life. The pursuit of certain of these goals to an extreme would doubtless be intolerable, and some goals are in fact inconsistent with others. Let us simply say that the presence of these signs of life in *some* degree is required for vitality.

With this discussion as background, we can return to the question of the possible futures for the village of Ford. Is Ford dying, as some observers believe? Or are there signs of vitality which suggest a healthy community life for the indefinite future?

We cannot expect the evidence to be clear-cut and decisive. It is impossible to be objective, precise, and quantitative in weighing the facts. We can, on the other hand, attempt to discern, by looking for the presence of vital signs, which of the possible alternative futures seems most likely.

Futures for Ford

There are, I believe, three possible directions for the village of Ford. From looking at the trends of the past decade or so, one could reasonably project an optimistic future—one in which Ford's population increases and its age structure does not grow older, one in which Ford enjoys a stable economic base and works toward collective ends through institutionalized activities grounded in a shared sense of place.

Alternatively, from looking at the community over the long sweep of history, one might just as reasonably project a continuation of the long-term decline in population and institutional vigour which began in the early nineteenth century. Ford could follow many other Highland villages into oblivion. It could disappear from the map, and after a generation or two, there would be few to mourn its passing.

The third possibility is that Ford might hold on to life by a thread; that it might enter a state of dying and remain there 'vegetating,' as it were, indefinitely. Its institutions and collective patterns may become weakened. Its conflicts and divisions could become heightened. Shared identity and commitment to place could fade. The capacity for localized decision-making could be lost almost entirely.

All these things could happen, gradually, imperceptibly, and yet enough could remain of the population and of the 'vital signs' to support some minimal form of human association. Slow death could well develop into an enduring pattern of association as it has for many other communities in the world which are hardly alive but which refuse to die.

My own conclusion, which I will state at the outset, is that there are enough signs of vitality in Ford to render a reasonably favourable prognosis. It seems doubtful, at least, that Ford will die out altogether, although, as we shall see, its future is really not in its own possession. Let us took first at the evidence favouring this relatively optimistic conclusion of survival before then turning to some inescapable qualifications.

The evidence for optimism lies partly in the figures discussed in the last chapter, which show a well-defined increase in population over the past fifteen years. The data there show that while depopulation has not ceased (and will probably continue to take away many young people), its effects have been offset by the numbers of recent incomers, most of whom are not retirees. Not only has the number of people increased, but the population appears to be growing slightly younger. The increase in numbers of people has meant an increase in new and improved housing—and not just for retirement couples.

Nor is the local economy dying. A substantial number of individuals appear to be making a decent living from hill farming in and around Ford. Agriculture is anything but dying when a total of over 17,000 acres is being farmed, supporting 4,250 sheep, 244 cows, 12 men, 10 women, and 21 children. Forty-three of Ford's 156 inhabitants are in farm families.

The same can be said of forestry and timber work. While the number of forestry-related workers may be declining, the industry still involves a large number of people in Ford: a total of 23 men, women, and children are in families supported by timber and forestry-related occupations. At least one man, Joachim Brolly, has found opportunities for rapid expansion in the timber business, and says he could hire more than sixty new men 'tomorrow' if they could be found.

A village is not asleep or dying when a sizable majority of its people are engaged in one or another collective activity which benefits the whole. The Village Hall may be less used than it was when it was the new pride of the community, but it is nevertheless in regular use for community affairs, and it was a lively place on the last Saturday of November 1981 when almost one hundred people crowded into it for a sale of work to benefit the forthcoming children's Christmas party. The Ford Gun Club, the SWRI, and Hall Committee are also still quite active.

A community is alive when its people are designing new enterprises and implementing new schemes which promise work for its members. Two fish farms (one unsuccessful), two nurseries, and a timber business have been started in and around Ford in the last ten years. People have shown strong imagination in creating work where there was none before: one man is a privately contracting deerstalker, apparently the only one in the West Highlands; another earns his income through a combination of various teaching jobs and his own painting. Another new fish-farming scheme seems to be aborning, this one, significantly, to be organized on a cooperative basis. Ford does not seem to me to be a place where most people are apathetic and have gone to sleep. It is alive and awake, and in its midst there are those who intend to keep it that way.

Quite aside from the issue of collective activities and shared institutional patterns as signs of community vitality, there is the question of shared identity which is place-related. This issue is especially critical in Ford where place-related identity could be undermined easily, if unintentionally, by the large number of recent incomers. It is possible to imagine a Ford which enjoys a reasonable population, the jobs to support it, the forms of social life and the amenities required to sustain village life, but a Ford which is nevertheless hollow, lacking in soul and shared identity. It is important, therefore, to ask what sense of place exists in Ford now, whether is shared, and how it is likely to change.

The subject of 'sense of place' does not seem to have been given much attention by analysts, whether philosophers or social scientists.[4] Relph points out that:

> Place and sense of place do not lend themselves to scientific analysis for they are inextricably bound up with all the hopes, frustrations, and confusions of life, and possibly because of this social scientists have avoided these topics.[5]

In attempting to deal with the topic himself, Relph suggests some provocative, if unproven, principles. To have attachment to places and feel deep ties with them are important human needs, he says, agreeing with Robert Coles, whom he quotes:

> Nations, regions, states, counties, cities, towns— all of them have to do with politics and geography and history; but they are more than that, for they somehow reflect man's humanity, his need to stay someplace and get to know … other people … and what I suppose can be called a particular environment or space or neighbourhood or set of circumstances.[6]

Relph and Coles both seem to feel that the attachment to place need not grow out of lifelong location in a single place, but from 'settings in which we have had a multiplicity of experiences and which call forth an entire complex of affections and responses.' Relph, following Heidigger and Vycinas, distinguishes between levels of attachment to place, using 'home' to describe the deepest level of connection, for 'home' is where one dwells, the place where one's being and identity begin. It is the 'point of departure from which we orient ourselves to the world.'[7]

The identities of places can come about in two ways, says Relph: they can grow naturally as people unselfconsciously come to share common knowledge of features and values associated with a locality, or they can be 'mass identities' (C. Wright Mills' term) created by image-makers and marketed as saleable images of localities, such as Disneyland, which are really pseudo places based on synthetic identities and stereotypes.[8] The ultimate in placelessness occurs when powerful central authority, or big business, or mass culture, in the grip of a faceless economic system weakens the identity of a site through surface, stereotypical messages which finally make all places look alike and 'offer the same bland possibilities for experiences.'[9]

In Ford, a very strong sense of place is expressed by most of the residents, whether they are incomers, natives, or long-term residents. (The exceptions, including the few who said they would really prefer to be some place else, did not fall into any *one* of these categories.) To evoke statements about place, I asked a number of different questions: What does Ford mean to you? How do you describe it to people from some place else? What do you like about it and dislike about it? What makes it unique or the same as other places? Would you prefer to be some place else? Where would you like to be buried? And, of incomers, what brought you to Ford?

The most commonly expressed imagery of Ford involves scenery, quiet country living, rainy weather, local history, trees, sheep, and people (variously characterized as friends, family, neighbours, or just 'my people'). Some examples:

I asked a long-term resident if she had ever thought of living elsewhere. She wouldn't move, she said, even if there were an alternative to Ford. She did not want an alternative: she was quite content with this place. Her sources of contentedness were her friends, her part-time job which put her in frequent association with friends. 'I'm in a rut, I suppose,' she said, 'but I'm contented. I don't even want to go on holiday. If I lived somewhere else, 1 would miss my friends, and the place—my rut.'

. . . .

The elder Mr. Murray explains that the family had never before visited Ford when they heard the hotel was for sale, but they liked what they saw and came to love the place. He said, 'Why live anywhere else when you can live here? We aren't making money, but it is a good life. The hours are long, but we close the hotel in the winter and have the place to ourselves. Everyone needs time to himself.' He has never considered moving anywhere else, because Ford has everything he and his family want. He once remarked that when he took a trip to America, what he missed most was seeing the sheep.

. . . .

A woman who used once to come to Dalavich on holidays eventually married a man from there, and they moved to Ford in 1973. She likes the general area because it is quiet and because 'everyone minds their own business.' She likes Ford better than Dalavich because it is closer to Lochgilphead. What she does not like about it is the lack of things to interest teenagers. And the weather. (She seems unusual in this respect.) Most people seem to have a perverse affection for the rain in Argyll, which is just as well considering the 80 inches they see every year. There are standard lines about the wet weather just as there are standard greetings for everyday interaction. One person will say, 'Terrible day.' Another will say, 'Aye, well, it keeps the dust down.' And another will say, 'Aye, well, it's drier in here than it is out there.'

A retired Forestry Commission worker likes Ford because it has mild winters and he can be close enough to a town without having to live in one. ('I don't like cities—they're all go,' says his wife.) He would not want to leave Ford, although, ironically, his wife, who is one of the few natives in Ford, would really prefer to live in a slightly larger village because of the conveniences. But he would miss the people in Ford, and he would miss working on the land, which he still does occasionally. She says she would miss the friends she meets daily in her work, although, she adds, people have changed and there is not the friendliness there once was.

. . . .

An older Scottish couple chose to return to Ford for their retirement because 'We really belong here. My family has been here for generations.' They have lived in the country and farmed nearby all their lives. The wife admits that she would like to be nearer to Lochgilphead because the shopping is better, some of her friends are there, and it is closer to a main bus route. But this is home. They plan to be buried in Kilmartin cemetery, which is the closest to Ford.

An English couple who retired here years ago describe themselves as 'born Londoners' who nonetheless have made a strong commitment to Ford as their new home. Most people, he observes, say they want to live in the place where they enjoy their holidays, and that is what this couple did, although not until they had spent considerable time here getting to know the place and the people. They describe it as 'still a holiday.' 'We have everything here to please the eye and enchant the senses.' They are ardent conservationists and work for the preservation of the natural beauty of the area. They question the desirability of bringing new industry in: 'Do we want industry brought to keep the young here?' This couple has been active in community organizations, but their sense of place is in the main rooted in the things that 'please the eye and enchant the senses.' Because his family originated in Lewis and spent some time in Argyll, the husband likes to imagine there is some ancient racial memory of the place deep within him: 'It's almost an instinctive feeling. I'm a different person when I'm in the south and when I'm here.'

Another, more recently arrived, retired English family says that nostalgia and family feeling brought them to Scotland. They feel they have been well received by the people of Ford. But it is really the place that attracts and holds them, judging from statements like, 'When I return here, I see these hills beside the loch, and I think, "These are my hills."' Sentiments such as this suggest a deep commitment to place has developed in a relatively short time.

· · · · · · · · · · · ·

For an older native single lady living at Torran in one of the renovated flats, Ford is a place filled with memories and ghosts. She recalls that her very sitting room was once the tool room for Torran Farm, and the bedroom was the bull's box. The flat across from hers was the byre, the place where cattle were kept. She smiled wryly as she reflected on her seventy-three years in Ford: 'If anyone had told me that I would ever be having tea in Torran byre. . . .' On the other hand, she has family elsewhere, and she visits them frequently. She admits that because of the family ties elsewhere, now that the brother with whom she lived in Ford is dead, she 'might not miss Ford' if she were to move. (I am not certain she is right; ghosts and lifelong memories have a way of travelling, too.)

Even for a small place such as Ford, a locality can mean many things to many people, but the most common themes which emerged from my conversations with people were the physical and aesthetic qualities of the area ('scenery'), a sense of its past ('history'), and a complex of associations with people ('friends'). For many, the Scottishness of the area was important enough to mention, especially in the case of many English incomers. (No doubt it would have registered as more important for the Scots as well had not most of them taken it for granted.) For some of these people, the land, the lore, and the history seemed to blend together and their appreciation of the place was as a totality.

It might surprise some to learn how deep a sense of place is held by some of the recent incomers. They spend time on the land, they read about local history, they work toward its enhancement and preservation. Ironically, I met one set of English incomers who voted for Scottish devolution in 1979 and then discovered moments later that members of the most Scottish of Scots families in Ford had voted *against* the measure, which would have granted greater independence from Westminster to Scotland. In other words, some of the English families in Ford have become more self-consciously 'Scottish' than many of their born-Scots counterparts.

In addition, some of the incomers seem to be more attached to Ford than a few of the natives, some of whom mentioned their desire to live closer to 'the towns,' even if it meant leaving Ford and their friends behind. The lesson to be learned is, I think, that sense of place, and the strength of that sentiment, are not *always* born out of lifelong associations and memories of place and people. That human need for a sense of place, for rootedness, can be so strong, that we sometimes, when the circumstances are proper, sink our roots deeply in a very short time. This is, apparently, what has happened with some of the incomers to Ford, and even some, although perhaps not all, of the commuters.

So the question of how deep the sense of place is in Ford can be answered: very. This statement may seem stark in view of the qualification which is necessarily placed around it: the feelings of some individuals about the place are in fact shallow. But even though we cannot test it at this point in any quantitative way, the generalization appears reasonably accurate. And to a surprising degree, the elements of place which people cite as important or meaningful seem to be fairly consistent, even if not uniform. For most of the people of the village, whether they be native, long-term resident, or recent incomer, and whether they be Scottish or English, Ford is a place for which they feel affection and about which they care.

With some exceptions among the commuters, most of their friends are here. They enjoy the surroundings and many cultivate a knowledge of local history and lore. It is a place where people are inclined to let their roots sink in. They make of it more than just a place to park. Being native, or having a long history of associations with the people and the surroundings provides excellent soil for the growth of roots, but the humus of accumulated years is not the only medium in which roots grow into place. The finding of good new friends and the closeness to land, history, and things that 'enchant the senses' seem to be sufficient for many. And some, I suspect, are in love only with the 'differentness' of the place and culture, especially if they are tied to former home environments, which many are. It will be ironic if this affection results in so tight an embrace that the life is squeezed from indigenous culture, but this is a process which often accompanies rural gentrification.

A place does not have to be objectively unique and distinct from all other places in order for a strong sense of identity to grow around it. Very small differences—a minor physical feature, an historical event of no great import, some imagined difference in the character of the people—can be taken and made into exaggerated qualities, unique meanings, distinguishing symbols of a whole complex of otherwise very ordinary traits and features. Such differences can become the basis of identity-related beliefs about a place and its people. ('Our people aren't like the people of nearby X. X community is just a totally different place from Y community.')

Ford's people share such a sense of uniqueness. It is expressed in their interest in local history, and in the amount of time people like to spend out-of-doors, on the land, in the hills, on the water and with each other.

Given these expressions about place, I reach the conclusion that there is a strong shared identity related to locality among the villagers of Ford. Part of feeling rooted is a concomitant caring about place, and as long as people care about a place as much as people in Ford do, it will remain more than just a population—it will be a living community.

The question of relative autonomy—the extent to which the village exercises authority over decisions which affect it--is perhaps the most critical in weighing its future. Those matters over which the people of Ford *can* exercise control are in fact influenced by them, but the truth is that the future of Ford depends primarily on circumstances over which it has no control. For although this fact does not often bore into the consciousness of the villagers, Ford is a tiny part of a vast world economy. It is not even the tail wagged by the dog; it is merely a hair on that tail. Moreover, the dog does not live anywhere near Scotland, let alone Ford.

The point deserves elaboration because, like so many of these observations, what is true for Ford seems also to be true for most small communities worldwide.

It is entirely accurate to say that Ford is peripheral, but it is not the isolated place the summer visitor believes it to be. (I recall a Dutch couple who strayed into the Ford Hotel for overnight lodging. They thought places like Ford were marvelous: they expressed pleased astonishment that people in places like this did not read newspapers or watch television. They thought it incredibly quaint that Ford could ignore the rest of the world and live as it did a hundred years before. I was unable to penetrate this wholly imaginary view of Highland life. They would not look when I tried to call their attention to the stack of newspapers at the end of the bar. They did not hear the monotony of the television in the next room. They came for the scenery, for the local colour, to enjoy that figment of the imagination the Scottish Tourist Board calls 'Scotland,' and they would not allow reality to intrude on their holiday.)

Indeed, because Ford *is* on the periphery, but is not isolated, it is less able to influence the decisions made in faraway places upon which much of its vitality hinges.

Major Warde-Aldam points out, for example, that the continuation of agriculture in the area depends in large part on government policies. Dependent as farmers are on UK subsidies and EEC 'Hill Livestock Compensatory Allowances,' it is easy to see his point. Economic philosophies come and go as political parties take turn about in government—who is there to guarantee hill farming subsidies for the indefinite future? If all the Fords in the Highlands conspired to block vote, and if they persuaded their Lowland Scots cousins to join with them—a feat which no one expects to see in this millennium—they could still be out-voted ten to one by people living on the other side of the Cheviot Hills. And if the United Kingdom spoke with one voice, it would be one among many in the Common Market, where policies affecting the Highlands are frequently hammered out.

Moreover, the presence of the HIDB has been a constant in the social and economic environment of the Highlands for over fifteen years. It has pumped millions of dollars into the development of enterprises and cultural and social amenities over this period of time, amounting to about $350 per man, woman, and child in the Highlands in the first eighteen years of its existence.[10] But the HIDB was a creation of a Labour government which is no longer in power. It is, according to one HIDB staff member, regarded with suspicion by landowners and businesses in the region who sometimes worry about its sweeping powers. For all the good it has done in the region, a government hungry for budget cuts may look closely at its budget, despite its relatively small size. The appointment as Chairman of a non-Highland Conservative, whose most recent experience was in Hong Kong, has raised a question about the government's plans for the HIDB. As in other areas of government practice and policy, the people of areas such as Ford have little to say in the matter.

Similarly, Ford influences neither the world market nor the domestic markets for sheep, cattle, venison, fish, nursery plants, timber, tourist services, or any of the other products and services upon which the livelihoods of its residents depend. It is, instead, at their mercy.

Increasingly, the tourist market is moving from the hands of small local entrepreneurs to urban-based companies and government agencies. While the Scottish Tourist Board does work diligently to bring in foreign tourists, it does so by the use of inane and inauthentic imagery, as though Scotland were nothing but scenery and bagpipes, employing, for example, the highly inappropriate Larry Hagman (inappropriate not because he is Mr Hagman but because he is better known as the fictional J.R. Ewing of US television fame) to sell the 'product.' Large tour bus companies are buying up hotels in the Highlands so that they can package their tours more dependably, efficiently, and cheaply through controlling all the elements of the system—transportation, accommodations, and meals. The consequence is to place the smaller hotels and guest houses at a competitive disadvantage because the buses will not bring passengers to them anymore.

One small example from Ford illustrates the centralization of the tourist business into larger, more heavily capitalized businesses. On my second visit to the village, my wife and I met a young woman from Edinburgh in the Ford Hotel where we were all enjoying a bar lunch. She was in Ford as part of her job, which involves travelling throughout Scotland, mostly in the Highlands, looking at prospective listings for her agency and reporting on them. She represented a private company in Edinburgh which books holiday home rentals, brokering between prospective tenants and property owners. In short, even bookings into small private guest homes are becoming centralized.

Whether families continue to move into the area as they have been doing for the past few years will depend not so much on what Ford does as it will upon such imponderables as the continuation of urban flight, the pervasiveness of back-to-the-land philosophies, the availability and cost of property in Ford compared with other areas, and the general state of the economy. Rural property in the Highlands and the way of life it is thought to represent are being made commodities which are very marketable at the moment. Agents in Edinburgh, Glasgow, and London will be much better prophets of this market than anyone in Ford. For the time being, estate agents and solicitors in Lochgilphead and Oban are enjoying brisk business.

The kinds of people who come to Ford to live in the future will depend on the availability of work, the convenience of transportation for commuters, and availability of services and amenities, the quality of education, and so on. They will depend in part also on the preservation of the natural beauty of the surroundings and the maintenance of the peaceful, 'easy-osy' atmosphere sought by many urban refugees today. But the creation of jobs and the control of all the other factors which influence decisions to move in or stay are the result of more than just local initiative.

The future of Ford also depends on its relationship to the town of Lochgilphead. This is true both because there are jobs there for people to commute to from Ford, and also because what people in Lochgilphead think of Ford will help make it what it becomes. If Lochgilphead continues its pattern of growth as an employment centre, and if transportation costs do not continue to escalate excessively, then the nearby villages, including Ford, could continue to receive the population overflow. But the connection between Ford and Lochgilphead depends to some degree on how the planners, estate agents, and decision-makers view it. If they believe that Ford is too far away, or that it is not a 'defined village,' or that it is a disappointing place to which to send prospective buyers of property, then the demise of Ford could become a self-fulfilling prophecy.

All of these matters—government policies regarding agriculture, forestry, tourism, and the HIDB; the whims of the marketplace; the attitudes of prospective incomers toward the advantages and costs of country living; the availability of work; and the connection to Lochgilphead and its fortunes—are unknowns in the equation by which Ford's tomorrows will be calculated.

While the connections between a peripheral area such as Ford and the centres of political and economic power can be traced, it is not possible to predict or prophesy changes in policy and influence which might emanate from these centres in the future. But my assessment is that unless there is some surprising development, or unless all the 'unknowns' take negative turns simultaneously in some cumulative way, Ford's future is relatively sound. It has more than an even chance of life.

On the other hand, the argument that Ford might die, or that it will vegetate indefinitely, is a plausible one. Any optimistic conclusion must be tempered with the knowledge that there are signs of dying as well as signs of life. What is the nature of this negative evidence?

There is, first, the long-term downward drift in population. This drift has been of too long duration and is too widespread throughout the West Highlands to be ignored. It is possible, for example, that the recently experienced increase in residents is merely an isolated spike on a long, down-slipping demographic line. If the best guide to the future is the pattern of the past, then decline may well continue over the long term.

There are signs of ill health in the village itself, matters which have not escaped the notice or concern of its residents. Some of these signs have directly to do with the indicators of dying and vitality discussed earlier, especially that regarding institutional patterns. One such sign, for example, is the closing of the Ford school in 1972.

The community rallied late in the day to save its school, but its closing was a foregone conclusion given the small numbers of pu-

pils in attendance and the government's need to contain the costs
of education throughout the country. The school was one of the
centres of community life and pride. Parents of children who once
attended it have told me repeatedly how much it meant to them
and how much they miss even the small things associated with it,
such as hearing the children playing in the schoolyard, or watching them collect on the bridge on their way to the school house:
they could visualize the future of their world in the collectivity of
Ford's youth. Now the children are taken away by van daily and
schooled elsewhere.

There are practical as well as nostalgic concerns about the closing of the school reflected in the thoughts of Kathy MacDougall
about what could become of Ford:

> It could become a derelict village. I think a com-
> munity loses a lot when it loses its school. When
> families think about coming in, they will look
> for a school for their children. Compare Ford
> with Clachan, which fought for its school and
> now has a two-teacher school.

The closing of the school may represent more than just the loss
of an important institution pattern in Ford. The lack of success in
resisting the closure could also be said to represent some weakness
in the ability of the village to engage in collective action at a critical
time when the community's interests were at stake. Nevertheless,
the village did organize itself, which is a more important sign than
the fact that it lost.

As we have already seen, Ford may also lose its church. The
possibility of its closing is viewed with anxiety, not only by its few
remaining communicants, but even by some of those who seldom
or never occupy its pews. It could be said that much of what was
vital about the church has already been lost; its contribution to com-

munity life was certainly greater when the minister could give it more of his attention and play a more active part in the village. To a certain extent, the closing of the church would be only a symbolic loss, but it is an important symbol to many nonetheless. And it is a centre of activity in the community for some, for whom it is even more important.

Nell Kerr put the matter well. She felt the closing of the school was a 'tragedy' and she now fears for the church. 'I think,' she said, 'that once the school goes and the church goes, the village will have a hard time laying the foundations of a good community life.'

Some segments of the economy upon which Ford's employment, income, and well-being depend have shown signs of weakness in recent times. Although Joachim Brolly and some of the other private timber contractors are either prospering or holding their own, the Forestry Commission continues to decrease the number of workers it employs. The timber industry is in a state of some confusion currently,[11] and there is discussion in government circles about 'denationalizing' the Forestry Commission itself in some way. The chief forester for Inverliever believes local forestry employment may decrease both because of the introduction of new machinery (a loader called a 'forwarder,' which can load twenty-four hours a day and accomplish more in a few hours than existing machines can in a week) and because the Commission is not likely to purchase new land for planting. The forester thinks the centre of gravity has definitely shifted away from Ford as far as the Commission's work is concerned. 'Ford is a pity,' he said, 'It used to be the centre of the Forest.'

Tourism is another economic segment important to Ford and the work patterns of its residents. It has taken a downturn, beginning in the late nineteen-seventies. Whether because of fuel costs, unemployment, inflation, or the greater attraction of alternatives, fewer people are said to be touring Scotland these days, and the farther from the major cities (primarily Edinburgh), the greater the reduction of tourist traffic. As a consequence, the Ford Hotel has seen fewer of its beds filled over the last few years, and fewer anglers seem to come to Ford every year.

Not only has the number declined, but the nature of the touring population seems to have altered somewhat as well. Other resort areas in Britain have noted the same shift from a clientele made up of 'a better class of people' in earlier decades to one consisting of middle class and working class people today. The more prosperous visitors of earlier days were good for the hotel business because they enjoyed the 'catered' style of living as a part of their accustomed class privileges. When for a variety of reasons holiday making became more popular among the less prosperous it was affordable to them only if they 'catered themselves' or found other, less costly holiday accommodations. The boom in bed and breakfast homes was one consequence of this class shift in tourism. In Ford, the bed and breakfast wave arrived only recently; the only two such guest houses which exist were introduced within the last six years. The presence of these guest houses does not appear to have drained an appreciable number of visitors away from the Ford Hotel, although they may have had some effect. The two are not precisely in competition with each other because of the appeal to different types of clientele. Nevertheless, the rise of one type of accommodation and the simultaneous decline of the other signals a class shift in the consumers of Scottish holidays. Many of the 'better class' choose to jet to foreign countries these days, perhaps just because the Scottish Highlands are so much more accessible to the middle and working classes.

The presence of 'self-catering' visitors has two other consequences for Ford. One is the increased number of dwellings owned by non-residents who occupy them only a few weeks out of the year. Some of these are strictly holiday homes, second homes of city dwellers who visit Ford only on certain weekends or on two week or one-month holidays. Others are intended as retirement homes, used meanwhile as holiday homes. The second consequence is the erection of small mobile homes on the lochside by farmers who leave them parked there year-round and rent them during the summer to self-catering visitors. There were 26 such mobile homes on the southeast side of Loch Awe in autumn, 1981, most of them shabby old camping trailers (caravans) occupied by temporary urban refugees who add little to either the local economy or the scenery. (In fact, their despoliation of the scenery will no doubt bring further decline to the tourist business around Loch Awe.)

When one looks at the decline of certain institutional patterns such as the school and the church, the precariousness of work patterns associated with forestry and tourism, and the possibility of long-term population declines, any optimistic projection of Ford's future must be qualified and cautious. Nor can one help but be more pessimistic about the future after listening to certain outsiders who are familiar with the community. The minister, for example, thinks the population will continue to diminish:

> There are some new bungalows in Ford, yes, but it is not likely to receive further depopulation from Lochgilphead. It is not a dying community, but. . . .

> Unless something happens out of the blue, I can't imagine it increasing. All but four families at Kilmartin are retired families. Ford is getting to be that kind of community. It is not really at this stage now because there are some employed with the Forestry Commission. But that appears to be the situation.

The minister's impressions may not be entirely accurate, but, whatever his basis, his forecast is one of decline.

Likewise, a physical planner with the Argyll and Bute District Council in Lochgilphead sees no growth ahead for Ford. The overflow from Lochgilphead, as long as it lasts, will be sopped up by closer-by Kilmichael and eventually by Kilmartin, says the planner, but not by Ford, which is too far away. Besides, to use the planner's inimitable language,

> Ford, bless its cotton socks, is not quite a defined village like Kilmichael, or even Kilmartin. It won't disappear, but there's not likely to be any more pressure for building in Ford.

One gets the impression that Ford has been written off by the government planners as well as by the minister and the forester.

Not only outsiders, but some of its residents, too, offer gloomy forecasts. Not all are pessimistic, but those who are seem to feel that the place is rapidly becoming transformed into a retirement village with no future unless new retirees replace old ones as the latter die off. One says it is an 'elderly community'; another believes it will become 'an old folks' home,' and another is worried about too many 'non-breeders' in the population. And I recall again my first conversation in the village when a resident characterized Ford as dying, saying that it would soon become a deserted ghost village filled with ruins like others in the area.

I find all these dismal prophecies exaggerated, however. Some are based on limited personal experience, some on misinformation, some on old information which does not bring the story of Ford up to date. My answer to the question: Will Ford survive? is a qualified 'Yes.' I see signs of continuing life in the village. I think it will continue indefinitely as a living, not a dying community. But I think it will change socially and culturally. Indeed, I believe that much of the pessimism of residents about the future has in fact been caused by the confusion of *change* with death.

Winds of Change

Ford has turned a corner in its long history and is not likely to be any of the things it has been in its previous eras. It will change culturally, the structures of social life will alter, and new divisions will continue to cut across it.

How is Ford changing now and what will it become like? A reasonable conjecture can be made from understanding the kinds of demands and wants which will be made by the new population mix of the village. Such a social-demographic analysis would suggest that there will be increasing pressure for more readily available services and services of high quality. Fortunately, good health care can already be found in Lochgilphead, where there are doctors, nurses, and regional hospitals. There may, however, be an increasing demand for services related to home health care. Likewise, because there are numerous school-age children in the new population, parents will be concerned with school issues such as educational quality, transportation, safety, and the like. And although library services improved in the nineteen-sixties, they are seen as inadequate by some of the people of Ford. In general, because many of the new incomers arrive from cities and are accustomed to the convenience and entertainments of urban living, they will carry some of these expectations with them despite the fact that they came to a place like Ford to escape from the city. They would like, as most of us would, to enjoy the serenity, personal friendliness, and pastoral qualities of country living without sacrificing the conveniences of town living. The geologist misses access to books, the wife of a forester misses shopping in large stores, a retired couple miss having the full range of electrical appliances, and the young people miss the dances, the movies, the record shops. The wants and tastes of the urbanized incomers will continue to be felt as pressure for improved services generally.

In a similar vein, we have seen already what kinds of effects the new population of Ford has on community organizations. It is an exaggeration to say (as a few in Ford do) that the incomers have taken over, but they have played a strong role in carrying on existing organizations and in innovating new ones. As numerous villagers point out, the incomers bring 'fresh blood and new ideas' to Ford. This innovative spirit is likely to continue as long as there are incomers (and it is just as likely to engender some of the resentment presently found among some of the longer-term residents). It

John at a news conference held to announce his selection
as the seventh president of Berea College in January 1984.
(Photo by Berea College Public Relations)

is even conceivable that newcomers could become more involved in the church, if it is granted a reprieve and its mission is rejuvenated. The experiences that people bring with them of activities and organizations in other locales will have some effect on the structures of social life in Ford; new ideas will be experimented with, and some will be discarded while others become institutionalized.

On the other hand, there is a large element of the population of recent incomers which does not participate much in the organization or social life of the village. If Ford becomes a 'bedroom' community for more commuters, the proportion of non-participants may grow. Still, the recruitment of people to voluntary associations is usually a struggle in most communities, and the pattern in Ford may not be so different, or become so different, from elsewhere.

It is likely that the hotel pub will continue to be an important focus of village life, but it may become a place where the new divisions in the community become more visible. Going to the pub is a cultural pattern more familiar to natives and less recent Scottish incomers; it seems to attract younger persons and those whose work is in or near Ford more than it attracts commuters, older persons, English incomers, and those whose family life appears to absorb all their attention. There is something very Scottish about the pub, and there is no reason to believe that this cultural atmosphere will weaken. And if more people work outside the village, it is probable that fewer will feel they have time to spend in leisurely evenings at the pub. The focus of life for a number of these new people—the commuters—will be work and family.

What will the role of the estates be in the future of Ford? Our earlier history of the estates surrounding Ford makes it clear that they were much more important in its past than they are at the present time. I once asked Robin Malcolm of Poltalloch how he thought the relationship of the laird to the local community had changed. In his answer, he dated much of the change from just before World War

Two. The changes are rather dramatic: the laird used to be the local authority, deciding where and when and how schools, churches, and houses would be built. Now these decisions are in the hands of local authorities, selected public bodies and the staffs appointed to assist them. In addition, at one time everyone in the village would have been working for the laird, and their services would have been let out to other users as their time was available and their skills in demand. Now, except for a handful, the villagers are independent of the laird's employment. Some aspects of the ancient feudal system still hold, but for the most part, the estate merely represents another large-scale landholding in the neighbourhood.

In the case of Ford, what has happened to the estates in the past has had direct influences on the nature of village life, as we have seen. There is presently only one major estate operating there. If Ederline were to be sold to an owner who chose not to farm it, or if government policies made farming infeasible, the economy, and work patterns of Ford would be affected drastically. If the lands of Ederline, Auchinellan, or Creaganterve were to be sold to the Forestry Commission, hill farming could virtually disappear, but such an event is unlikely under current government policies. If these estates were to be broken up and sold piecemeal for retirement, second-home, holiday or other residential purposes, again the farming sector of the local economy would be sharply affected. On the other hand, the resale of small portions of estate lands could lead to an increase in the incomer population.

The greatest likelihood is that estate lands in Ford will continue to be used for farming, no matter into whose hands they fall, as long as the EEC and UK government subsidies continue to make hill farming a break-even or marginally profitable activity. It is not likely that any imaginable changes in ownership patterns would alter the authority patterns between the estates and the village of Ford; as Robin Malcolm points out, those changes occurred years ago.

Ford will change culturally in subtle ways. Old customs and patterns are changing (as they always have been) to the extent that some feel a loss of culture even now. As more incomers arrive, especially urban people and non-Scots, new ideas and customs and habits arrive with them. What they do *not* bring is just as important. They do not bring with them a culture which duplicates what was there before—a replacement culture which fills in the missing elements lost as the natives leave or die. With a population as mobile as this one (over half the people in residence in 1981 having arrived within the previous 12 years), it would be difficult to imagine Ford duplicating itself culturally over even one generation. Even without the effect of incomers on local culture, ways of life in Ford are changing as a result of its connectedness with the world at large. The introduction of television is just one example.

It is therefore not surprising to hear people lament the passing of ceilidhs. Many of the individuals who contributed their talents are now dead, and many of the newcomers, although they enjoy the consumption of Scottish music, story-telling, and dancing, cannot furnish these talents themselves. And even many of the natives would, one suspects, be tempted to stay home and watch television. Nor is it so surprising to hear that most people now knock before entering someone else's home, this is the product of urban ways displacing country ways. The old-timers say that nothing is safe from theft anymore, and this is a lamentable fact, one which again results from high mobility, increased closeness to towns and cities, and the presence of more strangers passing through. (As one man put it succinctly 'Glasgow has come too near us. Loch Awe has been flogged to death.') Perhaps it is true as well that the older pattern of 'visiting' has fallen off. An elderly widow opined that the new people tend 'to stay to themselves. They don't visit. That's the style of people they are.'

Thus is Ford changing and thus will Ford continue to change. It will be a different place in the future from what it is now, and people will continue to miss the ways of life with which they have become familiar in their lifetimes. But this is nothing new—Ford has always been changing, and it is easy to imagine the good folks of several generations ago lamenting the passing of the Gaelic (as they no longer do in Ford but do further north and in the Western Isles), the declining use of the drove road, or the disappearance of the horse.

Culture change is a normal, if saddening process. If it takes place at too fast a rate, it can produce tensions and dislocations which divide a community seriously. It could conceivably exacerbate the division which already exists in incipient form in the village of Ford. But it is possible for people to share the ingredients of a sense of place to a sufficient degree that differences in ways of life are tolerated, that new ways blend with old, and that a people can work through their tensions together. It remains to be seen whether Ford will accommodate its own differences on the one hand or fall into more separated segments on the other. Whether its sense of 'Scottishness' can be shared or whether it will be divisive seems to me a most critical issue.

The making and keeping of a community requires more than merely maintaining a population in a locality and providing them basic services. It requires that people representing political and economic authority outside the community become the authors of policies and programmes which nurture life and do not presume the death of small places. Moreover, a community, as contrasted with a mere population, cannot persist that does not nourish shared perceptions and basic values, shared experiences, a shared sense of place which manifests itself in shared activity and collective action on behalf of the whole.

Ford could die. There are sufficient signs of dying to cause concern. But it is living now and its vital signs could continue and grow stronger. The question facing Ford is whether it will devolve into a set of people living side by side, acting together only in emergencies, sharing only their surfaces, or whether it will continue—and will be encouraged by public policy and private initiatives—to be the community that it is now, 'laying the foundations of a good community life' for its inheritors.

Comparative Changes in Appalachia and the Scottish Highlands

John's studies of the Shiloh and Ford communities inevitably led him to an analysis of their similarities and differences. One of his analyses was published in 1985 as a contribution to the series *Perspectives on the American South*, edited by Charles Wilson and James Cobb, and bore the title "Place for Sale: Repopulation and Change in an Appalachian and a Highland Scottish Community." The changes in Shiloh were compared with changes in Ford that John had observed and reported in his book published the previous year.*

What had impressed him most on his return to Shiloh was not so much the modernization of the community as the transformation of the population through the invasion of newcomers. They had moved to Shiloh for a variety of reasons, but generally for what John referred to as "some kind of imagined improvement in the quality of life." Whatever their reasons, their very presence altered the community structure, not necessarily for the worse. The process of repopulation, John noted, was "a case of rural invasion and succession. Local families are leaving Shiloh in search of improved lives in towns and cities, and urban refugees are taking their places in the country, also in search of better ways of living."

Meanwhile, in the even smaller Scottish community of Ford, a similar process was taking place. Although many of the older residents of Ford believed the community was dwindling, it was actually growing as "incomers" moved into the area. "When you listen to people in Ford talk about why they came there," John wrote, "you realize that they, like their Shiloh counterparts, have come to find a place on Fantasy Mountain. And to give credit where it is due in both Ford and Shiloh, most of them have found it."

As in Shiloh, the presence of new residents was bringing about a change in the community culture. The new culture, John perceived, was being reconstructed "in accordance with the ideas that incomers bring with them about what village life ought to be like." Perhaps it is a normal consequence of what John termed "place exchange" in which rural aspirants to a better life flee to the cities and urban refugees flee to the countryside for the same reason. So long as there is unhappiness with current place of residence and entrepreneurial-stimulated fantasies of a better life to be found in the country— or city—the process of place-exchange can be expected to continue.

PLACE FOR SALE: REPOPULATION AND CHANGE IN AN APPALACHIAN AND A HIGHLAND SCOTTISH COMMUNITY

It is a commonplace that every community is in change and that every study of community ought to be a study of its change. It would be difficult for me to do otherwise, for change is what I have witnessed even in the relatively brief time I have watched the two communities upon which I report here. The change processes I will describe in the two distant geographic settings of Appalachian America and Highland Scotland could be considered, I suppose, examples of rural gentrification or rural invasion and succession. They have to do with the repopulating of the countryside and the cultural repaving of rural areas. These processes are part of a larger pattern in which people search for opportunity, motivated and aided in this search by a variety of commercial and informal brokers. Part of the search is a search for place.

What, one might ask, is the basis for comparison of these two widely separated communities? The place that I call "Shiloh" is located in western North Carolina, the village of Ford in the West

Highlands of Scotland. Despite the great separation in distance, there are similarities that invite comparison. Geographically, the West Highlands (the old county of Argyll) and the Blue Ridge section of North Carolina share in common their topography, their beauty, and their shrinking distance from urban centers. They are both peripheral areas within subregions of a country, both less affluent than the urban cores to which they relate, both somewhat culturally different from their surroundings. Western North Carolina is in fact said to have been settled in part by Highlanders and others of Scottish descent in the 18th century, although it would be unwise to press the matter of cultural purity and persistence as far as some do in studies of Appalachia and the South. Both Shiloh and Ford share today a particular form of linkage to the societies of which they are part. There is a peculiar bond between the city and the countryside that finds its expression in these two cases—a bond that, as I have said, involves a search for place. It is the sharing of this bond that is the basis of the comparison drawn here.

Shiloh Revisited

When I first went to Shiloh, the changes on which I focused had to do with individuals and families in the process of what I then called "modernization," and what I now see as a historically mandated absorption into an industrializing working class. At that time, in 1965, I made note of another change in Shiloh: the arrival of an increasing number of tourists and summer visitors. When I placed this coming-in alongside the then-extensive migration of natives to the cities, I made a note that these twin movements could be captured in the phrase "inside out and outside in." But I did not bring the "outside in" part of the phenomenon to the center of the stage.

In those days, of course, Appalachian out-migration was the big story. I knew of that important trend largely because of the published work of James Brown. I suppose it was because of the absence of published research on tourists and in-migrants that I did not dwell on it as a major theme in my writing on Shiloh. Fifteen years later there was still not much published, but the fact of in-migration was so obvious a fact of experience by 1980 that it simply could not be subordinated to other themes of change in Shiloh.

Shiloh is a cluster of several neighborhoods ranging around a single main road in a rural western North Carolina county. The cluster is sufficiently integrated by kinship, friendship, and economic ties that it is thought of by residents—as well as outsiders—as a whole community. The origin of the community is lost entirely to history. More than likely, it was settled by whites of varied nationality in the 1700s, some of whom would have arrived there by way of the North Carolina Piedmont, though some of whom may have traveled south along the Blue Ridge spine. It is extremely doubtful that this area was ever isolated from the rest of the country in terms of its contacts, although it may have been relatively uninfluenced by what went on elsewhere until the late 19th and early 20th centuries, when timber interests and missionaries moved in to harvest trees and souls, respectively.

Change surged upon Shiloh as a consequence of World War II, when roads were built and improved, schools were upgraded and consolidated, the extent of farming declined, employment in mining and manufacturing began and increased, and communications from the outside grew in quantity and nature as a result of the coming of telephones (in the 1960s) and television (somewhat later).

In 1965 I identified the coming in of outsiders as no more important than the passing through of tourists and the occasional summer visitor interested in a second home. These were seen as another source of the "modernizing influence of the outside on the inside of this relatively unknown and nondistinctive mountain place" (Stephenson 1968). On the other side of the ridge there was, I knew, an entire summer settlement of Floridians in a cove named, coincidentally, Pensacola, but I did not foresee adequately what would happen on the Shiloh side of the mountain. Nor did I appreciate what lay behind the resettling of Pensacola and what its effects on local structures and culture were, other than to provide a cultural challenge to "traditional" values and orientation.

When I drove into Shiloh in 1980, however, the first observation I wrote in my notes concerned the real estate billboards decorating the approach to the community. They were new, as was the sign pointing to the campground and recreation area that did not exist on my earlier visits. Driving down the main road, I noticed that a branch office of a national realty chain had opened since my last trip to Shiloh, and that the store had changed hands. I was surprised to see a new Presbyterian church not far from the old one, which apparently was still functioning, and then a brick building that boasted the existence of a volunteer fire department.

A few new homes could be seen from this road, but otherwise the housing looked much like it had 15 years before. When I explored the off-roads, I discovered that what could be seen from the main road was entirely misleading: there were numerous new homes up the coves, as well as new mobile homes and greatly improved older residences of long standing. Farther down the main road I saw signs marking new tract developments, one of which was built around a championship golf course, on the edge of which had been built a new Bavarian restaurant (owned by card-carrying Bavarians, I might add).

With the aid of the son of one of my former key informants, I mapped the entire community, identifying the occupants of every dwelling for comparison to a similar map I had made 15 years earlier. And with the help of the son of another informant, I extracted information on land ownership in the township covering a 13–year span. I interviewed the new realtor and examined the records of property sales in that office. I talked to numerous newcomers and longer-term residents. The story of change in Shiloh in 1980 had little or nothing to do with modernization; it had, rather, to do with the resettlement of the community by persons whose origins were outside the mountains and indeed outside North Carolina altogether.

I found that while my friend John Henry Sommers had moved his household from down on the creek up to the main road, the internationally known concert pianist Lilly Kraus and her physician son-in-law and his family had moved from an eastern city to a place down on that same creek. John Henry was proud of his new location, pointing to the town sign in his front yard and remarking, "You can't hardly get more downtown than *that*." The Kraus household was equally proud of its new homestead up under the trees and out of sight of the entire community.

I learned that the deaf-mute old man who once made a rockerless rocking chair for me was enjoying life in Morgantown, North Carolina, while his old ramshackle house off the beaten path toward the upper end of the creek had been bought and completely remodeled, complete with white picket fence, by a retired couple from Miami.

I discovered that the store had been bought by a couple from the city of Baltimore who read about the property in a nationally distributed realty catalog. During all his years in the General Electric plant, the man had dreamed about being a country storekeeper, and now his dream was a reality.

Ironically, the farther I drove from the highly visible areas near the main road, the more likely I was to witness the transformation of the community. For people like John Henry, moving to the highway was an escape from marginality and the social class putdowns associated with life down the creek. To the newcomer physician, the attorney, and all the retired couples from the cities, the realization of their anti-urban ideal was measurable by the distance away from the highway. So as the John Henrys moved in closer to what they saw as a progressive, civilized life, the urbanites took their places, both literally and figuratively. Crumbling foundations of old houses were shored up, rusting roofs were replaced, weatherbeaten boards were made shiny with paint, and new mailboxes were erected bearing family names unfamiliar both to me and to the natives.

Statistics confirmed what the eye could see. The tax records for 1980, when compared with those for 1968, showed that the total number of parcels of land had increased while the average size of each had decreased. They also showed that the value of the land had skyrocketed over this 13-year period. And they told that the proportion of properties belonging to owners who were not native to the township or the county had grown strikingly.

The tax records showed, for example, that the number of property owners increased from 1,106 in 1968 to 1,521 in 1980 (see Table 2.1). Seventy-five percent of this increase was made up of non-natives. In 1968 the proportion of taxpayers who were natives of the township was already low at 47.1 percent; by 1980, the figure had fallen to 35.0 percent.

Table 2.1 Owners of Taxable Property by Nativity and Residence Category, Shiloh Township, 1968 and 1980

Nativity	1968	1980	Increase	%	% of Total Increase
Township Native	521	532	11	2.1	2.6
County Native	27	86	59	218.5	14.2
Non-Native			[325]		[78.3]
Full-time Resident	59	148	89	150.8	21.4
Part-time Resident	69	171	102	147.8	24.6
Non-Resident	403	537	134	33.2	32.3
Unknown and other	27	47	20 7	4.1	4.8
Totals	1106	1521	415	37.5	99.9

Source: County Tax Records for 1967-8 and 1980, coded by Christopher Chrisawn, native and lifelong resident.

When the category of "non-native" was broken down, the numbers became even more interesting. The owners were first divided into "resident" and "nonresident," and the residents were further classified as "full-time" and "part-time." The largest percentage increase occurred among full-time residents, followed closely by part-time residents. Far and away the smallest percentage increase was among township natives, who increased their ownership by only 11 properties, or 2.1 percent. To summarize, native ownership was giving way to outside ownership, and the fastest-growing category of new owners were those who came from outside to take up residence.

Who were the newcomers, and for what reasons had they come to Shiloh? Some, of course, were speculators who did not live there and never intended to. They hoped simply to enjoy financial gain. Others had bought property to enjoy for short vacations, sometimes renting out their otherwise unoccupied houses in order to help meet the mortgage payments. Others had built or bought homes to which they would retire; some of them had reached retirement and lived in Shiloh year-round. The remaining category was also made up of full-time residents; these were the year-round dwellers with intentions of permanent residence, who came to work in the vicinity and find a better life for themselves and their families. They were of working and child-rearing age.

The ownership statistics from tax records showed what had already been revealed to me in a visit with the realty office. Sixty pieces of property worth a total of $1 million had been sold by the company since it opened its doors four years earlier. Where were the buyers from? The realtor opened a desk drawer and read off the home addresses of the clients: 23 from Florida; 3 from New York; 2 from Mississippi; one each from Connecticut, Vermont, New Jersey, Ohio, Michigan, Pennsylvania, Illinois, Missouri, Indiana, Maryland, and Lexington, Kentucky. Eleven were from North Carolina, of which five were from the county and only one from the township.

What reasons did people give for buying places in Shiloh? Generally, it had to do with the fulfillment of a dream—not always the same dream, but some kind of imagined improvement in the quality of life. People said they were tired of the city—the danger, the traffic, the noise, the racial situation. People said they had been in places like this while on vacation, and they had in mind to live out their retirement days in a kind of unending extension of long-awaited, full-time leisurely inactivity. People said they came here for solace and retreat, to get close to the land and be with real people. A few people said they came here to help the sick, the poor, the unlettered, the disorganized, and those deficient in high culture. All these people said they liked the place and, in varying degrees, the people, and that they felt at home here.

What they had bought was, both literally and figuratively, a place. (A place, one might say, on Fantasy Mountain.) From whom was the land being purchased? Much of it was in the hands of land speculators and developers. Ironically, most of the so-called spec property was handled by a native son who had sold his father's grocery business to devote more time to more interesting commercial pursuits. This was Craig Bowman, who was exceedingly bright—bright enough to know where the money was, and insightful enough to see exactly what was happening as a result of his own actions.

Craig knows that the land values in this township have risen faster than elsewhere in the county—that this is referred to as the "Gold Coast" of the country. Land sales here have surpassed Pensacola (across the ridge) now, according to him. "Many people," he says, "have sold out to outsiders at what to them is a high price, and have bought over in McDowell County or in Burke, changing their life-styles." Craig buys land and sells it for a profit. I asked him what the local people think about what he's doing. He says, "The local people always want to know whether the people I'm selling to will be nice people. So far, they've been satisfied." Then he became pensive:

> I would trade all the money for the way it was in the mid-fifties, but it's too late. There's an old saying: don't crap in your own backyard. But we've done it, and I've helped. We all justify land development by saying if we didn't do it, somebody else would. Sooner or later, nobody but a few of us who can afford it will be left here.

As if to prove his point, he later introduced me to a man named Ed by saying, "I want you to meet a member of a dying breed—a native."

The breed is not dying, of course, but it is becoming outnumbered. The natives who have not moved to McDowell or Burke counties—or Charlotte or California—are still finding employment within commuting distance at places such as Baxter Laboratories, American Tread, Hickory Springs, Blue Bell, Glen Raven, Armored Garments, the golf course, the Highway Department, and the Forest Service. They still fish and go to church and observe Decoration Day and visit back and forth in ways reminiscent of Shiloh in 1965.

But the structure of community life is tangibly different, and subtle cultural changes have not gone unnoticed. None but the most hopelessly romantic would deny that these changes represent community improvements for the most part, although there is a great deal of ambivalence expressed by natives. In 1965, Shiloh experienced near-trauma in creating a community improvement organization, because no one would agree to be nominated as chairman. In fact, there were no community organizations except for the churches and a softball team, and the only reason the community improvement group came into being was because of the efforts of a minister from Ohio. Now there is a volunteer fire department, organized by newcomers but run jointly by newcomers and natives.

There is a program for senior citizens, organized by newcomers. The new church was begun at the instigation of one man from "outside." A monthly music appreciation group was organized—again by newcomers. Child development and health services have improved because of the initiative of a physician who moved into Shiloh. He has also maintained an imaginative program of assistance to problem families, coupled with housing improvement. Last, but certainly not least, there is now a community center in Shiloh—an unthinkable accomplishment 15 years ago that has since been accomplished mainly because of the efforts of newcomers. (A YMCA-sponsored youth program was the next project in the works; this idea was being promoted mainly by the wife of one recently arrived chiropractor.)

Relations between the newcomers and the natives vary greatly; but in the main, the attitude is one of mutual tolerance, a keeping of distance, a muted disdain. Most of the newcomers expressed the feeling that they were well accepted by the natives, but they admitted that they rarely associated with them except in public places such as the stores and in meetings. They had ideas about local culture that were not especially complimentary. ("Nobody will ever act together down here." "They're not taught things about responsibility and motivation." "They don't know the world outside this little place." "The low level of education is appalling." "I didn't realize the apathy of the people." "They don't know about things so they don't want them." "People are afraid to say anything for fear it will come back on them. We need to introduce the democratic process here.") The newcomers say that people are friendly, but they don't socialize: they do not take meals with natives, for example, and they do not golf with them.

The natives do not hide their feelings well. One man, attempting to put his new neighbors in a good light, said, minimally, "They speak. And I speak to them." Another says that some are better than others:

Some of these outsiders is all right and others is just plumb hateful. They're unfriendly, don't want you to set foot on their land but want to roam all over yours. I sold a man ten acres above me here; I wish I hadn't. I needed the money. It's been sold twice since then and I never met the man that owns it now. He might be one of those hateful ones.

Another native talks about how the outsiders stick to themselves. He does have one close friend who is an outsider—he says, "He ain't no smarter than I am"—but as for most of them, he says simply, "The Florida people has about taken over." When I asked Hope Sommers if she knew of any other terms people used for the newcomers, she said, simply, "land-takers."

A retiree from Miami, watching the sun set from his front porch while he broke with local custom and drank beer openly in front of God and his neighbors, said that he had found the local way of life different from his, but not surprisingly different. He said people were easy to get along with: "We don't have any problems. It's live and let live. Nobody sticks their nose in your business." That may be all he asks for, coming from Miami. But I asked him how he thought local people felt about outsiders like himself. His answer was accurate and perceptive: "They like the money from Florida people, but then they resent them."

We see in this one small Appalachian community a case of rural invasion and succession. Local families are leaving Shiloh in search of improved lives in towns and cities, and urban refugees are taking their places in the country, also in search of better ways of living. The machinery of this complex exchange is oiled and operated by a combination of local and outside entrepreneurs—all brokers of one kind or another. And the consequence is an uneasy acceptance of change on the part of natives—an eagerness to take the

Shortly after moving into the President's Home at Berea, the Stephenson family poses for a photograph by Warren Brunner with the beloved mountains in the background. L-R: Rebecca, John, David, Jennifer, and Jane.

money and run, coupled with as yet ill-formed questions about messes of pottage. The changes involve getting the community organized, forming more substantial community associations than Shiloh has ever known, and paving over local customs with the thoughts and habits and energy of urban sophisticates who came here to look at the scenery, lift up the benighted, and get away from the high prices and urban confusion they left behind.

While the natives may struggle with ambivalence toward their new neighbors, the newcomers seem on the whole quite happy with their decisions to relocate in Shiloh. While they may be aware of the distance at which they are kept by the natives, that pattern of distancing is nothing new to them, and it is more than acceptable as a part of community life; it is probably even preferred over the alternative. The newcomers feel accepted, and they *feel* at home. The full-time residents have made commitments to this place. It is now *their* place. They feel affection for it and love its physical aspects, and they want to care for it and "improve" it.

There can be little doubt that the newcomers' influence on Shiloh is making it a better community in many respects, if we measure community vitality by the degree of locality-based association and mutual problem-solving. If, on the other hand, we were to define the strength of community in terms of shared identity or shared sense of place, the picture in Shiloh is more confusing. My impression is that the newcomers may now have a stronger sense of place than do the natives, who are uncertain what is happening to their place. One native, in attempting to analyze what was taking place in Shiloh, said unsentimentally, "You've got to have progress, but after you reach a point, you lose what you had and you can't get it back."

The place has changed, every native seems to agree. One commented, "Neighborhoods are not as closely knit. Life is faster paced. People don't keep up with each other—they don't care that much." Another, describing what he meant by saying that the pace of life had changed, said, "Decisions are made quickly now. It used to take three days to decide whether to cut your hay. And you don't make deals on handshakes anymore, either." These are people reporting their perceptions of culture change—changes in a place they are not certain is even theirs anymore, a place becoming so filled with outsiders that some of the natives are feeling a bit crowded. Mountain humor, like humor everywhere, often has an edge to it, as when one man said to me, "If you're thinking about moving down into here, I'd say you'd better hurry while you can still wedge in."

As Shiloh changes into whatever it is to become, it will slip quietly into that future with the aid of native land brokers and culture brokers. Craig Bowman is an example of the local land broker who learns to live with his episodic nostalgic urges. Jim Hartley is a culture broker who plays a role in the transition because he understands the old Shiloh. There are California plates on his pickup.

There is a surfboard lying in the yard—probably the only one in the county, and it belongs to a native. Jim wants to stay permanently in this valley, but he leaves the door open to opportunities elsewhere, just in case things do not work out here. He could probably live anywhere, make a decent living as a builder/carpenter, and be happy. Everyone—native and newcomer—knows Jim, and everyone likes him. Jim does not suffer from nostalgia; he is not tormented by images of a departed past. He represents the kind of cultural and interpersonal linkage that will make the transition of community identity a relatively smooth one.

The Village of Ford

Comparisons between Shiloh and the West Highland Scottish village of Ford are instructive, although on the surface one would see little reason to seek parallels between them. Their histories are highly divergent, there are important differences in class structure and culture, and their settlement patterns are dissimilar. Even their weather and their topography are different, not to mention the national histories of which they are tiny parts.

Ford is quite small, with 156 people in around 60 households. Its history is considerably older than that of Shiloh. Records make mention of the place in the 17th century, although it was most certainly a human settlement earlier than that. Ford became important as a stopping place and a river crossing for the numerous cattle drives by means of which Highland cattle were delivered to markets in central Scotland. Located at the head of Loch Awe in Argyllshire, Ford grew adventitiously at the intersection of two townships and three then major estates. Once dependent on these estates for support and employment, the villagers now find employment in diverse settings usually not related to estates: tourism, forestry, hill farming, plant nursery work, fish farming, gamekeeping, and a number of occupations outside the community such as teaching, nursing, geology, and architecture.

Shortly after my arrival in Ford, I was told by an informant that I would have difficulty finding many natives in the village because everyone living there has arrived within their lifetimes. This prediction was not greatly exaggerated. Eventually, I identified seven natives among the 156 people in the village. The native population, it was said, had been dwindling for many years.

Yet the general population in Ford in 1981 was increasing. A look at population figures for the township of Kilmartin (in which Ford is located) showed that until recently the population had been steadily decreasing since 1801. This historical decline paralleled the pattern of population change in the Highlands generally. The infamous Highland Clearances, begun in the 1770s, resulted in massive forcible evictions, relocation, and emigration so that the native population could be replaced with sheep, which were more profitable to the large landowners. The potato blight, the failure of agriculture in the Highlands to respond to "improvements" and rationalization efforts, and the attraction of employment alternatives outside the Highlands continued this heavy outflow throughout the 19th and 20th centuries.

Entire glens that once might have contributed hundreds of fighting men for some Highland cause are now empty of people. Kilmartin Parish itself declined from 1,501 people in 1801 to 327 in 1971. In one of my first visits to Ford, an informant expressed serious doubt about the future of the village, predicting that it would die within a very few years as other villages had died before it. When I saw the long history of decline in the census figures, I knew no reason to doubt her prophecy.

But Ford was far from dead, as it turned out, both in terms of population and by other measures of community vitality. The Scottish Women's Rural Institute had thoughtfully taken an exact census in Ford village in 1966, a count with which I could compare my own census in 1981, and the comparison showed that the population had increased between 40 and 50 percent. It was clear that this growth was not attributable to natural increase—the young were still leaving Ford just as in earlier generations, and the birthrate had declined, if any-thing—but rather was brought about by a surge in the number of im-migrants, or "incomers," as they are known in Britain.

Who are the incomers and why did they come to Ford?

Before answering this question, it is important to make a dis-tinction between recent incomers and those who have been resi-dents of Ford for many years. Because the recent surge seemed to begin around 12 years earlier, I chose this as the date by which to distinguish early from recent incomers. Of the 59 present (1981) households in Ford, 33, or 56 percent, were those of recent incomers; 19, or 32 percent, were those of earlier incomers; and only 7, or 12 percent, were those of natives. Now, who were the recent incomers?

They were people such as the Greenshields, retired English schoolteachers, who had traveled earlier in the Highlands and looked for a place like Ford in which to live out their later years.

Mr. Brotherston had an ancestor from the Lothian area (near Edinburgh), so that there was a somewhat remote Scottish connec-tion in the family.

They were people like the Parks, lowland Scots who had worked on the western islands and then moved to Ford where Roger found work on a new fish farm. Roger and Nan say they love the High-land nature, scenery, land lore. They cannot imagine living in the city now. Ford is home.

Bryan Johns is an architect in the nearby town of Lochgilphead. The Johns moved to Ford from Edinburgh. He is a member of the Ford Gun Club, and he teaches bagpiping in the high school at Lochgilphead. When first footing takes place at Hogmanay (New Year's), Bryan is there with pipe and kilt, leading the group from door to door, wishing everyone a happy new year and bringing a small gift to bring good luck as the ancient custom dictates. The

Johns like Ford now, although at first they did not feel readily accepted by the village, and they would only move to Lochgilphead or some other town to reduce the inconvenience of country living.

Ian Willis came to Ford from Lancashire (England) to take over a nursery and make a go of it. To the Willises, Ford represented economic opportunity combined with a pleasant countryside environment and comfortable human relationships.

Other recent incomers are teachers, secretaries, nurses, and government employees in Lochgilphead. One is a businessman in Oban; another is a geologist who works anywhere in the world the oil business takes him. Others are shepherds and farm workers and forestry workers. Most came to Ford, like the retired couples, because they knew of the area from earlier travels or from friends, and they always wanted to live in a place in the countryside where the pace was slower, the people friendly, and the scenery beautiful. Others (the shepherds and farmers, especially) came to Ford because of job opportunities.

When you listen to people in Ford talk about why they came there, you realize that they, like their Shiloh counterparts, have come to find a place on Fantasy Mountain. And to give credit where it is due in both Ford and Shiloh, most of them have found it.

For almost all the recent incomers to Ford feel very much at home here. They feel a strong sense of place. Miss Greenshields once said that, whenever she goes on a journey away from the Highlands, when she comes back and sees the mountains she feels that "these are my hills." The Greenshields all voted for Scottish devolution in the 1979 referendum, which made them, by that measure at least, more Scottish than many of their Scottish neighbors in Ford, who by and large voted against it. The MacNays, also English ("born Londoners"), are rooted strongly in Ford, finding there "everything to delight the senses," and good friends and neighbors in the bargain. The incomers are among the most active in the local historical society, and incomers played a vital role in preparing the local history written several years ago. Few of them, incidentally, showed much desire to be buried near their original homes.

The impact of the recent incomers on the village is difficult to overestimate. They express their commitments to their adopted home in a number of ways, including participation in community associations. Mr. Brotherston's sister plays the organ at church. Incomers are active on the Village Hall Committee, which plans a large number of community programs throughout the year. Incomers began a youth program, an exercise program for women, and a new play school. Incomers helped with the planning and installation of the village's television antenna. Some of them are active in the Ford Gun Club, which has been a village institution since at least 1880.

Many recent incomers also participate in pub life at the Ford Hotel, which is the center of village life for the largest number of residents, especially during the winter when the tide of tourists is out.

The incomers have had an undeniably invigorating effect on the village. Although some older community institutions have disappeared or weakened, the incomers have helped bring new ones to life. At the same time that the former urbanites celebrate the virtues of country living and the English celebrate Scottishness, however, they bring change with them. These differences in habit and outlook are not always appreciated by the natives and early incomers. It is as though the olden ways of life are weakened by the very act of glorifying them, or as though what is cherished but not fully understood is smothered in the embrace of affectionate strangers. Whatever is left of native Highland culture in Ford is being papered over with the images of Scottish culture that people bring with them. The culture is reconstructed in accordance with the ideas the incomers bring with them about what village life ought to be like.

New divisions within the community have also accompanied the changes in population. Long-term residents understand something about the nature of invasion and succession, but not all of them like its consequences. A common complaint was, "They come to live here and then tell us what to do." I was told that the incomers are resented because they buy property at high prices that local people cannot afford, which has caused natives to leave. The incomers are described often as unfriendly, superior acting, demanding, aloof, and overbearing. They are referred to as "white settlers," a term usually applied to the English, against whom there is a strong historical prejudice among Scots, but which in this case is applied to a number of urban Scots as well. Some of the incomers are aware that they are thought of as "white settlers," but most are either unaware or choose to ignore it. The resentment is never expressed openly and is never manifested in conflict except when it takes the form of some other issue. The division is there, ever present, but below the surface of human relationships.

The village of Ford is not dying; it is becoming transfigured, but it is alive. In general, if one were to look for signs of community vitality, one might try to uncover evidence of the following:

> 1. The presence of shared, purposeful activity related to the collective interests of those inhabiting the locality.

> 2. The presence of locality-based institutions, or organized patterns of living.

> 3. The presence of shared identity rooted in a sense of place.

> 4. The presence of at least some minimal degree of authority over part of the decision-making that affects the locality.

> 5. The presence of shared overall goals and values regarding the community.

On all these counts, Ford shows vital signs. Community associations are reasonably strong, there is evidence of shared place-related purpose and of shared place-related identity. Decision-making autonomy is not strong in any absolute sense, but it is as strong as it could be, given Ford's linkages to larger economic and political systems. Ford is not dying; it is, however, going through another watershed change in its long life.

Changing Places

What is happening in Shiloh and Ford is no doubt taking place in a number of other settings. Howard Newby (1980, 1987), for example, has published thoughtful studies of the effects of incomers in farm villages of East Anglia. A Scottish anthropologist has almost completed a study of tourists and second-home owners in Sennen Cove, near Penzance, in the south of England. The process proceeds apace—although without benefit of study—along almost the entire Blue Ridge spine in Virginia and North Carolina. It is not unknown in places such as the fringe counties of eastern Kentucky.

Nor is what is happening today a new invention of our time. The surge of movement into the countryside in search of new permanent residences has swelled in recent years, but the precedent has been there to build on for many decades. In the case of western North Carolina, historians track the earliest movement of tourists and second-home owners as far back as the 1820s. Apparently, these were mostly South Carolina planters' families in search of relief from malaria during the summer season. In the case of the West Highlands, travelers' accounts are fairly common from the early 19th century; and by the late 1800s, the area had been "Balmoralized" along with the rest of the Highlands, with estates given over to sporting pastimes, and the lochs overrun with anglers. (The Game Book from the main estate at Ford showed that in 1903 there were 1,120 birds and 2,370 rabbits shot and 1,162 fish taken from its various lochs.) Loch steamers ferried tourists around the Ford area for about a hundred years beginning in the 1850s. The Ford Hotel is said to have opened in 1864, but inns of some kind were there before that date. The earliest guest book for the hotel I could find began in 1924; it showed visitors from all over Britain and the continent—and one from Arizona—but mainly from England. The point is that many people first learned about Ford by spending summer holidays there, and that second home ownership—if it can be called that—began in the 19th century when wealthy Londoners bought up estates and converted them from farming to sporting ventures for purposes of recreation and personal prestige.

What began in both western North Carolina and the West Highlands of Scotland as exclusively an upper class pattern of extravagant leisure consumption became more available to a nonaristocratic but still "better class of people" before the turn of the century, and gradually has become accessible by large numbers of middle and working class visitors, second-home owners, and new permanent residents.

To return to an earlier point, what is happening in these two communities and elsewhere is not really quite rural gentrification. Today's newcomers are not members of the gentry class. They range from professional class to working class, and the majority are hardworking white collar, managerial, and subprofessional.

Likewise, what is happening is similar to invasion and succession, except that the ethnic and class nature of these invaders is quite different from the classic Chicago case, nor are there anything faintly resembling concentric zones, nor are the consequences of the process anything like what the Chicago model would predict.

If the process must be given a name, I would suggest the simple phrase, place-exchange. It is a process in which rural aspirants to a better life flee to the cities and urban refugees flee to the countryside for the same reason. In both cases, new lives and identities are sought by persons unhappy with their present sense of place. Sense of place lends itself to commodification just as readily as anything else, so that place becomes marketed, brokered, imaged, and hyped just as do rock singers, cigarettes, automobiles, and politicians. Success is promised the young in the cities, and rustic peace is assured everyone who comes to the countryside—peace and a chance to uplift the benighted.

The extent and consequences for small communities of the place-changing process are not fully known; I have only hinted at them in these sketches. Nor can we guess how long the process will continue. Most of the changes are far beyond the means of local communities to control; they can respond only in the same ways that people respond to changes in the weather: they accommodate as best they are able.

In these two instances of repopulation, the transformations have been peaceable, but latent divisiveness remains a subliminal threat to community vitality. The process of in-migration has been at work for a longer period in Ford than in Shiloh, and yet the division is still there, fueling stereotypes, subtly poisoning personal relationships, and making for a good deal of mutually understood—and, so far, amiable—hypocrisy.

The phenomenon of place-exchange will probably continue for as long as there is a general unhappiness with place—a state of being in our world that appears to be quite strong at present. The need for a satisfying sense of place and an identity related to place is not well understood or even recognized, but it is obviously very powerful at times. And where there is a need that can be identified, marketing ingenuity and investment capital are not far behind. My guess would be that we are far from seeing the end of notices in the Shilohs and Fords of the world that announce, in one way or another, "Place for Sale."

PART 4
The Evolution of a Philosophy of Education

In 1970 John was offered an opportunity that would bring about major changes in his professional life. Dr. Otis Singletary, recently appointed president of the University of Kentucky, wanted to create the position of dean of undergraduate studies as a counterpart to the already existing dean of graduate studies, and he offered to appoint John to this new position. John's acceptance of the offer was not immediate. Although he had maintained a strong interest in undergraduate education since his first teaching appointment at Lees-McRae College in North Carolina some nine years earlier, he was not eager to accept an administrative position that would substantially reduce the time he could devote to his own teaching and research. After considerable soul-searching, he decided to accept the new post, which had the potential for introducing major changes in what he felt was a neglected undergraduate program.

School Consolidation and Its Consequences

One of his early projects after moving into his new role combined several interests: Appalachia, social change, and education. Actually the project had been initiated before he assumed the deanship when he learned that a new consolidated high school was to open in the North Carolina mountains area near Lees-McCrae

College. Seeing the possibility of studying the effects of the new school on students, he proposed a comparison of the students in the new consolidated school with those in a similar nonconsolidated school located in another mountain community some 40 miles away. The project, which in 1970 was awarded funding from the U.S. Office of Education, focused specifically on student achievement, aspiration, and adjustment.

The creation of a large school to replace a number of smaller schools was generally seen as part of the modernization process, but it was an aspect of modernization about which John entertained serious doubts. While providing more and presumably better physical equipment as well as a greater variety of courses and certain economies of scale, the consolidation process also weakened, and in some cases destroyed, the identities of small communities for whom the local schools were centers of social activity and nuclei of neighborhood cohesion.

With federal funding, John was able to extend the study over a longer period and to hire a graduate research assistant. Like many federally funded research projects, the consolidation study had more than a few problems, many stemming from miscommunication between the granting agency and the researchers. It is evident from John's letters in the University of Kentucky archives that the experience was not an entirely happy one. Nevertheless, the project was finally completed and the findings published in a 1973 report to the U.S. Office of Education.* The major findings of the study were that few significant differences were to be found between the students of the consolidated and nonconsolidated schools, at least with respect to student achievement, aspirations, and adjustment. The justification for school consolidation, John concluded, would have to be on the grounds of operating economies and efficiencies in the use of resources, rather than improving student accomplishments, ambitions, and adaptation.

CONCLUSIONS TO SCHOOL CONSOLIDATION
AND ITS CONSEQUENCES

In this chapter we return to the questions which prompted the study initially. To begin with: *Does school consolidation result in increased levels of academic performance and higher occupational and educational aspirations than would be the case in a nonconsolidated school?*

Insofar as we are able to bring data to bear on this question, the answer is "No." At the risk of ignoring the exceptions pointed out in Chapter III, students at the CHS [consolidated high school] do not generally show higher increases in achievement, job aspirations and expectations than students at the NCHS [nonconsolidated high school]. This conclusion must be hedged with a number of qualifications, of course. The absence of comparable reading achievement scores is disappointing, especially in view of the finding in Chapter IV which shows that the pattern of change in reading achievement in the CHS is different from that for GPA [grade point average]. In short, it is lamentable that we may not have been able to use the best, and certainly not the only, measure of achievement.

Moreover, as already pointed out, we are looking at three-year trends, beginning with the opening year of the CHS. It is quite possible that this school will have a different kind of impact in the future, when its program and staff are more fully developed, than it had in its early years.

The conclusion that the CHS did not perform as might have been desired also needs to be qualified by calling to mind once again the small sample sizes. Together with measurement error—concerning which no estimate has even been attempted—the small sample sizes leave a great deal of room for random fluctuation, and it is possible that a larger sample or repeated small samples would not show the same patterns reported here.

With all these qualifications, however, the answer still seems to be that the new school shows no outstanding advantage over the nonconsolidated school.

Does school consolidation result in higher or lower patterns of adaptive success than would be the case in a nonconsolidated school? Again, with some of the same qualifications already stated, the answer appears to be "No." The new school appears to be neither strikingly better or worse than the nonconsolidated school from the standpoint of creating major adjustment problems or providing a "good fit" for students. Lower status students may be somewhat advantaged by the new school in this regard, because they did show better signs of successful adaptation on two indicators than their NCHS counterparts. On the other hand, other CHS students showed up relatively poorly on two other indicators of adjustment, so that the overall answer seems to be that there was no major difference in adaptive success.

(It was true that dropouts were more likely to occur—as well as transfers—in the CHS. To the extent that this can be read as a sign of adaptive failure, it is a mark against the new school.)

Dropout rate aside, perhaps the finding of no appreciable difference in adaptive failure and success could be regarded as a plus for the new school. This is true at least from the standpoint that students were no *worse* off for the difference.

Does school consolidation reduce, maintain, or increase inequality in the attainment of school success? The findings in Chapter IV, again with the usual qualifications, are consistent with the findings of Coleman, Jencks, and others. By and large, extra-school influences appear to be at work in ways which overshadow school factors. In most cases, where initial differences existed between students of different abilities, status background, and outlooks, they were maintained four years later. The new school seemed to do very little to reduce inequality of school success, whether the success had to do with achievement, aspirations, or adaptation. The exception, as pointed out in Chapter IV, is grades, where gaps between subgroups of students tended to narrow over time.

But the issue is clouded by the finding that this narrowing did not occur in the case of reading achievement.

In short, the new school appears from these findings to be relatively powerless to overcome the influence of such factors as ability, status, and commitment to certain values.

Are students with particular levels of ability, status backgrounds, and outlooks especially advantaged or disadvantaged in the attainment of success in the three areas of achievement, aspirations and adjustment? Judging from the data presented in Chapter IV, what were there termed the "low females" seem especially disadvantaged compared to other students on several of the adjustment variables. On the other hand, this was the same category which was especially advantaged regarding GPA. They were, in sum, making higher grades but enjoying school less.

No other category of students—at least as classified for this study—seemed particularly advantaged or disadvantaged on more than one or two of the success variables. The possible exception to this conclusion is the "low males," who showed improvement in HOS [health opinion survey] absences, and PSA [Personal and Social Assets] ratings. But if anyone had expected that the lower status students generally would be advantaged by the new school, relative to their higher status peers, he would be disappointed by this finding. Likewise, if anyone had expected higher IQ students, or students more modern in their outlook, to be especially advantaged, he would not find strong confirmation in these data.

One is driven to the rather fatalistic conclusion that it does not really matter what takes place within the walls of the school, and that it matters even less whether the walls themselves are old or new, small or large. The life chances of students do not seem much under the control of the schools, which constitute one more complex sorting machine in a world full of sorting machines. In the words of Peter Rossi:

> By and large, no clear picture emerges from the
> research to indicate that a particular type of
> school, pursuing a particular type of educational
> policy, has a higher record of student achieve-
> ment than other kinds of schools pursuing dif-
> ferent educational policies.[1]

With all the limitations of the study, and with the qualifications
we have repeatedly placed on the findings, the results of this case
study in consolidation are consistent with Rossi's observation.

Should we then, as a matter of informed policy, recommend uniformly against consolidation? There is some irony in the fact that
now, when findings seem to pour in concerning the lack of effect of
school factors on educational outcomes, the consolidation and reorganization movement is so well established that it is well-nigh
unstoppable—if, indeed it is viewed as desirable to stop it. The number of school districts continues to decline yearly and no one projects
any significant slackening.

A blanket condemnation of school consolidation is certainly not
in order. No one would suggest, for example, that the people of the
county in which this study took place would be just as well off with
their former schools.[2]

There may be many reasons, aside from the kinds of educational
outcomes which have been the focus of studies to date, why consolidation is justified. In the minds of promoters of consoldidation
it may be that these educational outcomes are not even primary. In
the case of the study county, leaders who organized the push for
consolidation saw it as a means of unifying the county, of breaking
down the narrow sectionalism which the old schools had helped to
promote. They also used the new school as a means of maintaining
the impetus toward economic development, by showing prospective industries that the old schools were in bad physical condition,

even to the point of being unsafe. Something had to be done. Why not consolidate?

And as other studies have reported, there are certain economies and efficiencies in the use of resources which consolidation allows.

Many such claims for consolidation may be justified, and therefore, for reasons having nothing to do with the effect on the products of the educational process, consolidation is likely to continue. But from the findings of studies to date, including this one, promoters will find difficulty in justifying such reorganization in terms of improving outcomes for students.

Challenges to Liberal Education

As he moved into the role of dean of undergraduate studies at the University of Kentucky, John was faced by a persistent dilemma of the philosophy of higher education. Should higher education emphasize the liberal arts that provide a solid and comprehensive base of knowledge? Or should greater attention be accorded the professional and technical skills that prepare students for careers?

John was a strong believer in a liberal, or general, undergraduate education, such as he, himself, had received at the College of William and Mary. At the same time he was acutely aware that for many students (and their parents) in the 1970s a college education brought with it expectations of higher-income jobs that required specialized training. The problem was not a new one, but it was being posed with greater intensity by an exacting society demanding a higher monetary return on investments in higher education.

One solution to the dilemma was envisioned as a program of experiential education which would grant academic credit to students for supervised work in "real world" situations. Such a program, it was hoped, would retain the elements of a general education while providing opportunities for students to acquire marketable job skills. To implement such a curriculum, the University of Kentucky applied for and received a grant from the federal University Year for Action program. An Office of Experiential Education was established under the dean of undergraduate studies. Subsequently, John was able to launch the experiential education program with the support of a surprisingly large segment of the faculty.*

The fundamental issue of the nature of undergraduate education continued to occupy John's thinking as was evident in his article, reproduced in this collection, "Efficiency and Vocationalism—Renewed Challenges to Liberal Education," published in 1974.** In this article he perceived liberal education to be threatened not only by the increasing demand for vocational preparation but also by

Following his inauguration as the seventh president of Berea College, John is greeted by former presidents Willis Weatherford and Francis Hutchins, with faculty member Robert Menefee at the right. (photo by Berea College Public Relations)

pressures to measure the economic benefits of higher education. In his criticism of those two movements, John took pains to point out that he was not opposed to career training and the measurement of educational productivity in themselves, but he was concerned with the narrowness of their approaches.

With respect to measuring the effects of higher education, he denied any opposition to appropriate evaluation but argued that it should not be limited to those dimensions that were most easily counted and whose value was viewed solely in economic and vocational terms.

And in the case of vocationally-oriented programs of higher education, he explained that he was not opposed to the pursuit of vocationally relevant goals in higher education, but he did not consider them to be the most important for the advancement of civilization.

EFFICIENCY AND VOCATIONALISM: RENEWED CHALLENGES TO LIBERAL EDUCATION

> . . . [The] effort to improve choice by the use of management methods has produced the newest movement on campus—the management of movement. The signs are all around us. Look at the titles of recent books: *Efficiency in Liberal Education; Efficient College Management; The More Efficient Use of Resources*. The advertisements in educational journals reveal a growing market for consulting services in management. (And) consider the important new organizations such as NCHEMS [National Center for Higher Education Management Systems].
>
> Earl Cheit, "Coming of Middle Age in Higher Education," November 1972

> … the humanities are coming to be seen as a luxury the country cannot any longer afford, whatever their value. If taxpayers, parents and students themselves are going to have to pay more and more for education, they will increasingly demand evidence of measurable economic benefits.
>
> James Hitchcock, "The New Vocationalism,"
> *Change*, April 1973

I

The message contained in these quotations is clear: the burden of demonstrating the "value added" by liberal education is squarely on the shoulders of its purveyors. It is being placed there by both managers and consumers of higher education. Whether current attempts to justify liberal education are adequate to assure its continued existence as a major component of undergraduate education in the United States can be questioned seriously. These times call both for more eloquent and numerous public arguments for the continuing validity of liberal education values and skill and for more thorough efforts to define and measure the impact of learning experiences on the acquisition of those values and skills.

No special genius is required to recognize the two major social forces which trap liberal education in a kind of historical pincer movement. One, as implied in Cheit's words, is the greatly heightened sensitivity to efficiency criteria in evaluating all higher education programs. The other is the "new-vocationalism," the increased value placed on college education by students and their parents in terms of career preparation.[1] The first set of pressures issues from the top: from trustees, legislators, agencies and upper-level managers. The second set of forces issues from below: from the client systems of students, parents and taxpayers, as Hitchcock recognizes. Caught in this new and natural but as yet unclearly defined coalition, liberal education stands a good chance of being garroted. Such instruments of execution for general education are not new; this is only the most recent threat. But unless the necessity for advocacy, for justification and for its proper accounting are recognized, and unless we see more evidence of valuable educational impact than we are now witnessing, then the siege of liberal education may be brief and devastating.

The same kind of concern which Thorstein Veblen expressed in the second decade of this century for the future of graduate education should concern us now about the future of the liberal arts. He was convinced that a pragmatic business mentality seriously threatened free, creative, independent scholarship in "the higher learning." His prophecy, published in 1918, was that:

> . . . those principles and standards of organization, control and achievement, that have been accepted as an habitual matter of course in the conduct of business will, by force of habit, in good part reassert themselves as indispensable and conclusive in the conduct of the affairs of learning.[2]

Veblen recognized that it was the business interests which connected the two themes of accountability and vocationalism. It was business, largely, which was responsible for the incursion of pragmatic interests into the university and college. Fifty-five years before Hitchcock, Veblen wrote that "All this advocacy of the practical in education has fallen in with the aspirations of such young men as are eager to find gratuitous help toward a gainful career, as well as with the desires of parents who are anxious to see their sons equipped for material success. . . ."[3]

Veblen, by the way, felt no obligation to justify the higher learning in utilitarian terms the businessmen would accept. "The man of the world—that is to say, of the business world—puts the question, What is the use of this learning?—and the men who speak for learning, and even the scholars occupied with the 'humanities,' are at pains to find some colourable answer that shall satisfy the worldly-wise that this learning for which they speak is in some way useful for pecuniary gain." Veblen feared that scholars were already too ". . . infected with the pragmatism of the market-place . . ." to resist such temptation.[4]

In spite of the Victorian prose in which they are couched, Veblen's insights leap at us as though from yesterday, not from more than five decades ago. The recent literature in higher education chronicles our growing preoccupation with cost-benefit studies, studies of the income value of degrees, advocacy of career education at all levels, declining enrollments in liberal arts programs compared to professional programs, the new pragmatism in student values, and the application of management science techniques to the teaching-learning "industry." One is tempted to conclude that absolutely nothing has changed from Veblen's time, except that the "business men" have now invaded the undergraduate schools as well as the graduate schools. But there is at least this difference: there is no Thorstein Veblen today. Nor are there very many spokesmen for general and liberal education at all. (And even the presence of such statesmen might not be enough to sustain liberal education for our time.) For as Hitchcock observes: "Certainly at present humanities and science professors tend as a body to lack the will and the conviction to challenge such a trend, whereas they did challenge it rather effectively fifteen or twenty years ago. There is a widespread conviction in the universities that liberal arts education has failed and needs to make way for something else, whatever that might be."[5]

Thus at the very time the case is being presented against the economic value of liberal education, the faculty are themselves suffering a failure of conviction about the noneconomic value of their enterprise.

It is not a simple matter of "arguing away" the forces impinging on higher education today. Even if difficult for some to live with, the new cost consciousness (Consciousness IV, as Cheit calls it) and the new vocationalism are inexorable, understandable and capable of justification. The consuming public and the taxpayers feel their credulity is being strained: they want to be shown that the rising costs of higher education are worthy. This is neither new nor greatly different from other kinds of consumer concern. The demands for an accounting—whether made by finance committees of governing boards, by donors, by legislators, by state or federal agency officials, by state coordinating councils, or by the student market—are understandable and, in many senses, justified. Whether the public's unquestioning romance with higher education in the "golden years" declined because of student unrest, or because of the entry of higher learning institutions into non-traditional activities, or because of financial anxieties, is a moot question. Whatever the answer, the result is the same. Whatever the causes, the need to justify ourselves is here.

Likewise, market demands for increased career training are here, and no glib puffery is going to make them vanish. For whatever reasons, idealism, altruism and the intense belief in the possibility of a just future for the world have given way among young people to anxieties about their own individual futures. Increasingly, what is "relevant" to students is preparation for work. In Hitchcock's words:

> The greatest irony of the educational history of
> the past decade is the fact that relevance has now
> turned full circle and is coming to apply pre-

cisely to what five years ago almost everyone
agreed was fundamentally the wrong function
of higher education—'processing students for
the system.'[6]

Whether the explanation for this change lies in theories of ideological fashion ("radical chic"?), or results simply from a rapid rise
in the cost of living, or is the natural concomitant of the Nixon years,
the change is upon us. The new careerism is not going to go away
by virtue of any academic rite of exorcism.

II

Several items of information have emerged within the past year
which serve to heighten these concerns about the future of liberal education. These events add to what we already know is developing at
federal and state levels around the concept of career education. They
supplement our awareness of advancements being made in program
budgeting and management information and reporting systems at
NCHEMS and other management organizations. The events which I
wish to point out offer no support for the argument that the management movement and the new pragmatism have "peaked out."

1. The first item of information actually has the status of strong
rumor, learned in the course of a recent visit to an institution in a
midwestern state. The state legislature, I was told by several persons, seriously considered passage of a bill which would have defined as a measure of institutional output (to be used in budget
review and subsequently allocation of state monies to state-supported institutions), the proportion of graduates who found employment in fields related to their majors within six months after
graduation. (The bill did not pass.) The message for general education in the state institutions is all too obvious.

2. The second item is the publication of the Committee on Economic Development report, *The Management and Financing of Colleges*, in October 1973. The membership of the Research and Policy Committee which forwarded the report comprised primarily business leaders and academic administrators. Their purpose was to recommend ways in which higher education "might move toward a solution of its problems and serve the interests of society more effectively." The problems which they regarded as part of the crisis include financial troubles, student dissatisfaction, faculty unionism, skepticism about the value of degrees to job-seekers, and legislative questioning about the priority of higher education.

Most comments of this CED document draw attention only to the recommendations about financing public and private education, particularly the controversial proposal to increase tuition in all institutions to fifty per cent of instructional costs. Other recommendations covered such areas as academic freedom and due process, authority and decision-making structures, the adoption of management principles and techniques found successful in business and government, and the establishment of proper goals and objectives for purposes of better accountability. There is a great deal of value in many of these recommendations (and sometimes even more value in the memoranda of comment, reservation and dissent contained at the end of the report). The report even recognizes the distinctive nature of colleges and universities in contrast to businesses and industries and it shows an awareness of the difficulties of stating goals and objectives and measuring impacts in ways that take into account the peculiarities of production in education factories.[7] The need to recognize institutional diversity is likewise underscored.

A troublesome aspect of the CED report lies in what is implied rather than what is said. One wonders whether some of the authors of the report do not really believe that too many people are wasting too much time and money in "nonproductive" educational pursuits. For example, while the report shows proper concern for clear and specific goal statements for higher education, the illustrations offered of nonspecific (bad) goal statements and specific (good) statements tempt one to conclude that typical liberal education goals are bad (nonspecific) and vocational professional goals are good (specific). To quote from the report:

> An all-to-common (*sic*) deficiency of goals statements is indulgence in vague and even vacuous generalities. An effective educational program cannot be planned and executed if the institution's goals are described simply in terms of such general purposes as 'preparing the student for a productive career,' 'stimulating the intellectual life of the student,' or 'creating good moral character.' These are obviously of basic importance, but they must be taken for granted under the broad purposes of education.
>
> If a college is to develop its distinctive mission, its goals must be described in specific terms, such as 'preparing not less than one-fourth of the elementary teachers needed by the state over the next five years'; 'qualifying students to enter accredited schools of law, medicine, and public administration'; 'providing the basic elements of a scientific and liberal education for those intending to seek the Ph.D.'; or 'promoting the acquisition of knowledge and training in the basic skills essential to [specified types of] technical vocations.'[8]

It may be that part of our problem is that we *already* take for granted the goals of liberal education, which are so often represented as the vacuous catalogue rhetoric that CED criticizes. The answer, therefore, may not lie in setting aside that rhetoric altogether in favor of vocational and professional goals, but in working toward the specification and measurement of those vague-but-valid promises of liberal education. Theodore Yntema's comment on this section of the report (page 86) is extremely significant in this connection: "Operational specification of goals is especially important (and usually absent) in general education." (He opines further that "The vested interests, the reward structure, and the traditions of the faculty make it almost impossible to develop appropriate programs of general liberal education. If the public does not rally to the support of general education, university and college faculties might do well to ask whether they deserve such support.") With the exception of the Yntema footnote, the burden of the CED recommendations regarding goals seems to be to shelve the liberal arts and get down to business.

"So," to quote Veblen, "the academic authorities face the choice between scholarly efficiency and vocational training, and hitherto the result has been equivocal."[9]

3. There was another publication event in 1973 which doubtless went unnoticed by most scholars. In February, *Program Measures— Technical Report 35*, was issued by the National Center for Higher Education Management Systems at WICHE.[10] Building partly on earlier reports,[11] this document is an ambitious attempt to provide quantitative indicators of various program elements which might be used in a higher education planning and management system. The particular elements to which these program measures are addressed are elaborated in an earlier NCHEMS document, *Program Classification Structure*.[12] It suggests ways to quantify the various activities and results of effort that occur in colleges and universities

so that administrators, managers and so on can know what is happening, where, with what result. Such information is obviously quite useful to decision-makers.

It may not need to be said that *Program Measures—Technical Report 35* and the PCS are precisely the kind of importation of "management principles and techniques" which CED had in mind in saying that higher education should learn from business and government.

What aspects of program elements (or areas of activity) should be known and measured? *Program Measures—Technical Report 35* offers seven information categories: objectives, target group, beneficiary groups, activity, resources, financing, and outcomes.[13] Now outcomes is a fairly critical category. To quote the report:

> Information about outcomes includes the outcomes achieved or the products generated by the activities of a program element. Outcomes information also enables an administrator to evaluate the effectiveness of a program element in terms of the degree that the outcomes met the objectives of the program element. What did the money buy?[14]

Outcomes is, as it were, the proof of the pudding. The value of knowing the consequences of some area of activity—instruction, for example—would be easy to sell short. What instructor would not like to be able to go to his chairman or dean and say, "Look, my course had this impact on this number of students and the value of my instruction is therefore such-and-such"? And the dean in turn to his vice president and so on up to the governing board, legislature or whatever. (The availability of such knowledge would, of course, be threatening to the incompetent, but threatening the incompetent is a policy which sometimes recommends itself.) Given proper statements of objectives and adequate measures of their achievement, an accounting for our activities in terms of outcomes makes sense not only to managers and consumers but to us purveyors as well.

So much for the good news. The bad news is that, even by the admission of the NCHEMS staff, the outcomes measures in the instructional program area are less than adequate. The amount of space in the report devoted to outcomes in the instructional program is discouragingly small when compared, say, to the space occupied by resource measures. To give some idea of the *kind* of outcomes measures considered appropriate for "general academic instruction," look at the list offered by NCHEMS:

> Degree or certificates granted, by type
> Students accepted for transfer to another
>> institution
> Percent of graduates receiving job offers within
>> a certain time period, such as 90 days after
>> graduation
> Average first salary of graduates
> Student credit hours not completed, by course
>> level
> Students passing the course as a percent of those
>> originally enrolled

Of course, it was realized by the NCHEMS staff working on the educational outcomes project that "many variables will be identified for which no measurement technique can be immediately developed," and that this fact should not cause currently unmeasurable variables to be ignored.[15] Consequently, Appendix D of *Technical Report 35* contains a very interesting beginning of an "Inventory of Higher Education Outcome Variables and Measures," which actually had its origins three years earlier. What is discouraging about this project is that for either or both of two reasons—commitment of insufficient resources or problems inherent with the subject matter—progress in this area has been far outstripped by development of measures in other areas such as resources and by development of nonlearning-related measures in the area of instruction. Given the current pressures for accountability, it is axiomatic that what is measurable will be what is measured and that what is countable will be what decisions regarding allocation will be based on. It just happens that what is most countable is related to the pragmatic, the economic, the vocational, while what is least countable at present is the impact and contribution of liberal education.

We must, then, find some means to encourage and support work by persons such as Alexander Astin, Robert Pace and the staff of the NCHEMS outcomes project for which funds are currently being sought. Moreover, liberal educators must be ready to assist in the development of such output indicators and to insist that they be involved. The Commission on Liberal Learning of the Association of American Colleges recognized this need in 1971 and "urged WICHE to involve liberal educators in drawing up the list and content of educational outputs and in the devising of measures for evaluating performance as well as establishing the criteria for judging their appropriateness. . . ."[16] The commission's recommendation bears repeating. Far from being resistant to such faculty involvement, NCHEMS would encourage it: ". . . it is imperative that institutional administrators and faculty members get together with the educational evaluators or 'accountants' and attempt to strike a better balance between (the) two extremes of 'trivial precision and *apparently* rich ambiguity.'"17

4. Next in this list of recent events which serve to heighten anxieties about the future of general education is the report issued by the National Commission on the Financing of Postsecondary Edu-

cation.[18] The commission, established by federal law and appointed by the President and Congress, was given the task of reviewing existing programs of financial support for postsecondary education and recommending "new financing methods and policies that would most effectively serve the national interest." Fourteen months and $1.5 million later, the Commission delivered an impressive 442-page document which will undoubtedly have great influence on subsequent policy decisions in the area of federal, state, local and private support of all post-high-school education.

The substance of the report lies in the analysis of some 64 different financing models and in the laying out of consequences of implementation of the most feasible of these models. Note that the commission was concerned not only with policies relating to higher education but with the much broader category of postsecondary education, which includes vocational and technical education beyond high school and which spans proprietary as well as public and private non-profit institutions. The scope of this definition reflects movement of interest toward career and vocational education on the part of Congress and the Administration, a shift which grows out of a renewed federal emphasis on national manpower needs.

Again, as with the CED report, most of the discussion we shall hear of the CFPE report is likely to concentrate on the alternative financing models described. It should be a valuable document in providing method, logic and procedure for setting the terms of arguments which will probably rage for the next few years.

Chapter 2, "Objectives for Postsecondary Education," may or may not get much attention, on the other hand. The eight objectives drafted by CFPE were derived after lengthy discussion with students, educators, public officials and others, and are said to be a statement of the "'national interest' with regard to financing postsecondary education." Note that the commission is concerned with structural means and not ultimate ends of education: "These objectives do not deal with the ultimate purposes of education—knowledge, self-fulfillment, and socialization, for example—but with how postsecondary education should be structured, in the broadest sense, to serve those purposes." These objectives were finally chosen by the commission:[19]

1. Student access
2. Student choice
3. Student opportunity
4. Educational diversity and flexibility
5. Institutional excellence
6. Institutional dependence
7. Institutional accountability
8. Adequate financial support

This list is "balanced" in much the same sense as the CED concerns, but it is fairly strongly oriented to consumer interests and better management of resources. The inclusion of "institutional excellence" might be thought an exception, but upon closer inspection even it seems to be slanted toward the encouragement of that same set of pragmatic and vocational interests which so concerned Thorstein Veblen:

> Excellence must be the primary objective of postsecondary education in all of its forms, with excellence in the service to students its overriding concern. Excellence is not, however, to be judged by a single standard. It is as important to provide excellent training for laboratory technicians and auto mechanics as it is for engineers and chemists. Excellence is a responsibility of all institutions, public and private, the least as well as the most selective.[20]

While attention is drawn to *training*, there is no mention of education, liberal or otherwise, in this treatment.

CFPE recognized the difficulties inherent in measuring the attainment of the stated objectives, but took the initiative in suggesting some beginnings. Regarding excellence, two measures were offered:

> a. Academic quality according to surveys of faculty opinion
> b. Success of graduates in obtaining employment in the fields in which they were trained.[22]

The quarrels with the reputational approach to measuring quality are standard enough to have become almost ritualized. The successful employment criterion is essentially the same as advocated by NCHEMS *Program Measures—Technical Report 35*, the midwestern legislature already mentioned, and (in principle) the CED report. To say that the kind of excellence implied is not entirely consistent with the best traditions of liberal education is a considerable understatement. Whether by intent or by oversight, the CFPE report seems simply to ignore the role of liberal education in postsecondary education in the United States. To quote from George W. Bonham's commentary on the CFPE report, "In one of the current vogues of the New Pragmatism, the age-old question of 'what is learning for?' has been widely replaced by 'what is learning worth?'"[23]

5. Last in this list of items of disturbing information learned in the past year are certain statistics on student attitudes and intentions provided by the American Council on Education/UCLA Cooperative Institutional Research Program. If there had been any doubt in our minds about the shift of student interests toward jobs and job security, these findings would remove them. The ACE Office of Research has collected information from entering freshmen in all cooperating institutions for many years. It is revealing to compare freshmen who entered universities in 1970 with those who

entered in 1973, a scant four years later. In the table below, "probable major fields of study" have been combined into four categories: Humanities, Natural Sciences, Social Sciences and Professional. (The percentages do not total 100.0 because certain categories such as "Other" and "Undecided" were omitted from this tabulation.)

Probable Major Fields of Study of Freshmen Entering Universities in Fall 1970 and Fall 1973 by Percentage

Probable Major Field of Study	1970	1973
Humanities	22.6	14.0
Natural Science	11.4	16.8
Social Sciences	9.2	10.0
Professional	38.1	44.4

("Humanities" combines English, history, political science, humanities [other] and fine arts. "Natural Sciences" combines biological sciences, mathematics or statistics, and physical sciences. "Professional" combines agriculture, business, education, engineering and health professions [non-M.D.])

Sources: ACE/UCLA Cooperative Institutional Research Program, Summary of Data on Entering Freshmen for Fall 1973; ACE Office of Research, Summary of Data on Entering Freshmen (Fall 1970).

As one might have guessed, interest in the humanities has declined at the expense of professional and pre-professional training during this period.

The same source of information shows similar trends in choices of probable careers among entering freshmen. The proportion choosing "Artist (including performer)," for example, went from an already low 7.3 percent to only 3.6 percent. One of the more remarkable statistical shifts, however, occurred in the objectives which freshmen considered to be "essential or very important." For, while keeping up with political affairs, developing a philosophy of life, and influencing social values declined somewhat during the four years in question, the item "Being very well off financially" rocketed from 36.6 percent to 52.4 percent.

Such trends as these, while not definitive, certainly appear to express, to use Veblen's phrase, "the aspirations of such young (people) as are eager to find gratuitous help toward a gainful career."

At one time a question might have been raised whether students are not the allies of the faculty rather than of the accountants. After all, it was students who not long ago raised the issues of relevance and freedom in the curriculum. Surely their efforts at humanizing education show their kinship with liberal education values.

It would be a mistake, however, to regard student efforts for curricular relevance, freedom and humanization as—necessarily, at least—a plea for a liberating education, as certain arts and sciences professors might think of it. Much of that labor in the vineyard of freedom was unquestionably expended toward the

John joins a group of students in a fund-raising phonathon in February 1985.
(photo by Berea College Public Relations)

end of upgrading the quality of the learning experience. But much of it was not. Considerable student effort was predicated on such unexamined assumptions as that freedom (the absence of restraint) is a good to be pursued in and of itself; that a person is demeaned unless he or she is permitted total freedom of choice; that one is repressed and alienated unless permitted to determine his or her fate even in small matters. "Freedom" was not much understood, not much discussed, only shouted and harangued over. Now that radicalism is not so much in fashion, and the price of food and shelter has risen, it becomes clearer that the students who once appeared to be the natural enemies of legislators are now their seeming natural allies.

III

A case can be made that we have brought our own distinctive contributions to the problem we face, as Hitchcock and others have pointed out. Moreover, there is something beneficial to be gained from responding to the demands of the "accountants" and the vocationalists if the tasks are approached properly. We need the exercise which the process of self-justification requires. If we cannot convince many others of the continuing value of liberal education, then perhaps our arguments are merely self-serving contrivances anyway. The future of liberal education depends in part on persuading the inventors of schemes of accountability that they have a responsibility for measuring total effectiveness as well as for determining mere efficiencies. But part of the responsibility for the defense of general education just as clearly rests with the general educators.

Therefore, lest we professors bestow spurious sainthood on ourselves, we should heed the 1971 report of the Commission on Liberal Learning, which observed that:

> Most recent innovation in liberal arts education
> has been confined to the manipulation of the
> form and structure of that education. With rare
> exceptions—and these exceptions a sharp com-
> mentary on the unexceptional—the substance of
> that education has not been rephrased in ways
> that seize either the imagination or the sense of
> relevance of students in the colleges or of soci-
> ety at large.[24]

The report of the commission not only blames illiberally educated politicians and illiberally educated students for the moribund state of the humanities, but also claims that "The liberal arts are captives of illiberally educated faculty members who barter with credit hours and pacts of non-aggression among their fiefs and baronies."[25]

Thus it is certain that in this "middle age" of higher education the faculty share in the responsibility for coping with new management needs and new student/consumer demands. It is especially obvious, one hopes, that educators and administrators must play a role in setting the terms of their own accountability and their own response to vocationalism, or the emphasis will become lopsidedly business-, management- and consumer-oriented. Between the accountants and the vocationalists, liberal education may be threatened as never before.

To conclude this essay on a more personal note, I find it important to separate this plea for an effective and persuasive defense of liberal education from a defense of the status quo. We desperately need more eloquent spokesmen to restate the value (both economic and noneconomic) of liberal education. We need the best minds available for the tasks of measurement and accounting appropriate for liberal education. But none of this is to argue that we are doing the job well and should be left alone. I am terribly disappointed with the present state of affairs in liberal education, and it is people such as myself who, among others, must stand indicted for it. I am deeply frustrated and impatient for change, for improvement. Far from opposing account- ability, I embrace it almost eagerly. I only plead that we account for the right things and that we look for the impact of the college or university experience in more areas than just the most easily countable and eco- nomically/vocationally valuable.

Likewise, I do not wish to oppose the pursuit of vocationally- relevant goals in higher education. I am simply not satisfied that this is enough or the most important part of our job. I believe our civilization's fate depends to a considerable degree upon our abil- ity to protect and nurture those seemingly useless pursuits which maintain the critical conscience, the capacity for building alterna- tive futures, the development of esthetic response, the ability to reason and the ability to create, among other values in the liberal education tradition.

John Ciardi once commented, "I know of no sane poet today who persuades himself that the action of his art and imagination has any significant consequence in the practical reality of Dow-Jones averages, election returns and the state of the nation."[26] A world without poets might well be cost-effective. In that world, I would like to say, with e.e. cummings: "listen: there's a hell of a good uni- verse next door; let's go."[27]

Experiential Education and the Liberal Arts

In a subsequent publication*, John and co-author Robert F. Sex- ton, who was director of the University of Kentucky Office of Ex- periential Education, discussed the integration of experiential edu- cation in a liberal arts program. The challenges to general educa- tion discussed in the previous article were presented once again, most of which could be boiled down to a central issue, according to the authors: "Are we getting our money's worth from higher education?" It was a question not easily answered by the liberal arts proponents, especially when many liberal-arts faculty were themselves confused about the purposes of the liberal arts.

Stephenson and Sexton were not equivocal about either the purposes or value of a liberal arts education. "Basically," they stated, "the liberal arts provide a means for the individual to understand his or her relationship to the larger environment. . . . In sum the liberal arts have sought to awaken the intelligence and open the doors of self-awareness and to create the ability and desire for self-renewal through self-awareness and self- education."

But for a new generation of students, these goals were not adequate answers to the question of "What good is it?" especially when the implicit measure of "good" was expected to be in monetary terms.

In part the failure of students to appreciate the value of a liberal arts education derives from their lack of experience with situations that require a broad and firm knowledge base. This lack, Stephenson and Sexton argued, could be met in part by the inclusion of experiential education as part of the liberal arts curriculum. As defined by the authors, experiential education involved the placing of students in situations that would "permit them to become an integral part of the institution or learning environment, hopefully performing real work with real value in a manner similar to other nonstudent participants in that environment." Under the guidance of the instructor, the student would be expected to analyze and reflect on the experience, drawing on the knowledge base provided by the liberal arts. And while the experience would or could contribute to career preparation, the authors maintained, the justification of experiential learning "is its relationship to the reflective objectives of liberal-arts higher education."

Stephenson and Sexton were, of course, aware of the utilization of field experiences in the professional training of students in a variety of fields, such as medicine, education, and social work, but this approach was not (and is still not) widely employed in liberal arts curricula. They were also aware of the problems of implementing a program of experiential education in a liberal arts environment, but still felt that it offered a "promising direction" that had not yet been adequately explored.

Deciding to explore this direction, John and his colleagues applied for and received a grant from the Lillie Endowment to organize seminars on ethical issues that were conducted in conjunction with an internship program. During the 1976-77 academic year John and Griffith Dye, a philosophy professor, held a weekly seminar on ethical issues related to specific issues in various public service organizations. They later published an article on their experience.** They felt that in general the combination of the ethics seminar and the internship had a positive effect on nearly all of the students. It was, they concluded, the pairing of the internship with the seminar on ethics and public service that accounted for the success of the program.

> "It represents the critical juncture of the world of the practical, hard realities with the realm of principled, theoretical abstractions. Without the latter, the former represent mere opportunities and obstacles to be used or got around in a game whose objective is winning at any cost. Without confronting the former, however, the abstractions represent idle and irrelevant nitpicking."

EXPERIENTIAL EDUCATION AND REVITALIZATION OF THE LIBERAL ARTS

Our purpose is to explore the relationship between two aspects of higher education: the liberal arts and experiential learning. On the one hand, we are dealing with that aspect of education which is rooted most in tradition and is the university's strongest link with the past; on the other hand, we have an educational method that is, in some respects, a latecomer. Our suggestion is that a marriage of liberal-arts objectives with the methods of experiential education can result in a strengthening of liberal education at a time when circumstances severely threaten its future. The first part of this essay deals with the nature of these problems for the liberal arts, the second part, with the potential of experiential education.

The Concept of the Liberal Arts

For most of the twentieth century the term "liberal arts" has been used to connote the learning that led to the creation of the "educated" person. This part of the curriculum, in the form of distribution requirements, and a major, contained the basics of the university's nonvocational program. When combined with a major, which presumably would prepare the student for a career, the liberal-arts requirements were to contribute to the totality of the educated person.

The goals of the liberal-arts curriculum remain about the same today, despite efforts in recent years at refurbishment through name changes, and the validity of these goals continues. Basically, the liberal arts provide a means for the individual to understand his or her relationship to the larger environment. Traditionally, we have considered the tools for this understanding to be a knowledge of the heritage of Western and/or Eastern civilization, an exposure to the nature of man and the nature of historical and social forces, and the ability to analyze information independently and with the broadest possible vision. In essence, the goal is to help individuals control events or, failing this, to understand rather than be baffled and influenced by the whim of circumstance. In this context, history, literature, and philosophy are to give the student the knowledge of his heritage and of human nature. Sciences and languages are to provide experience in the rigor of intellectual discipline and the nature of logical thought. The social sciences fill the need for systematic analyses and the testing of hypotheses on the nature of group process and actions, for understanding both self and others. And the arts provide awareness of and sensitivity toward individual expressiveness and an understanding of the interrelatedness of beauty and functionalism; and, some would contend, they form the cathedral where man's ultimate achievement may be observed.

In sum, the liberal arts have sought to awaken the intelligence and open the doors of self-awareness, and to create the ability and desire for self-renewal through self-awareness and self-education. In the extreme, the lack of a relationship between the liberal arts on the one hand and vocations and careers on the other has been typified by John Stuart Mill's statement that "men are men before they are lawyers or physicians, or manufacturers; and if you make them capable and sensible men they will make themselves capable and sensible lawyers or physicians."[1]

But in fact, the goals of liberal education have never been completely divorced from the goals of society. It has always been assumed both explicitly and implicitly, for example, that this breadth of vision, this perspective, and these tools of analysis and reflection are needed by people who will successfully attack society's problems. In the sixties, when universities were polarized around the question of how far their commitment to the world outside academia should extend, the claim that academics should not take sides nor become involved was never consistent with the broader rhetoric supporting higher education. Sidney Hook, for example, makes a strong plea for the use of creative intelligence inspired by the humanities to perform the primary function of "taming power." As for utility, he contends that "the [educational institutions] must teach not merely the facts, but how to test them, how to relate them to problems, and how they bear upon relevant alternatives."[2]

But this vision of the liberal arts has come upon difficulties in the last few years. These difficulties may not have been perceived clearly by those within the system, and in many cases may be expressed only as problems of personal identity, but they are nonetheless real. At least five circumstances can be identified to explain this malaise: the so-called new vocationalism[3] and its relationship to a highly technological society; the influx of new learners with new needs into an old system; the ethical dilemma posed for the nation by political events surrounding the Watergate miasma; the growth of the management and accountability movements in higher education; and the confusion of identity and purpose among liberal-arts faculty themselves.

Increased Vocationalism

Much has been written lately about the so-called new vocationalism. There seems to be little doubt that today's students are more concerned with identifying and training themselves for satisfying careers than was the case in the 1960s. This trend can be seen in the general thrust of federally sponsored commission reports and of federal programs based on such concepts as career education. It is also reflected in student attitudes and choices of academic majors, which show that students are turning away from the more esoteric academic fields and toward those that are more marketable in a tight economy.

This shift in national policy and consumer attitudes finds its expression in such starkly utilitarian pronouncements as one official's, to the effect that "if learning cannot be useful, then it is not learning,"[4] and in such critiques of the liberal arts as Marvin Feldman's in the *Conference Board Record*.

> Our reverence for "liberal arts" is rooted in myth.
> It is graduates of technical or vocational colleges
> who create the options that make our society
> civilized. Without them life would be ugly,
> empty, and drab.

> Without artisans, the concept of liberal arts is sterile and vapid. We are often told that liberal arts serve to liberate the artisan from the necessary narrowness of his special skill. But it is also true that the liberal arts need the nourishment of practical expression, and thus the practical arts are the basis of liberal values.[5]

Kingman Brewster's response to the growth of vocationalism is particularly vivid.

> There is an almost frightening avalanche towards law schools and medical schools. And the country doesn't have that many good law schools and medical schools. So that this is a kind of bottleneck, which does mean that college, instead of being a place to discover yourself, and to take some exploratory trips in fields of knowledge that may not be related to your career, now is kind of pre-professional, and slightly grim in its professionalism, because of this bottleneck into law schools and medical schools.

> And that bothers me because I think a general education, a liberal education, is still the best way to develop between the ages of seventeen and twenty-two. And it would be too bad if that were squeezed into a professional groove of some kind.[6]

The colleges and universities with the strongest commitment to liberal-arts education have not yet responded creatively to this development. As President Landrum Bolling of Earlham College has said, liberal-arts colleges have not yet "come to grips with the dilemma between abstract knowledge and vocational competence."[7]

Sidney Hook made the same point almost thirty years ago in *Education for Modern Man.*[8]

The New Learners

Education in the liberal arts has also been affected by expanding enrollment since the early 1960s and by the resulting change in the nature of the college undergraduate population. It is one matter for the president of an Ivy League school to speak fondly of the humanizing objectives of the college experience to a group of students attuned by their social backgrounds to the value of learning; it is quite another matter when the subject is addressed in the open-admissions university of the 1970s with a student body composed of new learners, minority students, older students, and lower-income students, unaccustomed to these traditions. To the new student a degree means a job and increased income; practical and career-related courses are most important. Although, at least to us, it is beyond dispute that the humanities remain important, it is also obvious that new motivations are necessary to encourage many students to pursue these subjects.

Ethics in Public Life

A less tangible impact on the liberal arts, but perhaps the most distressing one, has come as a result of the ethical questions posed by the Watergate episodes. Media coverage of hearings and trials probably created an uneasiness among some academics about the nature of their ethical obligation. Political commentators were quick to point this out. Tom Briden, for example, in a nationally syndicated column entitled "What Was Wrong with Their Education?" mentioned the obvious doubts that legal educators were experiencing, but went on to emphasize the need for undergraduate education to consider right and wrong behavior. "But by the time anybody enters law school, he ought to have had some acquaintance with moral questions. In four years of undergraduate study, some professor, some course, some readings should cause him to ask himself whether a thing is right rather than whether a thing can be done."[9]

While it would be absurd for academicians to assume that they are totally responsible for the sins of their students or that they are accountable for the ethical behavior of all college graduates, many professors nevertheless feel that one of their jobs is, indeed, to profess. The academy by and large holds that no one set of values should be advocated by the liberal-arts curriculum, but it is at the same time committed to creating persons who will make the right decisions. This seems an uneasy resolution to the profound question of whether higher education should or should not—perhaps we should say "can or cannot"—be value free. This is an ancient dilemma, but it has been brought more sharply into focus in our times, largely because of events in public life.

New Forms of Management and Accountability

The drive for greater efficiency in the use of scarce resources has created what Earl Cheit calls the management movement in higher education. Elaborate models are now available for the analysis of faculty activity, the measurement of productivity, the attainment of carefully specified management objectives, the impact of resources on curricular change, and the flow of students and faculty through institutions. Such management devices, once found only among business corporations and some government agencies, are increasingly being adopted by planners and managers of educational institutions searching for means to adapt to the new "steady state" of the seventies.

This movement is encouraged in no small degree by pressures from vital elements in the external environment: parents, taxpayers, donors, higher-education coordinating boards and systems officers and legislators. All seek answers to the central question: Are we getting our money's worth from higher education? The question will no doubt become sharper as inflation continues throughout the decade.

When the money's-worth question is turned on the liberal arts, the answers are not easily forthcoming, especially in terms that humanists find agreeable. What, for example, are the measurable outcomes of a liberal education? What can be cited as evidence of value obtained (either by society or the individual) that will make liberal education compete successfully in the minds of legislators who must divide the education dollar between professional programs and liberal-arts disciplines? What competencies can be promised from a study of the *Aeneid* that compare well with those promised by studies of human anatomy, soil science, or constitutional law? What have the humanities to offer that pays off in knowable, countable, consumable, or spendable units?

Clearly it is a time when advocates and purveyors of the liberal arts should be raising their own issues about learning objectives and desired impacts, rejecting the notion that discussion of the aims of education in our time can only lead to stale platitudes. The alternative is to leave to business-minded managers and accountants inside and outside institutions of higher education the task of redefining the uses of the liberal arts, through such practical measures as the rate of successful entry into the job market.

Confusion of Purpose

Irving Kristol recently observed that "the question of the relevance of the humanities to young people only arises today because so many professors of humanities don't really believe in them. They don't believe they are teaching [all the] important or even the most important things."[10]

The hesitation about the profession of values makes its own contribution to the crisis of the liberal arts. The question of whether the humanities should be value free may have arisen naturally in response to the radical challenge to values on which there was assumed to be wide consensus. A retreat to the supposedly high ground of ethical neutrality is a normal response to value confrontation. It does, however, leave us with the question of what is left that is humane about the humanities and what is liberal about the liberal arts.

To this dilemma we can add the almost certain anxiety and confusion with which some faculty must react to the threat of declining enrollments. A few may choose to weave a cocoon out of the status quo, hoping that the current bad market conditions will eventually go away; most faculty, we would imagine, are wondering whether they have been doing the right thing, and wondering what, indeed, that right thing is.

These self-doubts among faculty members who should be the key advocates and interpreters of liberal education are recognized in Charles Hitchcock's observation: "There is a widespread conviction in the universities that liberal arts education has failed and needs to make way for something else, whatever that might be."[11]

Whether the liberal arts will survive intact in their present form is not the question, for they almost certainly will not. The pressures for accountability and evidence of improved management are more likely to grow than diminish. Unless the thrust of federal policy in the direction of career education subsides and unless students and parents return to an unquestioning faith in the nonvocational values of higher education, there will continue to be unrelenting demands on the liberal arts to "make learning useful." To the extent that new learners are responsible for the shift toward a career-oriented clientele, that orientation is likely to grow rather than weaken as we make progress toward equality of access to higher education. And finally, the current anxieties and dilemmas of identity and ideology among liberal-arts faculty do not seem likely to undergo spontaneous remission. These circumstances are enough to define the situation of the liberal arts as problematic; what defines it as a crisis is the fact that at the very time the liberal arts are weak and disoriented, the consequences of living in a utilitarian, virtually nonethical and nonhumanistic society are becoming clear, particularly in our public life.

Modes of Teaching and Learning in the Liberal Arts

Turning from the concept of a liberal-arts education and a consideration of its current traumas to the teaching of the liberal arts will lead us to a consideration of the potential role of experiential education in the learning process.

The lecture, of course, continues to be the device most often used to reach undergraduates in the arts and sciences, partly on the assumption that a person of learning can convey knowledge orally in large doses and that students will retain it. A somewhat more personal and dynamic approach is the seminar or discussion section, with an increase in readings and papers and interaction with the knowledgeable faculty member. Both lecture and seminar rest on the premise that the student's mind is a willing receptacle for information, which will then be turned by hard work and study into genuine learning and understanding.

A step closer to the concept of student involvement in the teaching-learning process is the independent-study project, which is sometimes used to structure field research academically but most often involves library research done at the student's initiative. In the sciences, the laboratory is in some ways comparable to independent study, because it confronts the learner directly with research material.

The student may spend more time outside the classroom in the social sciences, where a period of observation—in some cases, field trips—is widely used. Under close supervision, the student's observation of a policy-making board or a social worker in action, for example, is expected to help him or her relate to the "real" material, that is, that which is presented in the classroom. In other areas, such as geology, forestry, anthropology, and archaeology, the labora-

During a visit by John's parents in 1985, three generations of Stephensons sit for a group photograph. L-R: Louis, David, and John.

tory is actually somewhere in the field, as might also be the case when language students travel and study in the country whose language they are mastering.

What is represented in these examples of settings for teaching and learning appears to be a kind of continuum involving such dimensions as (1) dependence on the use of the classroom; (2) dependence on oral transmission of information; (3) dependence on the instructor as the source of knowledge; (4) dependence on the student as the generator of integrative principles; (5) degree of opportunity for application of theory to practice, abstract to concrete, general to particular; and (6) need to assume student motivation and self-direction for effective learning.[12]

As we define experiential education, it would come at one end of this continuum of teaching devices. The student in the experiential learning situation ideally would be expected to spend fairly large amounts of time on a regular basis outside the classroom. The location of the work, whether in a formalized institution or a less structured situation, should permit the student to become an integral part of the institution or learning environment, hopefully performing real work with real value in a manner similar to other non-student participants in that environment. This immersion is important, because simple observation—that is, from the periphery of the environment—might not be enough to help the learner understand the inner or hidden meanings, the cues that reflect real versus superficial activity.[13]

In this learning environment, the learner is expected to apply the same analysis and reflection demanded by other learning approaches. (It is important that academic credit is usually not given for the work or activity itself but rather for the reflection upon it.) It is here that the relationship with the instructor is crucial. For it is through the interjection of outside stimuli—conversation with the instructor, reading, the integration of both into verbalized reflection—that the learner sees how action and reflection are combined in the total intellectual process. In some cases, this process may be extended over a long period of time, with intense structured preparation for the fieldwork (preseminars) and follow-up. Or, the preparation and reflection may be integrated into the same time span. No matter what the method, the goal is the integration of facts, ideas, and experience into a synthesis of understanding.

Experiential Education and the Liberal Arts

Rather than further defining experiential education in general terms, it should be more fruitful to examine in depth its specific relationship to the liberal arts.

At the outset, we should deal with a commonly held assumption that experiential learning, internships, practical and so forth are basically professional or vocational. There is, of course, no doubt that there are career advantages in experiential situations. In some fields (for example, medicine, education, and social work) it is a pedagogical truism that field experience is an integral part of professional training. There is also little doubt that the internship, when employed by any student, provides the opportunity for career exploration and gives a potential employer the opportunity to recruit an employee. In addition, several disciplines, including some in the humanities, are beginning to realize that the student with a real work situation on his or her résumé ("assistant to a legislator," "public relations specialist," "management intern") is more competitive in a tight job market. As a college degree becomes more and more commonplace, these advantages will become more important.

But it is our assumption that it is not just career advantages that support, or in some cases justify, experiential education as a component of a student's general studies or liberal-arts curriculum. On the contrary, what does justify experiential learning is its relationship to the reflective objectives of liberal-arts higher education.

We suggest, for example, that one of the goals of the humanities curriculum is to help the student understand the nature of man and his environment through the study of history, literature, and philosophy. At the same time, instructors in these fields have probably wondered whether their students, who may have little concern for the disciplinary methodology that beclouds the presentation of this general understanding or who may have little aesthetic appreciation or sense of identity with past personalities, are learning materials by rote for the purpose of passing examinations and never reflecting on the broader implications of that material.

For several years, for example, one of the writers has tried to interest students of American history in Southern politics by suggesting T. Harry Williams' biography of Huey Long. In the beginning, the book was a disaster, partly because its length and detail were oppressive to most students, who had a limited understanding of the relationship between politics and administrative manipulation. Quite logically, they questioned why they needed to read nine hundred pages to get the information they thought the book contained; the understanding the book could have provided was simply unavailable to all but a few.

But a breakthrough occurred when the writer developed seminars for full-time undergraduate interns in state-government settings. All the interns were located in situations where they did real work for administrators of government agencies that related directly to the governor. The interns were aware, in a routine fashion, of the implications of practical gubernatorial power through their internship assignment, not their seminar. When the seminar reached the point of reflecting on the role of the contemporary governor, *Huey Long* was assigned. The book took on new relevance and meaning for the students. They could identify immediately with both Huey Long and his administrative environment. "My agency would have reacted differently in that situation!" "The Governor pulled that maneuver on our department" were their reactions, indications that each student had a peg on which to hang the information. Moreover, the wealth of detail and analysis in the book, formerly a hindrance, now became an advantage; a thorough analysis of the milieu of one governor and one state's political and administrative structure, in the context of practical experience, brought understanding.

The interns, therefore, each had a personal experience with historical understanding; they placed themselves and their agencies in the context of historical experience. And this was not, we should note, a matter of their relating theory to reality. They realized that this book, this "history," was in fact reality; historical consciousness dawned upon them when Huey Long became as real as their current governor; the only difference was that they read about one and observed the other personally.

This anecdotal example draws us toward a larger question. According to Ralph Tyler, a dean of American educational theorists, the belief that the mental process of abstraction comes before application is a middle-class belief related to social-class or employment differences. From this it followed that all persons, despite intellectual differences, were to be taught abstractions in the mode of training potential professionals. He argues that the notion is faulty, especially when applied to persons whose socioeconomic background is not middle class but oriented toward pragmatic vocationalism. (Our experience suggests that the middle class have difficulties as well.) This suggests that we will not reach the new college student with our standard approach, if indeed we are now reaching the old. Abstract curricula are meaningless to many of today's students unless we provide them with some reason, some motivating factor to appreciate and use the abstraction. This motivation can be a field experience.

But experience can be chaotic and meaningless unless the mind puts it into meaningful order. Reading *Huey Long* caused the student to reflect on his experience and added the "order" of historical context. The college learning experience should simultaneously provide the means of generalizing upon one experience to come up with a myriad of experiences and a conceptual framework for those generalizations. Another way of stating this is that the idea, the abstraction provides the individual with a reason to explore an experience, and when the idea and experience are thus observed they both have meaning. Having meaning, they will be remembered, used again and again, interact with other ideas and experiences that have been generalized, and finally enter the total being of the individual.

We have argued that an experience becomes more meaningful when combined with abstraction. In experiential learning situations, the reverse can just as easily be the case. The abstraction (the theory, the generality) can be tested in a nontheoretical environment, its validity can be assessed in a concrete instance, its extension to this particularity examined, and the practical applications determined.

One would hope that the theory, when merged with experience, will also be remembered better and used in the future.

It is one thing, for example, to read in Max Weber of the distinction between charismatic and rational-legal authority and quite another to see, as an intern, the exercise of leadership in the rule-bound process of lawmaking in a legislature. In fact, it is one thing to read about the application of Weber's ideal types to reality and quite another to attempt that application oneself. While Kant's observation that nothing is more practical than a good theory cannot be disputed, it can also be said that nothing reinforces a good theory and cements it to a mind like a living application of it. The best teachers, from Socrates and Christ to the present, have understood this principle and have imported their applications into their "classrooms" as analogy, illustration, parable, case study, and simulation, all of which are techniques only one step away from using live experience as the "casebook." As Paul Freund says of teaching about abstractions such as values in context, "They become part of a whole, to be apprehended kinesthetically, as you learn to play a composition on the piano. In context—not by dogmatic repetition but by working through problems with values in mind."[14]

The field experience designed to relate theory to practice has its risks and pitfalls, of course. Chief among them is that the theory, which may be sound, may be thrown out completely by the student because the observed real world does not confirm it. The marketplace, in other words, does not guarantee the purchase of a high-quality academic abstraction. Colleges of architecture, for example, are attempting to create in their students an appreciation for the total environment of man in his created landscape, as well as a sensitivity toward long-term aesthetic needs. However, when this appreciation and sensitivity are tested in the real world, economic, political, and social factors may demand that architectural firms set such considerations aside in favor of plans that contribute toward further pollution of the man-made landscape. One suspects, furthermore, that in schools with cooperative education programs for architects the student sometimes returns to the campus determined to challenge the validity of the abstraction and to demand that functionalism and profit be the foremost ingredients emphasized in the academic program. What is to prevent students from returning to the academic cloister with disillusionment, cynicism, and exclusive regard for the world of practical affairs when they test theories of peace against the facts of war, theories of democracy against the facts of unequal distribution of power in public life, theories of economic development in a world of cutthroat international rivalry, theories of truth in a world of propaganda, and theories of justice in a world of injustice?

There is no reassuring answer to this question, but it must be pointed out that the same dangers exist when students leave the college or university after four years, degrees in hand, to confront those same realities. But because these students will never return, there is no way to reinforce (or restore) their faith in the original concepts and principles. We suggest, therefore, that from the educator's point of view it may be more advisable to have the theory tested under supervised field conditions, in which the instructor and the student can rebuild, defend, or refurbish it, than to have the theory destroyed forever as a result of one bout with a hostile, nontheoretical situation.

There are other relationships between experiential learning and the liberal arts. One of these concerns the purposes related to moral choice, ethical decision, and citizenship in a participatory system. Sidney Hook, for example, maintains that making a choice among alternatives, all of which may be somewhat unattractive, is the constant dilemma of man. He argues as follows: "As I understand the philosophical bequest of the humanities to the modern world, it reinforces our awareness of the indispensability of human choice in every moral situation, and the dignity of human choice as constituting the glory and tragedy of man. Indeed, the operating effectiveness of human choice is what we mean by freedom. In the end, power can be tamed, if it all, by the human spirit which alone is the carrier of cosmic value, and by the use of intelligence in the service of human freedom."[15] Hook argues further that the responsibility of an individual with an educated intelligence demands that he analyze the information coming to him and perhaps swaying him by "sophisms, propaganda and brass bands." "And it is precisely here that the educational agencies of a democracy have an enormous responsibility. They must teach not merely the facts, but how to test them, how to relate them to problems, and how they bear upon relevant alternatives. They must also stir imagination and sensibility in envisaging the effects of proposed modes of conduct on the human situation."[16] The same argument was put as a truism by Whitney Griswold: "The liberal arts inform and enlighten the independent citizens of a democracy in the use of their own resources."[17]

Of course neither Hook nor Griswold is arguing for the use of experiential learning as such. But it is our contention that the moral choice, the relationship of intelligence to problems and to the impact on people, and the ethical virtue Hook ascribes to the humanities, are those that Americans currently feel are unrepresented in our college programs. And this may be because of inadequate pedagogy used to relay these virtues. In essence, the making of intelligent choices can not be learned in a vacuum, for no decisions are made in the context of an ideal value-oriented environment. Decisions—the determination and solution of problems—are made in the context of dynamics influencing the individual in the most graphic and personal ways. Decisions have potential for negative impact on home, family, career, and life itself. Of course, it is the academic hope that the "context" will be provided by the understanding gained through the humanities and sciences; these will provide the framework for taking in information and basing decisions on it. But, as we have seen dramatically, there is no guarantee that the abstract context will hold up, or that it will be remembered, or that the intellectual value orientation will not be thrown out at the first confrontation with hostile circumstances.

We therefore return to our earlier argument: that the integrated context of learning and experience may provide not only the means of remembering the learned abstractions but also a way of reinforcing them during and even after the time in which they are being tested by the hostile condition. We contend further that the values Hook advocates fall largely into the areas of appreciation and sensitivity, which cannot be adequately tested in the mind of the undergraduate learner as he sits through a lecture on Plato or the abuse of power. They may be tested, however, outside the classroom in a supervised experiential situation in which the learner forces a personal confrontation between his or her values and decisions (an intellectual and internal confrontation), assesses the results, and returns intellectually to the abstraction either for new insights, for reinforcement, or to modify the abstraction so as not to change its essence but to see how he or she can work within its general limitations while making the hard choice.

Using Hook's position that the goal of education is to be able to understand the relationship between ideas and problems and their impact on man, we also suggest that these relationships cannot be questioned through traditional teaching. Despite the importance of historical awareness, we have seen that the new learner, without an inherent attraction to abstraction, may have to be confronted by the problem before the abstraction becomes germane and can be used to make the decision. Therefore, a field experience, where the problem is explored in a controlled but real environment, should be preferable to a situation in which the same person makes the same choice ten years later as a presidential assistant.

Liberal Skills and the Technological Society

In discussing the nature of the liberal arts earlier, we mentioned the necessity for controlling technological as well as political power. One of the central challenges is to discover new methods for the training of technicians and professionals—and even ordinary educated citizens that do not produce "minds in a groove," to use Whitehead's phrase. A demanding economic environment and the historical development of a technocratic society have brought the realization that skills, as well as concepts and perspectives, must be produced by the educational process. Some would suggest that higher education in the 1970s faces a choice between abandoning the liberal-arts curriculum in favor of vocationalism or reaffirming the liberal arts in hopes of interrupting the ascendant curve of "blind" technology.

But perhaps the choice is not so extreme. It would be interesting to explore the possibility of developing "liberal skills," in addition to the "liberal knowledge" that dominates current curricula. It may turn out that these skills are best approached through nontraditional means, such as field experience.

Let us dwell for a moment on the notion of liberal skills. A case can be made, we believe, for the proposition that, although the traditional concepts of liberal education are valid for our time, these classical concepts require reinterpretation, recasting, and perhaps a new vocabulary in order to address contemporary needs and understandings. We might profitably ask ourselves what competencies are likely to be required of educated persons approaching the last quarter of this century. The answers will vary according to the ways individuals read the near future. One set of answers has been suggested by H. Bradley Sagen in his provocative discussion of the "professional model of undergraduate education."[18]

Sagen argues that while it remains true that knowledge is a proper end in itself, educators must understand that there are proper uses to which systematic knowledge can be put and that adding the practical component to pure knowledge, as in the professions, is a key to revitalizing undergraduate education.

He observes that "if we continue to teach only the scholar's conception of knowledge to undergraduates and fail to convey the importance of perspective and consequences, we may well also fail to control complex technologies and social systems."[19]

Among the "task-oriented competencies" that Sagen argues should be sought through undergraduate education are these:

1. Professional problem solving; that is, coping with "the kind of problem for which the solution does not begin with a review of the literature." Application to real problems will require multidisciplinary approaches, dealing with conflicting values, working under the pressure of time with inadequate resources and information, and so on.

2. Organizational and interpersonal skills of the kind needed to cope with corporate, governmental, and urban settings in which most of us will spend our lives. Component skills in this area would include leadership training, empathic skills, and self-developmental competencies.

3. A related skill is "the ability to interpret complex information to those less well educated," or, in other words, learning how to teach others.

4. Other skills mentioned include decision making, dealing with large quantities of complex information (for example, by use of the computer), the process of design, and legal reasoning.

Sagen does not intend that his list of competencies be taken as fully developed; each of us would offer our revisions, additions, and perhaps deletions.[20] But this list does serve to illustrate a basic point: that we are capable of making guesses about what skills will be required for us to face the future as educated persons. These skills are anything but alien to the time-honored and still-valid aims of liberal education, without which, "the results will be first, a nation of technicians who lack the capacity to predict the potential implications of their actions; and second, a nation of citizens and leaders who lack the wisdom to judge wisely the proposals of technicians."[21]

Sagen's treatment underscores, furthermore, what we and others have suggested about more effective learning of such skills: that the liberal arts might learn something from professional education, that is, the latter's greater emphasis on learning through the application of knowledge to practice.[22]

Shelton Williams, in describing the policy-research field program at Austin College, points out this merger of skills and knowledge by explaining that the program is to "assist students in applying techniques acquired in liberal arts education to the study of contemporary social issues. These techniques include not only modern research skills but the analysis of the ethical bases on which policy is or should be based."[23] Daniel Bell explains the process in broader terms, emphasizing the need to "uncover the underlying intellectual structure in which one's work is embedded." He adds, "In this way, the context of specialism can be enlarged, and becomes an aspect of the liberal education itself."[24]

Some Thoughts on Implementation

Thus far we have generalized about the liberal arts and experiential learning. A few examples of the possible ways such experiences might be incorporated into the curriculum are now appropriate. The examples are presented with certain disclaimers. First, we are assuming that certain important advantages of field experience are sufficiently obvious not to need elaboration here. These advantages might include help in career choice for the students, financial assistance, a sense of the real world, or a commitment to service. Secondly, because most readers will be familiar with such instances of out-of-class teaching and learning as government-intern programs, intern placements in business or architectural firms, and independent field study, we will turn our attention to less ordinary examples. Finally, it should be clear that these are illustrative examples, not proposals, and that the list is by no means comprehensive.

One possibility for tying a modest amount of field experience into a program such as English might be to relate a field experience directly to the content of a specific area of literature. This might require some course restructuring, but today it is not uncommon to structure upper-level courses by social characteristics of the literature. We might, for example, work with a course entitled, "Social Literature of the 20th Century." The reading list for this course might include *The Jungle, The Grapes of Wrath, Cannery Row,* and several of Richard Wright's novels.

The objectives of such a course, in keeping with the aims of the humanities generally, would be to use the insights of the best writers in this area of literature to illuminate real human problems in the present, and vice versa, and to illuminate the insightfulness of certain writers through confrontation with actual human problems.

One plan might be to extend this course over two semesters. During the first semester the student would work in a setting similar to that of the setting of the literature: a migrant-labor camp or an agency serving migrants, another laboring situation, or in an inner-city setting similar to those in Wright's books. The student would, of course, be expected to do more than observe behavior in these environments and therefore would have to spend a considerable amount of time in them, perhaps a minimum of twenty hours a week.

Credit would be awarded, not for the field experience itself but for the total experience. The student would enroll, for example, for nine hours of credit for the total package, and might complete part of a reading list while working twenty hours a week in the fall term, and then he or she would move in the spring semester into a seminar on the same subject with more reading and papers. A diary or log kept during the work experience might also be the subject of considerable discussion in the seminar.

The same model might apply to students in courses in recent political history. In this case students might be placed in a political campaign, a lobby, a labor union, or a bureaucratic structure. The student's responsibilities might be more related to research for the sponsoring agency, especially if the internship had to be carried out on a part-time basis. The related seminar in this case would be an effort to reflect on the specific machinations of the placement environment, as they were reflected in historical data.

The academic emphasis would be on comparison and generalization. Not designed to impart specific historical information, the total process (field placement and seminar) would be planned to help the student "read" his environment in its historical context. An alternative model appropriate for English or history might be field research, including the collection of oral history or oral data. Such a project could be tied to the specific research interests of the instructor. This approach has been used and discussed widely enough not to need extensive treatment here.

These examples propose modest programs of fieldwork. A more substantial amount might be included in a field-based course that would investigate the ethical basis of decision making in business or government. This course might be scheduled as a full-time field involvement for all or part of a semester and would be interdisciplinary. Students would be placed with persons in positions of management or supervisory authority. These executive supervisors would be carefully selected and told of the nature of the assignment in advance and could even be defined as a community-based "field faculty." The students would also participate in an intensive seminar, with a teaching staff comprised of an experienced business or government executive, a professor of philosophy, and a professor of administration. The student's specific academic assignment would be to identify and analyze a number of critical incidents where decisions were made and to test that analysis in the seminar setting. The specific program would, of course, be broader than it might seem (that is, meaningful not just in terms of ethical considerations) in that the student would be contributing real and constructive work and therefore would be getting practical experience; he would be examining the organization in terms of its total structure; and he would be developing skills of analysis more akin to those practiced in everyday life.

A much discussed but little used field-experience approach for the liberal arts might be a policy-research institute staffed by students under faculty supervision, such as the Austin College program mentioned earlier. A team of faculty members would supervise a task force of students in a contract relationship with a public agency. The contract would call for a thorough analysis of the applicability of a particular policy; the subject matter might range from the feasibility and desirability of a proposed highway extension to the legalization of off-track betting.

The policy-research approach could be designed specifically to give students the opportunity to delve deeply into the technical ramifications of planning, surveying, and forecasting. It could also give the students the opportunity to formulate, with some hope of implementation, their own rationale for the ethical base on which decisions affecting the entire community could be made. The model has the further advantage of not being tied to a specific place (that is, office space in an agency); research could be conducted in the community and reflection exercised in the classroom. An obvious disadvantage might be the unpredictability, from semester to semester, of community needs for policy-research projects.

Although these are modest sketches, they do point out the range of applications of field experience to the liberal arts. To repeat, there are numerous experiences already in existence or placements available for individual students that would also be of use in the liberal arts. These include not only the established government-intern programs but also opportunities to do field research and practical writing in archives.

The main point, however, is that the field experience could be useful in the liberal arts, that it has not yet been exploited, and that the range of options are as wide as geography and the imagination will permit.

Conclusion

We have tried to show that, while the aims of education in the liberal arts retain their validity, their vitality is critically threatened by forms of anomie and environmental threat peculiar to our times, and that one means for seeking their revitalization lies in the use of that family of devices for teaching and learning that we have called experiential education. Exclusive concern with experiential education in this paper should not be taken as evidence of naive preoccupation on our part with narrow pedagogical gimmickery for its own sake. We merely wish to present the case that such devices should be tried in furtherance of liberal-arts aims.

We can go no further than to suggest what appears to be a promising direction, and we would not dare guarantee success. So much depends on the quality of imagination, the willingness of faculty members to work through the problems of concept and execution, the administrative assessments of costs and benefits, and the readiness of students to make the most of such opportunities—to name but the most obvious problems—that one would be foolish to peddle experiential education as the "perfect product." Indeed, the proper training of the intellect, as Cardinal Newman pointed out in 1852, can be guaranteed by no particular method. He wrote: ". . . it is not mere application, however exemplary, which introduces the mind to truth, nor the reading of many books, nor the getting up of many subjects, nor the witnessing of many experiments, nor the attending of many lectures. All this is short of enough; a man may have done it all, yet be lingering in the vestibule of knowledge. . . ."[25]

The objective for all of us, we trust, is to get beyond the vestibule of knowledge, by whatever means.

A Tradition of Excellence

In 1979 John relinquished the position of dean of undergraduate studies to become director of the Appalachian Center, recently established at the University of Kentucky. Although he developed a multidisciplinary program in Appalachian studies at the university, his role in shaping general education policy was considerably restricted. However, while serving in that position, in 1983 John was appointed special assistant to the chancellor for academic development. This advisory position provided him with fresh opportunities to pursue his interests in higher education policy. But before he could implement his ideas in this area, he was offered and accepted the presidency of Berea College in 1984.

John's inaugural address was delivered in October of 1984. In it he set forth various aspects of his philosophy concerning higher education in general and at Berea College specifically. Reprising his concern with technological change and its social consequences, John saw in the future the possibility of some happier developments, such as those brought about by medical advances. But there were also some serious problems facing higher education. As natural byproducts of technical and social innovation, John foresaw that new moral and ethical dilemmas would arise.

The address also made explicit a theme that had been implicit in earlier writings and was manifest in John's daily life—service to others. The Berea Charter set forth the college's fundamental commitment "to promote the cause of Christ," which provided the justification if not obligation of service to others. And "Whom shall we serve?" John asked. "Those in need," he responded to his own query. More specifically, he noted the historic commitment of the college to the poor, who otherwise would not have been able to obtain a high quality education, to Black people still struggling to attain the full rights of citizenship, and to the people of Appalachia. How the service to these "neighbors" was to be provided other than through admitting their youth to the college was not stated in the address. But John's intent could be inferred from his citation of one of his predecessors, former President Francis J. Hutchins, who argued that "Berea should continue to intertwine and interweave the life of the campus with the life of the people who live in the region about us." It was the kind of commitment to service that John not only endorsed but promoted and practiced throughout his tenure as Berea's president.

INAUGURATION ADDRESS OF JOHN B. STEPHENSON
AS PRESIDENT OF BEREA COLLEGE
26 OCTOBER 1984

Mr. Chairman, members of the Board of Trustees, distinguished delegates, citizens of Berea, ladies and gentlemen of the faculty of Berea College, members of the staff, students and alumni of this great College, special friends and family, and honored guests:

I would like, if I may, to take a moment, before I begin my remarks, to recognize certain individuals present today who are important to Berea College and to me. First, my mother and father, whose lives have been great examples of Christian virtue, work, and service to others. Second, my wife Jane and my children—my family, who are the other indispensable part of this Presidency or any other. Third, Jane's mother, who may have been slightly astonished but who has been wholly supportive of the things that have happened in the last 22 years. And then there is Professor Wayne Kernodle of the College of William and Mary, who kindled my love of Appalachia and who thought I should go to graduate school despite my misgivings. To all of you I am forever grateful. I would also like to recognize Larry Hopkins, Member of the U.S. House of

Representatives, and to thank him for his presence today. Last, if Mr. and Mrs. Clyde Jones are here, I would like to recognize them by calling attention to the fact that they have been associated with Berea for 71 years, during the terms of 5 presidents. It is people like Mr. and Mrs. Jones who contribute the continuity for which this College is famous.

It is with both pride and humility that I respond to the call to serve Berea College as its seventh President. *Pride* because I cannot feel otherwise when I contemplate the magnificent history of which I have been invited to become a part. And *humility* because of the tremendous responsibilities and challenges which this very history places upon me.

Truly I stand in awe of my predecessors as I appear before you today. Knowing as I do the stature of the six great Presidents of Berea College who have come before me, two of whom are with us on this platform to share in the beauty of this moment of continuity and change, I can only feel humbled as I accept the responsibility which has been placed before me this hour.

Berea today is a legacy which we have inherited from those who went before. Not only from its Presidents, but from its generations of visionary and zealous women and men whose skills and toil have carried this institution through history like another ark of the Covenant, and from its students—those very special people who are the life of Berea both while they are here and after they leave to go into the world—these are the people from whom Berea College is inherited.

But greater still than the persons who have been the bearers of this institution is the College itself and the great ideas which it has manifested throughout its nearly 130 years of history.

> Berea, the improbable idea.
> Berea, the impossible task.
> Berea, the incomparable achievement.

It is this of which I stand in awe at this moment. I feel, as Governor Chandler said once when he stood here, that we should take our shoes off, for the ground here is holy.

We owe a debt for this inheritance. It is so large as to be beyond human scale, and it can never be fully repaid. How should we respond? As we would to any great gift, we should respond with a celebration of thanks. We should respond with great generosity of the spirit as we in turn give the gift to the next generations. We should accept as part of the burden of this gift the obligation to continue the prophetic mission which began when Paul and Silas went to the original Berea, where their message was received with all eagerness, and which was continued when John Fee and his band of believers came to this ridge, where their message was met with the same eagerness.

Berea was an improbable idea from the beginning. It consisted, as William J. Hutchins observed in 1920, of "dreams, which counted with other men for madness." In 1893, President Frost remarked in his inaugural address that "the task before us is an appalling one— to human eyes impossible." Even now, as we sit in the midst of this beautiful campus and enjoy the rich experiences which it presents to us, Berea College is difficult to believe. It is, as Thomas Wolfe might have said, one of those "dark miracle[s] of chance which make new magic in a dusty world." But, unlikely as it is, Berea is a great, an incomparable achievement, a great gift of history, and now we must carry it forward as we take our turn on the track of time.

As we take up this task it would be prudent to ask ourselves what kind of future we face. What kind of future not only for Berea College, but the nation and the world? And if we can see this future even dimly, what consequences can we foresee for education in general, for higher education in the United States, and for Berea College specifically?

As uncertain as forecasts of tomorrow seem to be, they are useful in focusing attention—and they are, lest we forget, sometimes accurate. We cannot escape the knowledge that certain trends and events must be taken seriously because they will definitely affect our futures: developments in biomedicine and genetic engineering, the perfection of so-called fifth-generation computers, the differential birth rate among ethnic and nationality groups in the United States, the aging of the population, and the escalation of the pace with which work is being automated are but a few examples of the ways in which the future is being altered at the very moment we ponder it.

We might well ask whether there are happy tomorrows ahead, tomorrows of the sort depicted by the cartoon futurists of the earlier decades. Perhaps there are, but even the happier aspects of invention, medical progress, and "convenience" innovations will necessitate adjustments and adaptations.

There are problems, for example, which we will witness increasingly because of the effects of technology on the nature of work.

There are problems in a future where there is an increasing gap between the haves and the have-nots, and between the knows and the know-nots, for the gap will increase between those who have the learning skills to keep up with technological explosions and those who do not.

It is obvious, moreover, that we can anticipate an increasing number of ethical and moral dilemmas which are the natural byproduct of technical and social innovation. It is a truism that the solution to one problem brings other problems in its wake.

There have been and will continue to be tremendous changes in the means by which power and influence over other people are exercised.

Moreover, as knowledge explodes, we are asking again what knowledge is, and, as knowledge splinters, what wisdom is.

And as the global economy becomes a reality, as we find ourselves woven into a network of transnational corporations, international loan markets, competing currencies, and rising national debts, we will probably experience more abrupt fluctuations in the economy. Are we ready for a redefinition of the good life?

As we feel the winds of change blowing, and as we see glimpses of a future which brings us as many problems as it does promises of progress, how do we respond? And in particular, what leadership and vision are provided by higher education in anticipating and resolving these dilemmas of change?

Despite the abundance of leadership talent and skill available on the thousands of college and university campuses in this country, circumstances of our time do not seem, to allow for much national leadership and vision from this quarter. Nor, unfortunately, do we see adequate visionary leadership from business, religion, or government, with the consequence that we are living in a society almost devoid of vision.

Most institutions of higher learning are currently too preoccupied with survival to be visionary. In the sixties they were preoccupied with the management of success and growth, whereas today they are caught up in the management of decline or stabilization. The emphasis has been on management and not leadership.

There have been and there will continue to be problems of declining or stabilizing enrollments confronting higher education institutions. Clark Kerr, former president of the University of California and former chairman of the Carnegie Council on Policy Studies in Higher Education has said that he projects a 10-per-cent decline in undergraduate enrollment which will not subside until 1997. The next twelve years, he says, "will be disastrous for some institutions, hardly noticed by a few, and difficult for most." There will be intense competition for students, especially talented students. The bounty wars and unethical recruiting practices already underway evidence an extreme preoccupation with the management of survival.

A second concern which preoccupies higher education leadership nationally during these times is the escalating cost of going to college. Especially among independent colleges and universities, cost containment is a major issue. This is not news; parents and students are even more aware than college officers of the rising costs of college. The future promises no relief: a recent report predicts that by the year 2000 the cost of tuition at a private college or university will have risen to $100,000 for four years. Again, this is a management issue, and preoccupation with it does not allow time for visionary thinking.

Competition for dollars to keep the more than 3,000 higher education institutions in the United States in operation has become intense, and will become nothing less than a mad scramble in the next few years. Private dollars are sought just as assiduously as public ones these days, by both public and independent colleges. I have some doubt whether there is enough to go around. Unfortunately, if this assumption is correct, not all existing colleges will survive to greet the 21st century.

Meantime, while we watch this national survival contest proceed, we face internal problems of a generally dispirited and unappreciated faculty which is starved for recognition and reward, and which is tortured by an archaic tenure system. There is, moreover, a strong need for, continuous updating and renewal among faculty, who find it difficult to deal with a knowledge explosion for which one-time graduate school training is not adequate preparation. The graduate schools themselves need reform, to avoid the pitfalls of overspecialization and to recognize the continuing educational needs of those who emerge from graduate schools with so-called "terminal degrees." Moreover, we are insufficiently concerned with the quality of new graduate student recruits and with the question of from where the next generation of college faculty is to come.

These are some of the problems with which we are grappling at present, and it is plain to see why they drain our energy away from larger issues of vision and leadership for the rest of society. Higher education has its own future with which to be concerned.

But this is not all. If we in higher education think we face intense problems now, and if we already face the future with clenched teeth and an uncomfortable sense of dread, we had better rope ourselves to the mast before the next wave of educational criticism comes crashing down. It is a wave which will arrive soon, and it is directed this time not at public elementary and secondary education but at college and university education.

We already know something of what will be said. The National Institute of Education has already issued its report on higher education just this week. And Ernest Boyer, former U.S. Commissioner of Education and currently president of the Carnegie Foundation for the Advancement of Teaching, recently announced his next study, *College: A Report on Undergraduate Education in America.* The results, to be published in 1986, will conclude that college students, are ill informed about the world, that there is an inability to wed the liberal arts and preparation for meaningful work, that there are problems with the current system of tenure, that business leaders are unhappy about the preparation of the graduates they hire, and that there are no activities besides athletics that bring all faculty and students together.

We are likely to see other criticisms as well, for national reports on education, like starlings, seem to arrive in great flocks. Judging from the warmup reviews we are already receiving, higher education will be accused of blandness and irrelevance. Institutions will be described as lacking in distinction, being without character, to use Warren Bryan Martin's phrase. We will be told that there is an absence of values from the college curriculum. It will be said that our teaching methods are largely unchanged from those of the Middle Ages.

It will be said, moreover, that some of the problems with elementary and secondary education can be traced to higher education, which neither provides the support nor the outstanding teachers for the schools it then criticizes. It will be pointed out that higher education has become old and creaky and in its ossified state is unable to adapt to rapidly changing needs, with the result that it is losing educational functions to business, to government, and to proprietary schools which promise to deliver results promptly and effectively in new areas of essential learning.

And it will be said that higher education is unable to prove that going to college makes a difference, especially a large enough difference to justify the cost. What, we will be asked, is the tangible value of going to college? The state of Tennessee already mandates the measurement of the value added by attendance at its state universities. The Southern Association of Colleges and Schools is already pushing hard for the inclusion of student outcomes criteria in its new standards. The purpose of these developments is to prove to the skeptics that going to college does make a difference. We are already on the defensive.

The consequence of the new criticism of higher education, justified though it may be in part, will be to further weaken any remaining public support colleges and universities now enjoy. Our publics, including business, foundations, government, and individual students and parents, are going to look for answers to increasingly tough questions before they invest further.

The new criticism adds an additional handicap to an educational enterprise already struggling for vision. It will be difficult enough to foresee future trends, identify the issues and dilemmas likely to attend them, and respond to them in a leadership fashion as higher education should. But under the pressure of the new criticism, our task will be like trying to chart a new course while battling a high and unfriendly sea. Visionary leadership is not what one normally expects under these circumstances.

How will we respond?

Most institutions will, I suspect, follow the time-honored tradition of muddling through.

Many institutions will change gradually in order to survive.

Some institutions will change radically as a spirit of total reform overtakes them.

Those institutions will be most favored, I believe, which already know themselves, which possess true distinction in mission and function, and which are well on their ways to meeting the charges against higher education before they are even brought.

I believe Berea College is fortunate in finding itself among the last-named—the favored.

Berea College has a strong sense of its own identity. It knows itself. It knows its commitments. These Great Commitments are as valid today as when they were first asserted, and they have infused the life of this College as it has introduced the world of learning and the world of service to more than 150,000 students in its lifetime. While, as President Fairchild said in 1869, "We do not expect to be carried to the skies on flowery beds of ease," we *do* expect the unique qualities which these commitments contribute to Berea College to make it easier to know who we are and what we should be about. Self-knowledge is surely the first requisite of success in meeting the future.

Berea's first and most fundamental commitment, established in its Charter, is "to promote the cause of Christ." From this principle may be derived all the others. It is from our commitment to follow Christ's example, and to show our love of God through our love for humanity, that we have dedicated this institution and ourselves to lives of service.

And whom shall we serve? Our neighbors, according to Christ's many examples, are those in need. From the very beginning, in 1855, those most in need of the kind of education we can offer at Berea have been able to acquire an education of high quality which would otherwise have been unavailable to them.

From the beginning, Berea reached out to Black people in their struggle to attain full participation as citizens of this country. It was a mission which made Berea distinct and which is still vital today. It is a commitment to which we pledge renewed energy as a part of Berea's promise that the dream shall not die. As President Stewart said, "The College is still as true as ever to the noble motto on its seal: 'God hath made of one blood all nations of men.'"

And not only all nations of men, but all genders of people as well are of the same blood. The time is proper for us to pledge ourselves also, out of this same tradition, to greater efforts in resolving issues of gender and justice in the world.

From its earliest days, Berea declared its intention to serve the needs of the people of Appalachia. President Weatherford is the most recent among Berea's leadership to reaffirm emphatically this historic commitment. The suggestion has been made that perhaps the mountain region has changed so greatly that it no longer demonstrates needs which Berea can help meet. Indeed, it is true today, as President William J. Hutchins observed 64 years ago, that the changes are "swift and momentous." It is just as true, however, to quote his words further, that "One sees these things with foreboding." While these changes have brought economic and educational benefits to some in the region, great needs still exist, *especially* in education. The fact that Berea's current freshmen rank in the 60th percentile academically and yet 60 per cent come from homes that cannot contribute to the cost of their educations shows that Berea is still needed in the region. Perhaps Frost did not put it too strongly when he said that "As a radical college we have a mission in educational reform." Our commitment to Appalachia remains as firm as ever.

This commitment will be met not only through what we offer on the campus itself but through a revival of Berea's great tradition of innovation in outreach. As President Francis Hutchins reflected in 1937, "In China colleges have walls about them. In some cases, colleges in the United States have invisible walls about them. Perhaps we have already undertaken too much, but I am bold enough to suggest that Berea should continue to intertwine and interweave the life of the campus with the life of the people who live in the regions about us."

Berea has also maintained its early commitment to the marriage of education and work. President Frost referred to the importance of learning "something of the dignity of manual toil, alongside college studies." He said, "Berea College stands with a spade and a spelling book in one hand, and a telescope and a Greek Testament in the other." Berea students still have their hands full, as they will readily attest, but the labor program is as much a part of a Berea education as is the program of general education. It has not always been easy to make this marriage work, but it does work, and it is to be celebrated.

Berea recognizes the need for a curriculum and a learning environment which is rooted firmly in the values inherent in the Christian faith, and such a curriculum is realized here. Berea has, furthermore, developed and will continue to evolve a learning program which is integrated, comprehensive, and synoptic. It is one of those rare "colleges of character," and it deserves to be emulated. It is a college which has kept its vision. It is still a great, transcendent idea, an idea larger than the physical manifestation of the campus, larger than the region and the people it serves, an idea which enlarges the souls of all who learn of it.

Berea College provides unexcelled opportunities for its students. But of even greater importance is the example it gives the nation and the world. *Berea has something to say to the world, something the world is listening for.* If there is lack of vision, if demoralization and fatalism are abroad in the land, if there is an unfortunate separation among life, learning, work, and service, if community is missing from institutional and societal life, then let Berea provide an example for the nation and the world of how we can keep our vision and face the dilemmas and issues of the world's future.

This college will of necessity face its own peculiar problems because of its unique commitments. It will not be a simple matter to maintain a required labor program, or to ensure that we continue to serve those of modest means. It will be difficult to keep the Christian faith at the center of our work while the secular and sectarian winds blow around us. But be assured that Berea's moral, ethical, and spiritual foundations will not be eroded in our quest to solve these problems. The Great Commitments will be our guide.

Howard Beers once wrote that "a future always waits to be designed." The future of higher education and of the nation and world is waiting to be written. It could be a terrible future if we do not anticipate it and control it wisely. We in higher education have a great obligation, an awful burden, but it is one we have asked for. Ours is the obligation to prepare students for their futures. But ours is also the obligation to help create the future we send them out to face.

This is more than a challenge. Merely surviving is a challenge. *This is a moral duty.*

We are all part of a noble calling, whether we are trustees, officers, faculty, staff, donors, elected officials, students, parents, alumni, or friends. President William G. Frost once said, "God's plan is a cooperative one." There is a role to be played by all of us in undertaking this task of designing the future through our work in higher education.

I have been asked to do my part through joining hands with others here at Berea College and becoming part of its miraculous work. Berea, the improbable idea. Berea, the impossible task. Berea, the incomparable achievement.

I pledge to do my part by providing the best leadership I can for this great work, and for the educational enterprise everywhere. I ask you to take your part in this work as well. And may we enjoy God's blessings as we do justice, love mercy, and walk humbly with Him.

The Place of the Independent College

During his term as Berea's president, John had ample opportunity to develop and express his philosophy of education. One expression was an essay prepared for the Prichard Committee for Academic Excellence, an organization recognized as being largely responsible for bringing about revolutionary changes in Kentucky's primary and secondary public schools. The executive director of the Prichard Committee was Robert F. Sexton, John's former colleague, who had earlier directed the University of Kentucky's experiential education program. Having achieved remarkable success in the passage of the Kentucky Education Reform Act of 1990, the committee had turned its attention to higher education. Perhaps it would be more accurate to say that it returned to the consideration of higher education in the state, for the committee had given the subject considerable thought at the initiation of its operations.

John, who had served as a member of the Prichard Committee, was invited to contribute to a set of essays published under the title *Issues in Kentucky Higher Education.** In his essay, entitled "The Soul of the College: A Requiem or a Manifesto for Independent Higher Education," John expressed concern for the future of small private colleges, such as Berea, which he felt were engaged in fierce competition with large state-supported universities for funds and students. Perhaps as a consequence of their struggle for survival, colleges and universities had neglected, if not, lost their function of providing society with a strong, reasoned voice on moral issues, careful and committed discourse on the right things to do, and independent critiques of our culture.

THE SOUL OF THE COLLEGE: A REQUIEM OR A
MANIFESTO FOR INDEPENDENT HIGHER EDUCATION

There is a spectre haunting higher education in America and in Kentucky. The distinctive qualities of the independent liberal arts college are being compromised in ways that the public by and large does not recognize, and the contributions of these qualities to society are weakened and may already be lost.

Let us begin with that word "independent." To the extent that there is any distinction at all in the minds of Americans between "public" and "private" higher education, the use of the term "private" is customary. But as others have pointed out, there is no "private" higher education; all higher education serves the public interest. The distinction which should be drawn is that between state-supported and independent higher education. But the truth is that the line between the two sectors is blurring as state-supported institutions become more like independent colleges in their increased reliance on nongovernmental funding sources, and as the independent colleges are forced to emulate the "publics" in programs, calendars and schedules, residence requirements, and yes, sacrifice of independence.

The question of the future of independent higher education would never have been in doubt in the 1930s. In that decade, as in earlier years, the clear majority of students enrolled in institutions of higher learning was to be found in independent institutions. Those institutions played a crucial leadership role, not only in higher education, but in American society generally. Since that time, and especially since the 1950s and 1960s, significant changes have influenced the way we "deliver" higher education in the United States, and even the way we think about it.

Public Policy and Change

The G.I. Bill had a transforming effect on our colleges and universities, presaging the even greater impact of the explosion of college-age students in the 1960s, as baby boomers caused campuses to bulge with unprecedented numbers of new students. Federal policy with regard to higher education placed great value on "access," and the rapid development of governmental need-based student financial aid programs contributed greatly to the sudden growth of state-supported institutions. Overnight, it seemed, new dormitories sprouted like mushrooms, and teachers' colleges were redesignated universities.

If anyone recalls the days of Sputnik, it will also be remembered that not only was access emphasized by federal policy but also by national competitiveness as well, the international advantage being gained by that country which produced the largest number of university-trained individuals, especially scientists and engineers and others who could feed the national purpose.

Outside government, there was during those days (and perhaps even today) what might be called "the big sell." Not only would the national interest be served, but individual's interests as well, through pursuit of higher education. Statistics showed convincingly, if somewhat spuriously, that higher education led to higher income, more education to better jobs.

Whose job was it to respond to such concerns as those just enumerated? Government, federal and state. Public policy regarding higher education translated into public funds, which translated into a strikingly large and sudden investment in government-supported higher education. In the 1980s, of course, the philosophy underlying public policy toward higher education was reversed. Further education was not the responsibility of government, because the benefits were now defined as accruing to the individual and not to society. The investment must, as a result, now be made by the individual, through student loans, through higher tuition, through coupling study with gainful employment. The corresponding reduction in the investment of public dollars quickly alerted public institutions to the fact that they would need increasingly to rely on private funds, thus breaking an age-old tacit agreement that the "publics" and the "privates" would graze in different pastures.)

Balance Altered

This tremendous and disproportionate growth of government-supported universities dramatically altered the balance between public and independent universities and colleges, probably forever. Competition for students and for funds became excruciatingly sharp. The result has been a period of scrambling, rearguard struggles for maintenance of quality, if not survival, on the part of independent colleges. One estimate has it that roughly 700 colleges have either merged or died over the last 20 years.

Strategies for survival have included adoption of job-linked educational programs, adjustment of academic calendars and schedules to meet the needs of increasing numbers of part-time students, the enticement of non-traditional students to make up for the decline in the number of 17- to 22-year-olds. (The invention of the new-standard "FTE" wasn't required until whole new students began to be replaced by parts of students.) Another strategy was to develop new funding patterns; as many colleges lobbied for their "fair share" of the trough, many were forced to increase tuition, and others greatly intensified their nongovernmental fund-raising efforts.

Plastic Ivy

One has to question at times whether, as a result of the imbalanced competition and the blurring of lines between state-supported and independent higher education, higher education in America has sold its soul—to corporate research interests, to someone's current definition of the national interest, to the job market, to whomever will pay the piper.

We are customarily too courteous to raise questions about what has happened to quality in higher education, but the truth is that there is plastic ivy on many of our campus walls. In the name of all the right things, we inadvertently have created a nation full of Wal-Mart universities and colleges. Not all, to be sure, and we can be thankful for those institutions that have had the understanding and support and financial strength to withstand the temptations to become like the current norm. There are still colleges, mostly small independent liberal arts colleges, which have tried stubbornly to cling to what they have always done best—offer intense, residential quality learning in a close community of scholars.

The public is not so blind or indifferent to issues of quality as some might like to think. And sooner or later the public learns when it is getting less than it was promised. Most of the negative public sentiment about higher education is in fact aimed at government-supported universities rather than at small liberal arts colleges, but the blanket of condemnation covers the colleges as well. Note that the language typically used in media reports on higher education refers to "colleges," when what is meant is state-supported universities. This unfortunate journalistic habit cropped up in a recent headline in a state (Kentucky) newspaper which announced that colleges in the state were increasing tuition, when in fact not a single college was mentioned in the body of the story. So all institutions are tarred with the same brush, whether or not good teaching is being sold short at the expense of questionable research, whether or not graduate students are teaching most of the lower division students, whether or not second-rate faculty are "processing" second-rate students in the manufacture of cheap degrees of questionable value.

Unfortunately, in the minds of most Americans today, the phrase "higher education" conjures up not an ivy-covered intellectual retreat, not a place of learning for its own sake, not a place where one practices valuing those things of eternal worth, not a place of values at all, but a place where knowledge is served like fast food—tasty, cheap, trendy, convenient, and not very enriching: the state-supported university.

Most people these days have their only experiences with such institutions, whether as students or sports fans. It's all they know of higher education. And from their point of view, it's all they need to know. "Private" colleges? They are insignificant little places for the snobbish rich who can afford to fritter away their years in trivial pursuits. They don't even bear thinking about. In fact, they are not within reach of the everyday consciousness of the vast majority of those who have any thoughts about higher education in the first place.

It is predictable thinking on the part of people in a state such as Kentucky, for example, where only 20 percent of students enrolled in higher education are enrolled in such little places.

My experience of 18 years on the public side tells me that high quality education can be found in the government-supported institutions. And, of course, there are small liberal arts colleges of questionable quality. Moreover, I feel strongly, having worked in both settings over my three-decades-plus in higher education, that there are roles for both in the future of this country.

But there is a serious question in my mind about whether many, or any, of our institutions of higher learning can provide for our society the more subtle functions it seems to me every vital society needs. To what sector of our society do we turn today for a strong, reasoned voice on moral issues? Where shall we go to engage in careful and committed discourse on what is the right thing to do as opposed to how to solve technical problems? To politics? Religion? The family? The media? I don't think so. To the colleges and universities? Perhaps at one time, but probably not now.

To what societal institutions do we turn for an independent critique of our culture? Who even possesses the independence required for such a dispassionate critical faculty? I fear that such independence has largely been lost in the scramble for survival and success.

How are we to be assured of the quality of education? Is it safe any longer to assume such high and selfless professional standards on the part of higher education institutions that they truly can be trusted to be self-correcting? How long will it be until accreditation associations themselves will come under scrutiny?

Potential for Independents

I believe the potential exists primarily among the independent colleges for the exercise of key societal roles quite beyond the preparation of students for careers, quite beyond contributing to politically expedient notions of the national interest, quite beyond the whelping on high-grade scientific technical problem-solvers. The word "potential" is important here, because these roles are anything but actual, let alone guaranteed at this time.

Potentially, freedom of ideas is best protected in institutions less beholden to politicians and taxpayers. Potentially, among the independents one is more likely to find a commitment to higher values which inform those who devote themselves to the long-term public good rather than to personal or special interests. Potentially, it is among the independent institutions that one is more likely to find a willingness to speak out on issues broader than institutional protection. And it is here that there is greater likelihood of finding forums for reasoning and platforms for speaking about great moral issues. It is here that the wisdom of society, not just the brains, is more likely to be stored and shared.

It is time for presidents and other academic leaders in the independent sector to lay aside survival concerns and play national and regional leadership roles. Which means that it is probably time to search for a different kind of academic leader.

It is time, as well, for the media and the public to learn to distinguish between government-supported and independent higher education.

It is time to become aware that the drive-ins are running fine dining out of business, that large institutions offering low prices and greater convenience to casual students now have the power, the authority and the public's allegiance. (While a strong athletic team may have no relationship to the quality of the educational experience, it can be worth unlimited advertising dollars.) They're cheaper in price—though not necessarily in cost, and they sell the same pieces of paper. Who's to tell the difference?

It is time to recall the highest purposes of higher education as expressed by visionaries such as John Henry Cardinal Newman and Thorstein Veblen, and some of the early leaders of Kentucky's higher education institutions, such as John Fee.

And it is time to return to a willingness to pay the price of the inevitable tension that exists between a truly independent higher education institution and society at large. Else our country will sacrifice high moral and intellectual vision in the name of short-term economic and political goals. And our best colleges will make the same sacrifices in exchange for mere survival, albeit with comfort.

This is a spectre that haunts us.

PART 5
Sermons

John's position as president of Berea College provided him literally with a "bully pulpit" from which he could express his views, not only on higher education but on a wide range of topics. He was not an ordained minister, but he was a preacher. From all accounts it was a role he enjoyed. He regularly preached at services in the college chapel, which provided him with welcome opportunities to communicate with Berea students, faculty and staff. Less often he spoke at community churches, at times in response to the invitations of his close friend Randy Osborne, who *was* an ordained minister. How many sermons John delivered is unknown. A number were recorded and a few were transcribed from the taped recordings. The subjects of his sermons were varied, but all bore the hallmark of careful preparation.

The first of the sermons reproduced here takes its title and inspiration from the Book of Joshua (4:6). As a prelude to the sermon, John and various members of the congregation had brought stones into the Danforth Chapel, which was celebrating its fiftieth anniversary. The stones were placed in a pile on the chapel floor as a deliberate replication of Joshua's celebration of the safe passage of the tribes of Israel through the waters of the River Jordan. Joshua had successfully followed the example of Moses in crossing the Red

Sea. As an expression of gratitude, Joshua called for representatives of each of the tribes to carry stones to their new lodging place. There the stones were placed in a pile, whose purpose Joshua clarified:

> And he spake unto the children of Israel saying: When your children shall ask their fathers in time to come, saying, What *mean* these stones? Then ye shall let your children know, saying Israel came over this Jordan on dry land. For the Lord your God dried up the waters of Jordan from before you until ye were passed over, as the Lord your God did to the Red Sea which he dried up from before us until we were gone over. That all the people of the earth might know the hand of the Lord, that it is mighty; that ye might fear the Lord your God for ever. Joshua 4: 21-24.

With typical Stephenson humor, John facetiously suggested that the reason the Red Sea crossing was so much better known than the River Jordan crossing was that Moses had a better press agent.

After discussing the origins and significance of the stones used in the construction of the Danforth Chapel, which he referred to as a "glorious rockpile," John concluded that they had meaning not just as a memorial to the generosity of Mr. Danforth but also to Berea's great commitments and to the high purpose and extraordinary mission of those who had come before. And as for the stones especially collected for the commemorative service, they should serve as tokens of rededication not just to the idea of Berea but also to the daily re-creation of thoughts and behavior expressing that idea.

The second sermon—"The Christian College: An Oxymoron?"—discloses John's concern with the role of Berea as a nondenominational Christian college. Is the concept of a college compatible with the idea of Christianity or, for that matter, any religion? It is for those who believe it is.

John approached the issue by exploring the functions of the early Christian organizations before there was a church. Drawing on his academic discipline of sociology, he advanced the proposition that organizations can be more than the sum of the individuals who make them up. Organizations, including the church, have a reality and identity of their own that supersede the collectivity of their members. They are "more than just the people," and can take on qualities and characteristics of their own. Christian organizations, including Berea College, are identified by their profession of Christian beliefs and their practice and teaching of Christian ways.

John warned against letting others determine what Berea College's Christian premises and goals should be, and argued for self-determination. Berea, a Christian College, he concluded, is not an oxymoron. It is a possibility yet to be fully realized.

The final sermon—"A Berea Covenant"—is also concerned with the religious obligations of the Berea College community and was delivered at the Berea College Homecoming of March 21, 1993. In it John compared the people of Berea with the people of Israel being led by Moses to the Promised Land. The Covenant between God and the Israelites offered an abundant life in return for obedience to God's commandments

Berea College, John suggested, was a special recipient of God's benevolence, which also implied the existence of a Berea Covenant. But was Berea keeping up its side of the agreement? It is a question left unanswered, but John points out the necessity of being continuously reminded of the Covenant, and its obligations. These include observance of the fundamental Christian commandment that "you must love one another," and the responsibility on the part of the people of Berea "to act justly, to love mercy, and to walk humbly with our God."

What Mean These Stones?

Have you ever noticed what an important part stones play in the Bible?

There are so many that it would be difficult to list all the references to rocks and stones in both the Old and New Testaments. Think, for instance, of the tablets of stone on which God wrote the Ten Commandments. Think of the many times God is likened to a rock in the Psalms. Remember that one of the disciples was named "Stone" by Jesus himself—"on this rock, Peter, I will build my church." And remember that one of the mysteries of the resurrection was that the stone sealing Jesus' tomb was rolled away. If it had not been for that rolling stone, we might even question whether the matter of Christ's second coming—or indeed the first coming—would have ever taken on great significance it has for us today.

And recall the story of the house built on sand and the house built on a rock. The point of the story is the same point that underlies all these references to stones in the Bible. Although nothing in this world is permanent, rocks are about as close as we can come in our human experience to representing endurance, durability, hardness, unshakability, unmovability, everlastingness. That is why, when we humans seek to memorialize someone or some event, we very typically do it in stone: gravestones, statues, carvings on cliffs, and buildings, such as the one we are gathered in here today.

That is also why, when Joshua wanted to memorialize an extremely significant event in the sojourning of the Jews in the Wilderness, he chose to do so with stones.

Lee Morris pointed out this passage in Joshua to me several months ago, and I thank him for that, because I had wondered where this expression came from: What Mean These Stones?

You know that there were two episodes during the long trek of the Jews on their way back to the Promised Land from Egypt in which the Lord pushed back water and made dry land for the people

John's parents, Louis and Edna, at a Christmas party in the mid-1980s.

to walk on. Moses seems to have had a better press agent and so the publicity has gotten out about the parting of the Red Sea. Moses parted the Red Sea first, as everyone knows, when Pharoah's army was in hot pursuit of his newly freed slaves. But Joshua asked the Lord for the same small favor when he got to the Jordan River, and the Lord was similarly obliging. (Joshua 3:15-17)

Joshua wanted people to remember that day, and so he asked twelve people, representing the tribes of Israel, to bring stones together at a place east of the river so that in the future, children would ask "What is this pile of rocks doing here? What does this mean?" And they would be answered as Joshua instructed: "Tell them that the flow of the Jordan was cut off before the ark of the covenant of the Lord. When it crossed the Jordan, the waters of the Jordan were cut off. These stones are to be a memorial to the people of Israel forever."

The walls of stone which surround us today are another kind of memorial. This house of the Lord is called Danforth Chapel, and it is, among other things, a fitting memorial to Mr. William H.

Danforth, the founder of the Ralston Purina Company, whose Christian convictions and generosity caused this chapel to be built fifty years ago this year. It is, you will agree, a magnificent pile of stones, combining architectural elements of strength, permanence, and beauty in good measure and in balanced proportion. It is a marvelous concatenation of Gothic vertical airiness and Berea simplicity. The eye, leading the spirit, ascends, but the hand can at the same time reach out to its neighbor in peaceful, comforting community. This is a place for the joyous soaring of the spirit and simultaneously the celebration of our kinship under God.

And if the stones on the inside of this chapel were not a sufficient memorial, those on the exterior of the building should really cause us to pause and wonder. I don't know how many of you know about the story of the stones that are embedded in the outside walls of Danforth Chapel.

Did you know that one of the stones in the wall behind me came from Lincoln's first tomb in Springfield, Illinois? That one stone came from Nazareth, allegedly from near the place of Jesus' carpentry shop? That one came from Mars Hill in Athens, Greece? From the Washington Monument? (And don't ask me who stole it from the Washington Monument. Some tourist, no doubt.) From the 8th Century B.C. palace of King Sargon II of Khorsabad, Iraq? From Eisleben, the birthplace of Martin Luther? From Canterbury Cathedral? Did you know there is a stone in this wall from India, a gift from Mahatma Gandhi, who did know about Berea College? A stone from one of the pyramids of Egypt? There are stones from Switzerland, Japan, Turkey, Tunisia, Sweden, Labrador, Italy, and Africa in this wall.

And it makes you wonder, doesn't it? What do all these stones mean?

And in this wall to your right, did you know there is a stone from the home of Alexander Graham Bell in Baddeck, Nova Scotia?

A letter was received in March from an alumnus of Berea College who was the person who transported that stone to Berea. His name is Robert Blake and he's an accomplished psychologist living in Austin, Texas. He reflects back on the trip he made carrying that stone. He says, "I hitch-hiked into Canada and was provided the stone, which I recall as terribly heavy to be carried by a hitch-hiker. I had bad luck in making progress toward Kentucky and without money decided I needed to rest, regardless of the circumstances." So he made it as far as Chicago and in Chicago decided to spend the night in Grant Park right next to Lake Michigan under the stars and to resume his journey the next morning.

"That left me out under the stars with a heavy rock of high symbolic significance. I can't reproduce what went through my mind but it must have been something like this, 'I want to sleep well and I never will if I have to worry about that stone.' Why I thought that it might be stolen I will never know, except for the high symbolic value that I attached to it. There was a bus terminal across the street from Grant Park and it provided the perfect solution. I placed the rock in one of the ten-cent lockers, inserted my dime, got the key and happily hiked into Grant Park, where to the best of my recollections I spent a very restful night and the return to Berea from Chicago was uneventful. The above is an approximation of what happened looked at from a 50-year perspective." And that's the message from Dr. Blake.

[Did you know] there's a stone from Thessaloniki, close to the original Berea in Greece? And one from Oberammergau, a gift of a man who once played Christ in the Passion Play? One from Williamsburg, from Cuba, from Panama, from a glacier in Jasper Park in Canada, from the Alsace-Lorraine in France (from John Frederic Oberlin's home), from a university in Kyoto, Japan, and from the garden of Gethsemane?

It does cause you to wonder. What do these stones mean?

And did you know that in this wall to your left there is a stone from Mt. William H. Danforth in the Antarctic, brought by Admiral Richard E. Byrd? And one from the Cathedral at Rheims? One from North and another from South Korea? One from the old summer palace in Peking, China? From the Roman Forum? From the chapel at Stanford University, a gift of Herbert Hoover? And one from the ruins of Carthage, brought by William H. Danforth himself? From Pike's Peak, Denmark, Trinity College at Cambridge, and the birthplace of Alexander Hamilton in the British West Indies?

I really do wonder, don't you? What is the meaning of these stones?

Here is a memorial indeed. This glorious rockpile was intended by its builders to remind every succeeding generation, including each one of us, of something significant—maybe something as significant to them as the parting of the waters of the Jordan River. Stones were gathered by many people from the far corners of the world to create an enduring edifice here that would serve as a reminder of something special. That something was and is the miracle of Berea.

For this chapel is not just a memorial to Mr. Danforth, but to Berea's Great Commitments, to the love of God and the belief in human freedom and in the dignity of all persons shown by our founders, to the courage and the idealism shown by the men and women who made possible the realization of an interracial utopia, a shining beacon of hope and opportunity, a labor of love and a love of labor, a devotion to service in the extreme to place and region, and an early recognition of the justice of offering educational advancement equally to women and men. A fitting memorial, these stones, to the high purposes and the extraordinary mission we have inherited from those who came before. May they serve to remind us and all who witness them to follow yesterday's heroic examples when we encounter injustice and indignity today.

And may these stones we have brought together here today, fifty years after the creation of Mr. Danforth's memorial to Berea's commitments and the glory of God, serve as tokens of our own rededication—not just to the idea of Berea, which I think we understand well, but to its daily re-creation through our own thoughts and behavior. Let this pile of rocks remind us to overcome our own prejudices, our carelessness in relating to others, our mistrust and cynicism concerning the intentions of others, our egotism and self-centeredness, our willingness to overlook sins against the spirit when we recognize them well. Let the hardness of these stones remind us forever of the need to be soft, gentle, patient, giving, and forgiving; the love of each other is what we owe to God.

And about these stones before us, shall we leave them here in the middle of the floor so that passersby will wonder—for a few days if not generation after generation—what is this pile of rocks doing here? Perhaps we should do just that. At least for the time being, we shall do just that. As our own kind of memorial, as a reminder of our own promises, a reminder to serve each other out of our gratitude for the love God has shown us. As a fifty-year token of the faith we continue to show in the mission of Berea College and of the gracious God who stands behind it all.

The Christian College: An Oxymoron?

There's a story in the Book of Acts I'm always mindful of when I get up to speak because it has to do with a sermon that Paul gave and an unfortunate episode that happened as a consequence of his—well, it went on a little too long. They were gathered together to break bread and Paul talked to them and he prolonged his speech until midnight, and there was a young man sitting in an upper window who fell asleep and fell out of the window. Fell down from the third story and was taken up dead. But, they brought him back to life and everything had a happy ending.

*The president's office of Berea College is located in Lincoln Hall,
one of the oldest buildings on the campus. Here John speaks with a visitor in 1986.
(photo by Berea College Public Relations)*

I'll try not to keep you too long today, but if you should fall out of your chairs asleep, why, we'll try to do our best to revive you.

Beth Klepinger was kind enough to send me an article from *Christianity Today* several months ago. The article was called "Playing the Oxymoron Game" and the writer of this article relates his experience with being together with some friends where they got into a contest to see who could come up with the newest oxymoron, which contrary to what Reverend Osborn says, doesn't mean "dumb cattle." It means a pointedly self-contradictory phrase, like "square circle." And the participants threw out examples like "jumbo shrimp," "postal service," an old favorite "military intelligence," and "airline food." And then came this stopper: "Christian College." I gather there are some at Berea College who would agree this is an apt oxymoron. I've heard it said at one time or another in the six years of my presence here at the college that "colleges can't be Christian." That's one thing I've heard. I heard it said once during our self-study, our long-range planning, that we shouldn't study the Christian commitment too carefully. And I've heard it said by several people, students and some faculty, that we're too tolerant of one kind of sin or another—take your pick—to be Christian.

I remember after lunch one day my first year here, a young man came up to the door just as I was leaving to go back to the office, and with just barely introducing himself, he said, "Mr. President, I think the higher-ups around here should know what's going on." And I said, "Well, what is going on?" and he said, "Do you know what they're making us read in freshman English?" And I said, "Well, what? What?" He said, "I don't know the name of it," he says, "but it's got swear words in it . . . and the Lord's name is blasphemed, and I think the higher-ups around here should know what's going on." And he said, "I thought this was a Baptist College," and I said, "Wait a minute. I never heard that." And he said, "Well, a Christian—whatever." And I said, "Yes, that's right." I said, "It's a college—because we study things. We look at ideas. We look at what people have written. And it's a Christian college, it means we even study sin, not for the purpose of emulating it, but for understanding it." And I said, "Who wrote the book?" He said, "I don't remember, but it was a black man—I think his name was Baldwin." And I said, "Have you spoken to your professor about the reason why this book was selected?" and he said, "No." And I said, "Well, let me recommend that you do that." I said, "It may have a purpose which fits perfectly in this Christian College context." But, a lot of people think that's a kind of sin we shouldn't even look at—we shouldn't try to understand.

Well, when people raise this question, "Is Berea a Christian College?" it seems to me naturally to raise a lot of other, related questions. Can any organization be Christian—churches, for example—

or can only individuals be Christian? I have a kind of, you'll have to pardon me, sociological answer to that one, that I'll get to in a minute. It raises a question in my mind about what the early organization of Christians was like, and that's why I went back to read that passage from Acts.

Before there was church, there was a gathering of Christians. What was it like? And was that a Christian gathering? It wasn't a church—that came later. What characterized them? Well, they had a common purpose, they shared their goods with each other, they helped each other. They ate together—a lot. They worshipped God together—attended the Temple. It was, as a later phrase says, "a company of those who believed." And I think I would call it Christian, even if it was not a church.

I guess another question that pushes itself on me at this point is whether Jesus was a Christian. I don't recall that he ever repudiated the Jewish faith. I don't think he ever claimed that title for himself—he was more a reformer within the faith. Ironically, it was only people who came after him who could claim "I'm a follower, and therefore, I'm a Christian."

Well, my point is not to play games with words, but to say that if you work at it, you can make it pretty difficult to earn the right to be called Christian. People propose a variety of different tests, not all of them consistent with each other, some of them impossible to pass. It's a wonder anybody, or anything, is willing to claim to be Christian.

Well, let me go back to the question of the Christian College—the oxymoron. Let's rephrase the question from a Kantian rather than a Humean point of view—by which I mean, instead of asking whether a college such as Berea can be Christian, let's assume that it's possible and then ask what it would be like.

First of all, an organization like a college can't be Christian in the same sense that a person, an individual, can be. There's a doctrine in the social sciences called the—I'll wake you up when this part of the homily is over. By the way, this is the sociology part. There's a doctrine in the social sciences called "the fallacy of misplaced concreteness." And the fear of committing that fallacy has led to an unfortunate rejection by many people of the very reality that we have tried to establish through the work of many social scientists over the years: the rejection of the reality of social facts themselves.

I think that I was fortunate—I grew up in an era when we read the works of people like Emile Durkheim, a French social scientist writing around the turn of the century. People like that were still being read back when I was growing up in the discipline, and he asserted that organizations and indeed whole societies were more than just the sum of the people that made them up. Out of the interaction of individuals, there emerges a new reality which is different from and has a force beyond the people from which it derives. It goes by many names: culture, norms, shared expectations, roles, organizations, societies. It has a power of its own; it's passed on from generation to generation, so we don't have to invent culture anew every year. And it spreads from place to place. It is real; it has identity and it has direction.

As a child, no doubt, you learned to put your hands together and recite this little rhyme: "Here's the church, and here's the steeple, open it up, and here's all the people." Well, the fingers are less than the hand, and the church is more than its people. And so is any organization, including a college, more than just its people. And it's possible for an organization, such as a college, to take on any of a number of qualities and characteristics. Organizations can, for example, be Christian. Not in the same fashion as individuals—organizations do not have souls—they cannot rise as a body to heaven—but they can have identity, purpose, intent, and direction, which are detectably Christian.

And so, we arrive at the question of how it is possible for a college to be Christian. How can one know it when one sees it? And most importantly for us, would we be correct in calling Berea College Christian? Well, this is a sufficiently large question for a whole series of homilies and I'm reminded of that same passage in the Book of Acts—we don't want to have to rescue the perishing today. But these thoughts occur to me in quick response to that question.

First, "by their fruits shall you know them." Is the climate of the college one of nurturing and caring? Does the college reach out in love to the poor and the forgotten? Does it work toward reconciliation? I think Berea attempts to pass these tests, though it could and should always do better.

Secondly, "does it institutionally declare the love of God through Jesus?" What does it say its intentions are? Does it, as suggested in the verse we read from Deuteronomy, teach these intentions diligently to the children and talk of them when sitting in the house, and when walking by the way, and when lying down, and when rising? Are they bound as a sign on our hands, and worn as frontlets between the eyes, and written on the door posts of our buildings? I'd say we go considerably beyond that—we even wear the cross on our bottles of bowl cleaner. Berea's intentions are made clear. From its 1859 charter to the label on last year's bowl cleaner—the reminders are all there to see.

Third, a college can be Christian without rigid behavioral prescriptions and without requiring that all individuals in it be declared Christians. Still, it cannot be without some expectations regarding the way that people are supposed to live together in mutual respect and love. And what are those expectations? What does the Lord require of us? There have been many tests put forth, but when boiled down to the essence, one can find it clearly stated in more than one place in the Bible, for example, in Micah 6: "And what does the Lord require of you but to do justice and to love kindness and to walk humbly with your God." Likewise, the passage we heard earlier. And if we need instruction in the meaning of those expectations, then we have the life of Jesus, the greatest gift of God to humans, to inform us.

Last, the Christian college, as many have pointed out, has a greater potential for achieving the ideal of community. As George Brushaber points out, "the unity of faith forms a basis for mutual caring." There can be gentle admonition, encouragement, cooperation, accountability, and a sense of responsibility shaped by the purpose of divine love. The real risks associated with growth, learning, and the crucible of ideas so essential to real education are best handled where this true sense of community is lived out.

Well, is Berea College a Christian college? It might be. It could be. It should be. It's certainly possible for Berea to be Christian, and that is its stated intent and has been the foundation of its community from the very beginning. It's how we give shape, day by day, to this mutual declaration of faith and works that will determine how well we measure up to the ideal. We should not let others prevent us from stating our premise and our goal just because that phrase, Christian college, is used in other contexts we judge less desirable than our own. No, this is not the kind of institution where we require that all faculty tithe, as one I just heard about last week. No, it is not the kind of institution where all faculty members are required to become members and attend the church which is the property of the president. It's not that kind of Christian college. Why can't we make that phrase mean what we want it to? We should wear it with pride and make it take on our meaning—Berea, a Christian college—it is no oxymoron. It is a possibility and you can help make it Christian. Let us then pursue what makes for peace and mutual upbuilding.

A Berea Covenant

The story of the Covenant is one of the most powerful in the Old Testament. God chooses Moses, a somewhat unlikely candidate for leadership, to lead the people of Israel from Egypt, to discipline them on their long trek homeward, and to explain, again and again, what's happening to them, where they're going, what their "New Deal" with God is, and even who they are.

Moses must have been terribly exasperated at times. He was forced to realize that the people who were supposed to be following him didn't understand what was happening or why. He repeatedly pointed out to them that they were a disappointment, a pretty despicable lot for a people presumably chosen by God for a special purpose.

"You made the Lord angry at Taberah, at Massah, and at Kibroth Hattaavah. And when the Lord sent you out from Kadesh Bamea, he said, 'Go up and take possession of the land I have given you.' But you rebelled against the command of the Lord your God. You did not trust him or obey him. *You have been rebellious against the Lord ever since I have known you.*" (Deut. 9:22-24)

And when he goes up the mountain for a private talk with God, when his back is turned for a moment, what do the people do but melt their gold and cast the infamous golden calf to worship. Moses was so mad he broke the first set of tablets of the laws and had to go back for another set!

For Moses, the "Deal," the agreement, the Covenant was simple: Do what the Lord wills you to do, and you will enjoy the abundant life. "Observe the commands of the Lord your God, walking in his ways and revering him. For the Lord your God is bringing you into a good land—a land with streams and pools of water, with springs flowing in the valleys and hills; a land with wheat and barley, vines and fig trees, pomegranates, olive oil and honey; a land where bread will not be scarce and you will lack nothing. . . ." (Deut. 8:6-9)

And what are the Lord's commands? Again, according to Moses, and later Micah, He expects three things: "And now, 0 Israel, what does the Lord your God ask of you but to fear the Lord your God, to walk in all his ways, to love him, to serve the Lord your God with all your heart and with all your soul, and to observe the Lord's commands and decrees that I am giving you today for your own good." (Deut. 10:12-13)

(Micah's version is even plainer: "He has showed you, 0 man, what is good, and what does the Lord require of you? To act justly and to love mercy, and to walk humbly with your God." (Micah 6:8)

But the reality that Moses faced is the one we face today, at Berea College and throughout the world. You can bring God to the people, and you can try to bring the people to God, but the brute fact is that people are people and not gods, and therefore they tend to forget their side of the Covenant, they forget to put God first and would rather give themselves all the credit for what God has provided. As someone has said, we are all warmed by fires we did not build, and we are sheltered by trees we did not plant, and we are watered by wells we did not dig. We did not create ourselves; we are not self-made. But we would like to believe we are.

Moses warned his people, and it should be a sufficient warning for us today: "When you have eaten and are satisfied, praise the LORD. . . . Be careful that you *do not forget the Lord*. . . . Otherwise, when you have eaten and are satisfied, when you build fine houses and settle down, and when your herds and flocks grow large and your silver and gold increase and all you have is multiplied, then your heart will become proud and you will forget the Lord your God. . . . You may say to yourself, 'My power and the strength of my hands have produced this wealth for me.' But remember the Lord your God, for it is he who gives you the ability to produce wealth, and so confirms his covenant. . . ." (Deut. 8:10-17)

Even when we acknowledge the Covenant, we are inclined to twist it so that it serves our ends and not those of God.

Even, maybe especially, the whites of South Africa used the Covenant as a metaphor, indeed a *mandate* for their dominance of Black South Africa. (Michener) This was a good example of what Moses warned against: pride in human power; the relegation of God to the background; the forgetting of God's ultimate power and purpose.

I want to suggest the Covenant as a way to understand the right relationship between God and Berea College.

We know what God expects of us (more than just the Ten Commandments). The founders of Berea College agreed to accept these obligations. Bereans became another "chosen people." And while

Kentucky Governor Martha Layne Collins and John are among the speakers at the groundbreaking ceremonies for Berea's new Tokico manufacturing plant in July 1987. (photo by Kara Beth Brunner, Berea College Public Relations)

we may not have moved into a land of milk and honey, we're doing well. We enjoy a wonderful campus, with fine buildings and well-manicured grounds. Somehow or other, Berea College manages to maintain 8,000 acres successfully, and over 40 miles of walking trails. Our faculty is exceptional, our Board of Trustees is strong, we've operated for countless years in the black financially, our graduates constitute a flowing stream of successful lives of service, helping to transform the world. Berea College enjoys remarkable heights of recognition in published ratings, and the statistical evidence continues to show that Berea is doing its job in meeting the higher educational needs of thousands of students in each generation, students who would not enjoy such opportunity were it not for the College. Sounds like milk and honey to me! I should think we would have to conclude that "we have eaten and are satisfied."

The question is, "Are we keeping up our side of the agreement?" Are we doing justice, loving kindness, walking humbly with our God? Or have our hearts become proud, and have we forgotten the Lord?

I would ask this question not only of those who work daily to make Berea College a reality, but all those who have been touched by Berea, the graduates, the participants in our service programs, all those who work or who have worked for Berea: Are they, are you, mindful of your covenant with God?

Well, how are we to be reminded of our Covenant? And how should we express our side of the promise?

First, we are reminded by the Holy Spirit. As Christians we acknowledge that through the life and death of Jesus Christ we have entered a New Covenant, a new "New Deal." The law that we are to follow is at the same time more simple and more complex than the law given by God to Moses and the people of Israel. We now live under the Law of Love. A new command I give you: Love one another. As I have loved you, so you must love one another. By this all men will know that you are my disciples, if you love one another. (John 13:34-35)

Jesus also promised that as a guide, interpreter, and reminder of this law, He would leave with us the Holy Spirit. If you love me you will obey what I command. And I will ask the Father, and he will give you another Counselor to be with you forever—the Spirit of truth. (John 14:15-17) So we are promised that if we love Christ, we will be reminded through the Spirit of truth, the Holy Spirit, how to keep our promises to God.

Second, we are reminded of the Berea Covenant by the Gallery of Berea Saints, our own cloud of witnesses. I think often of the portraits of the early Bereans that hang on the walls of the President's office and in Phelps-Stokes Chapel. That is our Gallery of Saints. It is the stories of those stalwarts that can remind us so easily of our enduring Covenant, if we will only attend to them. We do indeed need to listen to each others' stories, as we continue to recreate the collective story which is Berea, past present, future.

If I may paraphrase John Berger, writing in his extraordinary book *Pig Earth*, " What distinguishes the life of a [community] is that it is also a living portrait of itself: a communal portrait, in that everybody is portrayed and everybody portrays." "Every story, and every comment on the story—which is a proof that the story has been witnessed—contributes to the story and confirms the existence of the "community." The paint pot, as it were, from which this portrait is painted, is gossip, according to Berger, and we are certainly not lacking in this kind of paint at Berea! We are painting the story of Berea, recreating it day by day, through the contribution of our own individual stories and through our reinterpretations of the past. And through the telling and retelling of this story we are reminding ourselves of our obligations, our promises, our side of the Covenant with God.

Third, we have *each other* reminding us to be mindful of, sensitive to human need. Reminding us daily to ask, Who is my neighbor?

Sometimes my neighbor is not only the person who needs my help, as we are taught through the parable of the Good Samaritan, but the person whom *I* need—because *I need the practice of loving*.

The practice of love. The practice of patience. Practice in loving the unlovable. Loving our enemies.

I was helped in understanding why it is important to love our enemies in reading in the works of Shantideva, an 8th century Indian monk poet who is a favorite of His Holiness the 14th Dalai Lama. He says that praise destroys peace of mind by creating illusions, self-delusion [shades of Moses!], and that therefore those who demolish one's praise are in fact saving one from "falling into lower states." How can you hate people who are saving you from self-conceit? You should be grateful for them. In fact, you should be grateful for your enemies because they are the only ones capable of teaching you virtue and patience. As Paul says, it's easy to love the lovable. That's no test at all.

Therefore, recognize and love your enemies, for they are the persons who offer you what no one else can: chances to practice, practice, practice patience and love.

Thomas à Kempis wrote in the 15th Century: "We wish to see others severely reprimanded; yet we are unwilling to be corrected ourselves. We wish to restrict the liberty of others, but are not willing to be denied anything ourselves. We wish others to be bound by rules, yet we will not let ourselves be bound. It is amply evident, therefore, that we seldom consider our neighbor in the same light as ourselves. Yet, if all men were perfect, what should we have to bear with in others for Christ's sake?" (Ch. 16, p. 44, *The Imitation of Christ*) "May I prudently avoid those who flatter me, and deal patiently with those who oppose me." (Ch. 27, p. 131)

At Berea, we have been called as a special people, a chosen people, favored by God, led by our own Moses, John G. Fee, beginning in the 1850's to create a church which is now Union Church, a school which is now Berea College, and a community which now extends worldwide. *It was an impossible dream, it was an unbelievable task, it has been an incomparable achievement. God has kept his promise. Will we keep ours?*

Let us be reminded of our obligations to God through the presence of the Holy Spirit, through the examples of our forebears, through reminders from each other—those who are with us and those who are not—as we work out our salvation and the bringing of the Kingdom of God to earth here in Berea.

And let us be mindful that the task is never completed, the promise never completely fulfilled, no matter how much credit we give ourselves for success.

Keep in mind the story of a six-year-old girl observed by Robert Coles during the desegregation struggle in New Orleans 30-some years ago. Coles, author of some 50 books, now a professor of psychiatry at Harvard, became a virtual member of the household of a black grandmother and her grandchild during the time that the National Guard was brought in to keep the peace when the public schools were integrated in the 1950's. He recorded many conversations. He followed the days of this little girl, Tessie, who daily walked through crowds of hate-filled segregationists with her head held high, who was spat upon, and who was the recipient of curses and epithets most of us would find unbearable. The little girl persevered, one of a few grains of pepper in a huge shaker of salt. One day Tessie said to her grandmother that she didn't want to go to

John rides through Berea College farm fields in 1987. (photo by David Stephenson)

school. Coles could understand this, and he expected the grand-mother to be sympathetic. Instead, she remonstrated, telling her small charge that she had an obligation that was ordered by God and that she could not falter now. "You see, my child, you have to help the good Lord with His world. He puts us here—and he calls us to help him out." "You're one of the Lord's people. He's put his hand on you. He's given a call to you, a call to service—in His name!" Without a word of argument, the little girl continued her painful daily march through the hate-filled crowds. As you know, and as we now take for granted, integration eventually won the day, thanks to this small child and a handful of others like her. When it was all over—or appeared to be—Coles asked the little girl how she viewed her success. She said she wondered what her "next thing to do" would be. "We were supposed to get them to stop being so angry; then they'd quiet down, and we'd have the desegregation—and now it's happening. So we did the service we were supposed to do for New Orleans, and Granny says 'Next it'll be some other thing to do,' because you should always be trying to help out God somehow."

Thank you, Tessie. "A little child shall lead them," indeed.

May God be thanked for the fulfillment of his promises to Berea, and may we be daily reminded that we, in turn, are obliged as part of our Berea Covenant to "act justly and to love mercy and to walk humbly with our God."

PART 6

Despatches from Appalachia

One of John's concerns about his role as president of Berea was that his administrative duties would prevent him from maintaining contact with the people and communities of Appalachia. In the words of the psalm, John lifted up his eyes "unto the hills" for help, and he felt the need to visit them periodically to refresh his mind and spirit. And so he initiated a program of visits to keep in touch with the mountain region and to meet Berea alumni and students. Out of these visitations came a series of reports circulated to Berea faculty and staff that he called "Despatches from Appalachia." We do not know how many reports he prepared or the period they covered. The "despatches" reproduced here are selected from half a dozen that were written between September of 1987 and May 1989.

For those of us who knew him well, these reports are vintage Stephenson. In a folksy style, they express his love of visiting the places and people of Appalachia. They also embody his keen observations of social and economic changes taking place in the region. Not least, they reflect his justifiable concern for the ultimate outcome of the transition under way—a concern shared by residents of the region with whom he talked. His own assessments of the likely future of Appalachia appear to rise and fall, like the paths of those early settlers who crossed the mountains. Too realistic for

Pollyannaish optimism, he was constantly finding renewed hope for the region from encounters with community leaders who were both able and willing to work for a better future. Many of these leaders were Berea College alumni.

Unfortunately, John's program of visits to the mountains was disrupted by more immediately pressing administrative demands. His pilgrimages became less and less frequent and were eventually abandoned. With their disappearance, publication of the "despatches" came to an end.

Despatch from North Carolina

The first of the despatches reprinted here—entitled "The Invasion of the Leafpeepers"—reports on a visit to four North Carolina counties and is entitled "The Invasion of the Leafpeepers." "Leafpeepers" was the derisive name given in one county to the aggregate of tourists, summer people, and new residents in the area—the outsiders. They brought relative prosperity to the local area, but they also introduced new ways that were questionably better ways. As in some of his earlier writings, we see John's concern with the cultural invasion of modernism. In this case, it was not a concern widely shared by the residents, especially the students to whom he talked—and listened. "These folks may not like the leafpeepers," John noted, "but they see no reason why they shouldn't live like them." The students in a Yancey County high school with whom John talked were optimistic and confident. Unlike the young people of many Appalachian communities, many planned to remain after graduating from high school.

In Asheville, North Carolina, he met with a group of strong and progressive local leaders working to move the city into a better-designed future. Downtown Asheville was prosperous; higher education was responsive to community needs. But the city was not without its problems. Among them was the recognized need to get more people involved in long-range planning. And, John noted, even though there was a large black community, few blacks were to be found among the city's "movers and shakers."

Revisiting the town of Celo and seeing again friends first met more than 20 years ago, John was informed about the obvious: Celo was changing. Indeed, it was undergoing the "Great Change" from a small rural Appalachian community to a prosaic plastic contemporary society of which he had frequently written. Such change was not an encouraging prospect for him.

THE INVASION OF THE LEAFPEEPERS
NOVEMBER 1987

This is the way I remember a typical autumn day in western North Carolina: russet hues, warm daytime temperatures, refrigerated nights. Just about perfect. A good time to be back in the Blue Ridge, admiring the foliage. We are not alone in thinking this. Unbeknownst to us, in this part of Appalachia it is the season of the dreaded *leafpeepers*, among whom, technically, we should count ourselves.

I know some people here. I know the lay of the land. I don't know what people think about the future, what's happening among young folks, where the hopes and fears and satisfactions and unhappinesses lie. That's why Ed Ford and I have come here for three days: to listen and talk and listen some more.

Thanks to arrangements made by President Virginia Foxx (a former student from my Lees-McRae College days), we begin with a visit to a constitutional history class at Mayland Technical College. That's where we learn about leafpeepers and the threat they pose to the pursuit of happiness by the natives of this region. For this group of adult students sees the hordes of tourists, summer people, and new full-time residents from outside the mountains who have come into their counties in recent years as blights on the mountains.

John and Alex Haley, author and Berea College trustee, pause for a photograph before departing to visit several high schools in eastern Kentucky.

"You can't go anywhere around here without failing in behind some leafpeeper driving five miles an hour," says one frustrated young man. (Over in the next county they are known as *headbobbers*. Our informants are referring to strangers, outsiders who come to gawk, like Ed and me.)

Growth and development and rapid change in this area seem to have created a sense of loss, and a sense of loss of control. There is a perception of having been invaded. These students are critical of outside developers, too many billboards, too much booze, rising land costs, strip development, traffic. "It's getting to be just like downtown Charlotte," says one student.

These students, like many others less outspoken, are inclined find the source of local problems in the invasion of western North Carolina by people from elsewhere, frequently lumped together as

"Florida people." Some are more careful in their stereotyping than others; one person observed that the problem was "the northern people who go to Florida and then come here—the ones who are really from Florida are OK."

It is interesting to hear from these same folks about the things they value highly. I asked them to name positive things about living in the area. It is obvious they place priority on friends and neighbors and family relationships and values they consider typical of their culture. They like the outdoors, getting away from people, hunting and fishing, gardens, scenery—they like to look out at the mountains whenever they wish. They like living where they feel they *belong*.

In the future they want more cultural advantages, better employment opportunities, more social activities and county-wide zoning. One person wants to retire here, another wants to summer here and winter in Homosassa Springs, another wants to help her husband in his business and travel the U.S. One student wants to teach high school history either in Appalachia or in the inner city. Another feels trapped here since being discharged from the Navy; he wants to teach mathematics, moving to a warmer climate but keeping a summer home here.

Appalachia, my summer home. Are some of the natives learning from the Florida people?

Ironies and dilemmas: These folks may not like the leafpeepers, but they see no reason why they shouldn't live like them. They may not approve the officially sanctioned presence of alcoholic beverages, but they know it's good for business. They may make fun of Hollywood's arrival in Plumtree, North Carolina (for the filming of John Ehle's *The Winter People*), but they know it brings in the tourists. The tourists may be called leafpeepers and headbobbers by the natives, but their money is greener than balsam boughs.

Virginia Foxx has advertised an evening of informal discussion with the President of Berea College on the topic of education and the future of Appalachia. We plan to spend the evening hours in armchair conversation with ten or twelve people, and are astonished to find fifty people waiting for us. We move to a small, theatre-style classroom with banked seats, and I become a talk-show host. More Berea alumni appear. Gloria Snyder, who participated in the New Opportunity School for Women last summer, shows up with her mother. It is an exciting night, partly because of the number of people who came out, partly because of the intensity and sincerity of the discussion. These people hunger for talk. These folks are interested in solving problems, preparing for a better tomorrow, and working to improve the quality of education in their part of the mountains.

Asheville the next day is a great contrast to Spruce Pine and Mitchell County. Still not quite downtown Charlotte, it is definitely urbanizing and bears little resemblance to the overgrown farm and tourist town I recall visiting frequently in the early 1960's. Some interesting things are happening in Asheville, although not without the usual headaches and momentary setbacks. The downtown area is on the verge of a notable renaissance, with Pack Place, a center for education, science, and the arts, as its centerpiece. I am very pleased to meet Roger Maguire, who heads the Pack Place effort, and Smith Goodrum, who has taken over John Ehle's educational foundation and moved it to Asheville. Forward planning, through a group called "Asheville 2010," is carrying the city into as better-designed future. Higher education is strong and becoming stronger in responding to the educational needs of the city.

Even a brief visit reveals some issues as yet unresolved: a proposal for a nuclear waste dump in the area, the question of consolidating schools versus upgrading existing facilities, the issue of whether there is too much growth or too little, the question of how to get more people involved in long-term planning. And, perhaps especially noticeable to a Berean, the apparent separation between blacks and whites in Asheville. There is a large black community within the city of Asheville. This is a place to which I will return in order to meet people and gain a clearer understanding of educational need. There is a gap in my knowledge here: our day in Asheville is all white. Of the over-100 persons present at the Civitan Club luncheon where I speak (thanks to the arrangements made by alumnus Rick Gunter), none that I see is black, yet many refer to this, the largest Civitan Club in the United States, as consisting of Asheville's "movers and shakers."

We spend our nights in Celo, at what Berea alumni Brad and Alice Crain call their river shack, their getaway place on the familiar and beautiful South Toe River. It is hardly a shack. We are grateful for the conveniences as well as for the hypnotic burble of the river at night.

Celo is the home of close friends of 22 years. Many of them, like Dean Chrisawn, still live there. It was the home of Wade Biddix, recent graduate of the College who headed the golf team during his Berea years.

Dean says the place has changed. He always says this and it is always true. This time he is rather more definite and extreme: "Celo is not there anymore. Nothing brings the people together now except the churches."

What has happened is improved roads and telephones (new to the South Toe River when I first came there in 1965) and television and postal consolidation and county seat shopping centers and county seat job centers and school consolidation. And what has happened is that the leafpeepers have invaded Celo in great numbers and for the duration.

The processes that sociologist Roland Warren lumps together as "The Great Change" have hit Celo like ballistic missiles. I've written about this before, and I don't want to dwell on it here. The Change is not complete; it moves on, targets unknown, effects indecipherable. Who knows the ultimate outcomes of The Change? My guess is that the missiles are loaded with a bland and insipid version of the American Dream. I predict an explosion of average, least-common-denominator Americanism. A firestorm of sameness.

Hello, America. Goodbye, Appalachia.

School consolidation: On Election Day, 1987, we watch as Yancey County votes against the consolidation of middle and elementary schools. This is a temporary victory for those who oppose consolidation, and Ed and I see the victors in triumph at the vote-count in the South Toe Elementary School that night. But it is only a temporary setback for the Progressives, one feels, the movers who will eventually see their view—that advancement in education requires large expenditures of money and the relinquishing of outmoded facilities even if they represent "neighborhood schools"—become the predominant one in the county.

Next day we go to school again. This time it's John Stallings' Appalachian Studies class at Mountain Heritage High School in Yancey County. There are 24 four students, mostly seniors, in this class, in a school which according to Principal Jerry Holden sees about half its graduates pursue education beyond high school.

The attitudes of students in this class reflect a spirit of optimism, a strong feeling of confidence in themselves and in the future of this county. There are a few things they don't like, such as Florida people (they drive too slowly, they cause land prices to go up, they tell us how to live), and we are no longer surprised to hear this. But they feel good about many, many things, such as the rating of their school in the state, the friendliness of people, people you can count on. They feel safe and secure and still don't bother to lock doors. They like the pace of life. "The barbershop in Micaville is usually full, but there is often just one there to get a haircut."

There's a sense of comfort, of *belonging*. (Another echo of sentiments expressed two days earlier in the adjoining county.) Significantly, no one mentions the economy, or problems of joblessness and underemployment. Why? Maybe because, as the *Yancey Record* announced on November 4, the unemployment rate in the county stands at an incredibly low 2.5%. Maybe because of new industries in the area like OMC, which manufactures marine engines. It opened in Burnsville within the past few years and now employs over 600.

After a trip to Scotland, John joined the Lexington Pipe Band as a drummer. In his pipe band attire, he leads a group of students bearing the haggis into the college dining hall for an alumni dinner. (photo by Berea College Public Relations)

One consequence is that young people plan to stay in the area. Among John Stallings' students there is no "can't-wait-to-get-out" attitude. Eleven of the 24 say they want to stay right here in Yancey County.

Before leaving for Berea, Ed and I meet with a number of county leaders for lunch in Burnsville, including Bereans Dick and Mary Bailey and Mack and Dorothy Ray. Dean and Shannon Chrisawn are there, and Bill and Ginny Banks, and Bill Fender. I share my impressions of changes taking place in the county, and they help me sandpaper my views. They, like the younger generation about to finish high school, display a kind of confidence and optimism about the future which is not characteristic of many other sections of Appalachia.

Blue Ridge North Carolina is plainly different from the coalfield areas of central Appalachia. It has an air of rural prosperity. The people on this flank of the mountains know they are not without their problems—lack of planning and shared visions for tomorrow among them—but the kinds of problems they are dealing with are on a noticeably higher plane than those of some other mountain areas. There is poverty and there are educational needs in this section of Appalachia, but the proportions are markedly lower here. There are environmental and natural resource needs in northwestern North Carolina, but they are of a different order of magnitude and of a vastly different nature. (For example, at the time Kentucky was working—unsuccessfully—to constrain the use of the broadform deed, North Carolina was passing its ridge-top law to prevent developers from building high rise condominiums on the tops of mountains where the scenic views of others might be spoiled.)

But the need for leadership and vision and the ability to think ahead is real. The changing mix of population brought about by immigration only serves to heighten the importance of the need for sharper native vision. It is not only nature which abhors a vacuum. Where there is no vision the people may not perish as individuals, but they may well perish as a people.

Despatch from West Virginia

John's report on his visit in 1988 to Raleigh and Greenbrier counties in West Virginia provides a graphic picture of the complexities of the state's economic and social problems. In that year there were, indeed, hard times in West Virginia: high rates of unemployment, low per capita income, growing dependence on transfer payments, a crushing public debt, and a flow of outmigrants that appeared to siphon off the most promising potential leaders. But the problems varied from time to time and place to place. Perhaps their variation, which included aperiodic conditions of relief, served to raises false hopes of a lasting prosperity. But as John found out, state and local leaders were not unaware of their problems. What they lacked were attainable solutions.

As he usually did on his Appalachian excursions, John met with school administrators, teachers, and students. Contrary to existing stereotypes, John found the high school students in Raleigh County to be bright, talkative, and perceptive. Perhaps as a consequence of these qualities, the vast majority planned to migrate from the area after they had completed high school. The brain drain, John concluded, was real. Greenbrier County was more prosperous than Raleigh County, although hardly steeped in wealth. The Greenbrier students with whom John talked were more optimistic about the future. More of them expected to remain in the county after completing high school, and it was likely that more would receive their diplomas.

What heartened John most, though, was visiting a school principal—Karen Cadle—in Rupert, West Virginia. In John's words, "Cadle is the school administrator you dream about." Dedicated and determined, creative and loving, she inspired her students, their parents, and their teachers—and John Stephenson. In closing his despatch he wrote with emotion: "That's love. That's in Rupert. And that's in West Virginia."

IN WEST VIRGINIA: FROM COUNTRY ROADS TO INTERSTATES
MARCH, 1988

In the early and middle 1970's John Denver sang wistfully about West Virginia's country roads: "Take me home," he said. And at the same time the oil crisis reversed one hundred years of outmigration from Appalachia almost overnight, as mountain sojourners streamed back to the newly prosperous coalfields. Those country roads of West Virginia were taking people home by the tens of thousands.

Now, almost fifteen years later, the interstates, not country roads, are a dominating fact of life in this state. And people aren't coming home any more. Home may be where the heart is, but the dollar is elsewhere. The interstates are taking West Virginians away.

The front-page headline of the March 21 Lexington *Herald-Leader* foretells what we find in the next three days: "Hard times in West Virginia: Debt, Coal Woes Take Toll." Indeed, the air is thick with prophecies of doom while David Sawyer and I are in the state, and the facts, as best we can glean them, give such prophecies the ring of truth.

Unemployment statewide is the highest in the United States; per capita income is among the lowest. The state's population has been dropping for several years, and an increasing percentage of those left behind are dependent—the very young, the very old, the incapacitated—those, in short, who in many cases subsist on transfer payments.

As in other sections of the Appalachian coalfields, production is up overall and the market for coal is at least adequate, but the new technology is driving employment down. In consequence, state revenues are down as well: severance tax, sales tax, income tax—all down. The state's new lottery, everyone seems to agree, has not produced the income predicted.

Lack of revenue coupled with the increasingly dependent population has, in turn, created a sizable public debt, with many school

John speaks to a friend at the kirk in Ford, Argyll, Scotland, 1989.
(photo by David Stephenson)

systems and hospitals living from hand to mouth or worse. Scarcely anyone sees evidence that things will get better, especially for the section of West Virginia south of Charleston.

We begin our visit in the state capitol building on a Tuesday afternoon, asking questions of Drew Payne, Director of Community and Economic Development for the state. A Charleston native and a graduate of Hampden-Sidney, Payne's mind seems as clear as his desk. He is, to our thinking, surprisingly straightforward in rating the economic chances of various parts of the state.

The prospects of the eastern and northern panhandles are very good. In fact, Payne says his optimism about the eastern panhandle rates an 11 on a 10-point scale. He doesn't see much problem in Greenbrier County, but the prospects for the Beckley area, where we are headed this afternoon, are only so-so, and the hopes for economic development in southwestern West Virginia are close to zero.

Payne tells us what we might have predicted: coal production is up but employment is down. The industry is no longer labor intensive. Industries don't want to locate in counties like Mingo, McDowell, Logan, Wyoming, Boone, Lincoln, and part of Mercer. The roads are poor, the educational level is low, there's no flat land. There will be no high-tech development here. There's not much that can be done in these counties, in his view.

While Payne may appear to have written off the southwestern part of his state like a bad debt (his response when asked what will happen in these counties is, "They're just going to have to move"), he takes the long view regarding the state as a whole. He interrupted his own career, which had taken him to Washington, to come back to Charleston because he "felt there was hope." He believes rebuilding the state's economy is like building a house. When you call in the architect and begin planning, you don't expect to move in the next day.

In Payne's view, solving the state's problems begins with straightening out special interest and political squabbles over who gets to spend new revenue for what. For example, while the income from the new lottery was intended to go to education, economic development, and human services according to a formula which is still printed on the back of every lottery ticket, Payne says the entire amount now goes into the General Fund.

"The new revenues West Virginia raises aren't dedicated," he says. "They go into the General Fund, and the Legislature meets 60 days every two years to divide it up." Some of the revenue needs to be protected from this special-interest-prone body, in Drew Payne's opinion.

I am reminded by this meeting of the title of a recent book on stress-reduction: "The Situation is Hopeless but not Necessarily Serious." While Payne is straightforward in discussing the economic and educational problems of the state, there is no atmosphere of crisis here. Maybe it's not possible to live in such an atmosphere day after day.

Or maybe Governor Arch Moore's administrators are influenced to some extent by his official optimism. Moore's visit to the Rotary Club in White Sulphur Springs (in Greenbrier County) as reported in the *Mountain Messenger* on March 22, is upbeat, confident, hopeful: "The state is not going bankrupt. It just ain't so." He believes West Virginia has come farther in growth than any state in the union. Things are not so bleak as the media report. "I know the direction we're going," he is quoted as saying.

I think everyone would like to believe that someone knows where the state is going. Not everyone is so certain, however, that the Governor's publicly-expressed confidence is justified.

When we roll into Beckley early in the evening, we are met by union members leafleting in the parking lot of the Ramada. Inside, Kay Hall, the registration clerk, explains that a debate is to take place tonight among five of the seven candidates for state Supreme Court justice. One of the major issues these days is "right to work." Sitting Justice Darrell McGraw, winner of a 1987 Berea Service Award, has said he will not attend this "right to work" rally.

We ask Kay for directions to Lewisburg for our trip the next day. She gives us a map and recommends we talk to a gentleman in the lobby to whom she points; he owns the motel. Not only that, he is also a state Senator from Raleigh County, the Honorable Tracy Hylton. The Senator agrees to meet and talk with us at breakfast the next day.

Meanwhile, we eat supper and marvel to ourselves that here, ostensibly in deepest Appalachia, we are staying in a motel that flies a Canadian flag (one-third of the hotel's patrons are from Canada, says Kay), the billboard outside welcomes the Friendship Force from Bristol, England, and the dinner menu boasts three kinds of massage, including the holistic "Shiatsu accupressure massage."

The Ramada is well-appointed, and in fact this entire interchange on I-77 looks to be prosperous. If there is a coalfield depression, it is well-hidden from the transients, who see only the face of well-to-do middle America. This is Anywhere, U.S.A., planted in southern West Virginia.

The candidates' debate is a mixture of old and new mountain politics. Sponsored by the Beckley Chamber of Commerce, the "debate" is actually a series of stump speeches. Most of the time is spent in lambasting two empty chairs drawn up by one speaker to represent the two missing candidates, both incumbents.

Candidate Jones of Sutton, representing the old school, presents a brief life history, stressing his four-and-a-half mile walk to high school and the fact that he grew up on a farm. "I'm intelligent enough," he says. "My son is an engineer."

Candidate Hey, said to have the Senator's endorsement, is long-winded but witty enough to make it enjoyable. He says McGraw accuses him of violating one of the Ten Commandments: he covets McGraw's job. Top score for entertainment.

The new politics seems well-represented by Candidate Work-man, who claims to be rated Number 1 in the polls. I don't know whether Workman grew up on a farm or walked to school, but here is one candidate who is articulate on the issues. She seems capable of pulling off a first.

If any of these candidates wins, it appears that the Court will take a swing toward judicial restraint, toward support of business interests, and away from the "activism" which apparently charac-terizes the current Court. None of the five debaters seemed daunted by the presence of demonstrating union members milling about outside the hall.

Breakfast with Tracy Hylton is bracing and informative. He knows the state well. He not only owns the hotel where we are eat-ing breakfast, but he owns extensive coal interests as well. He does not disguise his feelings about organized labor: he is considering selling his coal company and starting a new, non-union company.

The Senator believes the economic problems of this area of West Virginia will only get worse. He blames the unions for a substantial part of the problem, although he also knows what long wall technology has done to coal employment, too. He blames the McGraws (Darrell and his brother, Warren, a state legislator) and former Governor Jay Rockefeller for what he terms "a degressive situation" in West Virginia: unemployment growing, tax base failing, population declining.

The lottery is a poorly managed "flop." The legislature is loaded down with political hacks. The economy has been controlled by unions for thirty years or more. Tenure and seniority in the schools are an obstacle to improvement. There are "more damn lawyers around here than you can shake a stick at." And too many people are dependent on welfare checks.

We are aware that on the previous day the Senator and his colleagues had been in a three-hour special session in Charleston. Eugene, the doorkeeper to the House chamber, had told us that the session had just approved a temporary increase in the state sales tax, from 5 cents to 6 cents. This bill turns out to be Senator Hylton's idea for solving the tremendous problem of debt that threatens to close a number of hospitals in the state. Does he think it will really be a temporary increase? "Once a tax is in place, it's hard to remove it," he says.

We compliment the Senator on his attractive hotel property. We tell him things don't look so bad in Beckley—at least here at the interchange. The completion of I-77 must have been a boon to the county, we suggest. But he assures us unsmilingly that things are not what they seem. The hotel lost $750,000 last year. It hasn't made money in 5 years. The occupancy rate is only 53%.

What are Hylton's opinions on the status of education? He feels the state is overextended in higher education and in medical education, with 28 institutions plus community colleges, and an insufficient financial base to support them. He thinks the public schools are too scattered (there are six high schools in Raleigh County), and says that county lines should not be used to designate schools for kids to attend. He also believes the state puts too much emphasis on students who are hard to educate: "Why let our bright students go to hell?"

Senator Hylton hopes the completion of Interstate 64 from Beckley to Greenbrier County will be an economic boost to his area. We wonder about this. Interstate 77, a vast improvement over the old West Virginia Turnpike, was supposed to water the economic desert, too. These newfangled two-way roads can take people out just as fast as they bring them in.

The Senator is a rich and powerful man. He has strong opinions. He walked one-and-a-quarter miles (on a country road, we speculate) to school for twelve years. I wouldn't want to be his enemy. But he is vitally interested in the well-being of his community, county, area, and state. He works hard to improve things, and he is not easily daunted. It is therefore discouraging to hear his estimate of the prospects for progress in southwestern West Virginia: "zero." Perhaps worse, he does not think most people understand that there is a crisis; they are too dependent on "checks."

After breakfast we drop in on Roger Wolz, the Administrator of the Appalachian Regional Healthcare Hospital in Beckley. His hospital is able to survive, although not easily. The region is overbedded, he reports, with four hospitals in the community and another nearby. His census so far this year: 38.3%.

As a relative newcomer he is tentative about his generalizations, but his view of the economic picture is expressed in a thumbs-down gesture. He compares it to Bell County, Kentucky, another coalfield county where he served as hospital administrator before coming to Beckley. The whole area, in his judgment, is in trouble because of its too-great dependence on coal. And the leadership is generally, in his words, "not so great," except in the important area of schools, where things are more "upbeat."

Ah, the schools. David and I meet next with the County Superintendent, Mr. Cantley, for a few minutes before we are introduced to 20 seniors who have been drawn from five of the six high schools for our discussion about the future. Cantley says the number of students in the county fell by 747 this past year. Around 2,000 have been lost in the past 4 years. He says young families are leaving, going south and east to states with right-to-work laws.

Larry Hatfield, Director of Pupil Personnel for the district, introduces us to the students. Larry is from Mt. Sterling, and seems happy to see someone from Kentucky. He leaves on us an impression of eagerness and vision for better things. Meanwhile, he is blunt about the fact that the state is so far in debt that in Raleigh County the teachers aren't certain they will be paid on Friday. (There was no such uncertainty the next day in Greenbrier, another story altogether.)

These students are the brightest and most talkative I have met in any of my trips into the mountains. Their high schools vary in the size of the senior class from 400 at Woodrow Wilson to 23 at Clear Fork. It's a certainty someone has handpicked them for this exercise. I want to take them all somewhere and start a college.

There are many things these young people liked about Raleigh County: size, easy access to everything, low crime rate, no pollution, nice climate, friendly people, recreational variety, small schools that give individuals a chance to excel, nearness to an urban area (Charleston). Despite these advantages, only one of the twenty could imagine himself or herself living in the area in twenty years.

I couldn't help feeling a little sympathy for Michael Wilson, the sole student who could see himself in West Virginia twenty years from now, when others were thinking about heading out for South Carolina, Georgia, North Carolina, Florida, Virginia, and so on. (Mostly to the South, but there was one young woman who wanted to go to what she called the Northwest, by which she meant Indiana, and a few who were looking to the far West.)

Interstate highways, get me out of here. I'll think about West Virginia's country roads from the comfort of my split-level home in an Atlanta suburb.

These predictions (not aspirations) are based on what appears to be a realistic appraisal of career opportunities in West Virginia, and the unlikelihood that the situation will change. These people have thought about the larger forces at work which create the local problems they see, and as much as they like the place they now live, they don't forecast great changes in narrow-self-interested politics at the state level, backward tax policies, inadequate funding for education, and stale thinking about the future. ("All the idea people are leaving the state," says one student.)

In short, although they would miss certain aspects of life in Raleigh County, these young people do not believe the conditions that will give rise to opportunities will be present in their lifetimes. There are three choices for life after high school, they say: leave the state, join the service, or go to college.

Eleven of the 20 have heard of Berea College, though it is clear few know anything about it and none plan to attend. They are going to West Virginia University, Georgia State, Concord, VPI, Emory and Henry, Marshall, Mary Washington, the University of Tennessee, Washington and Lee, or one of the state's community colleges.

We have seen the brain-drain first-hand in West Virginia. It is real. It is not slow like the flow of lava; it is a cascade of intelligent youthful leadership leaving the state like a sparkling mountain stream rushing to sea-level.

From Beckley we hurry to Greenbrier East High School in Lewisburg, taking a combination of interstates and country roads. We cross the New River Gorge over the longest arch span bridge in the world. So the sign says, and I believe it. The New River, one of

John at Commencement in 1991.
(photo by Berea College Public Relations)

the oldest in the world, flows south to north into the Kanawha, and it has cut a spectacular ditch over its millions of years.

"East" is one of two high schools in Greenbrier County. The other school is called just what you think. We learn that Greenbrier is another of those counties which contains a very significant internal division which entails geography, economics, education, politics, and mutual stereotyping.

Indeed, when students, mostly 11th graders, are asked about local problems or things they would like to see improved, one girl says, "Stop the stereotyping." Thinking she means the usual barefoot hillbilly image carried by outsiders, I ask for clarification and am told that within the county there are strong feelings about people from different areas. We find this strong geographic differentiation confirmed later: Rupert and Rainelle in the coal-mining west end, Renick in the north, "snobbish" Lewisburg toward the east, and White Sulphur Springs, which caters to rich tourists, in the extreme east.

There are some other surprises in what the students complain of: one thinks the arts should receive greater support, another says teachers should be paid more, one says the worst thing West Virginia ever did was to separate from Virginia in 1863, and only way down the list do we hear about the need for jobs. Even then, what we hear is a plea not for jobs but for *better* jobs, higher-paying jobs. As we had been told, Greenbrier is a different place from Raleigh County. Joblessness is not so severe a problem in this economy, at least in the east end of the county.

Where do these young people think they will be in twenty years? They are naturally less certain as 11th-graders (what a difference one year makes), but they think they are headed to Washington, D.C., New York, Boston, Pennsylvania, the East Coast, Virginia, California, New Mexico, Hawaii, Switzerland. Their geographic orientation is east and north, for the most part. Seven of the thirty think they will remain in Greenbrier County. On the whole, they are reasonably optimistic about the future of their area of the state.

Almost all are college-bound, as one would expect from a group that volunteers to come hear a "Berea College presentation," but they are, at this stage, uncertain where they will go. One says Berea, another Wake Forest, two VPI, one Clovis in New Mexico. Fifteen stay after the conversation to ask for further information about Berea. It looks like a gold mine for Berea Admissions Counselor Irene Holland. I telephone her in Charleston that night.

We thank Head Counselor Kay Mann for putting this conversation together and leave "East" to seek further adventure.

We are curious about Renick. What could it be about this little wide place in the road north of Lewisburg that makes it a victim of county seat ridicule? After a late sandwich lunch, David and I motor the eight or so miles to have a look. It's a very pretty place. We drive to the top of Droop Mountain and look back on it, a little village set like a jewel, postcard-style, in a beautiful valley reminiscent of Highland County, Virginia, where my old ancestor settled in 1745. I want to stay a few months and write a book. David says we'd better get back.

On the way back to town we can't resist the impulse to turn into the lane of eye-stopping Renick Farm, first occupied (by whites) in 1784 and recently rejuvenated by owners who are professionals in Charleston. Eleanor Ringel, one of the owners, who happens to work for the state legislature, is up to her ankles in mud and cow manure, but she gladly greets us and gives us a tour.

The farmhouse is a marvel of restoration. Eleanor is a marvel of knowledge and insight. She seems to know everyone in Charleston. She knows Lawson Hamilton, who maintains some of his Berea ties. She knows Brereton Jones and recalls when he was a Republican. She knows and has opinions about the entire state of West Virginia. They are ones we have heard before: no vision in the state, no leadership, the economy was never worse, southwest West Virginia is the worst off with the only jobs in coal or through political connections, and so on. She confirms the perceptions of local young people about county seat stereotypes: Renick is viewed as "country," and not in the "chic" sense.

We enjoy this impromptu visit. Eleanor promises to send vidalia onion sets to David. We conclude that if Renick is going to be a part of the rural gentrification process, it ought to be gentrified by people like this.

After dinner with Berea alumni Marianna and Doug Hanna (parents of current Berea student Peri Ann), we meet with ten adult students at the Greenbrier Community College Center. Marianna Hanna has arranged all our visits in and around Lewisburg, including this meeting at GCC, which is a branch of Bluefield State. We are in her debt, and in that of Vivian Crane, Director of GCC.

The GCC students see West Virginia as a "welfare state" that's losing its best people and which greatly needs fresh ideas. Teacher morale is low, political squabbles hamper economic development, vocational education is not related to West Virginia jobs, the state has no clout in Washington, there's too much dependence on coal, and drugs and alcohol are becoming problems. By the time we finish, I find I am preaching about civic literacy, leadership, and giving of self to the place one calls home. Not a bad sermon, although no one comes forward.

After this discussion, David visits long-lost relatives (his mother, Berea alumna Jo Ann Sawyer, is from here) and I repair to the General Lewis Inn for some writing, telephone calls, and sleep. Next morning we meet with county school officials in an old house in Lewisburg which was David's ancestral home.

Frankie Appel, Kelley Ford, and Ellsworth Buck are employed by the central office. Karen Cadle is principal of the Rupert Schools. We learn economic history lessons about different sections of the county and begin to understand some of the animus we detected

John talks with Berea College trustees, Jim Bowling and Juanita Kreps, 1992.
(photo by Berea College Public Relations)

yesterday. Loyalties are sufficiently strong that when consolidation was discussed at one time, an opponent warned consolidation advocates they should "come prepared for war."

These folks don't think the media are exaggerating the state's problems. "They may be understated." They are quite discouraged with state leadership in the area of education. In his state of the state address last year, they report, the Governor said this was to be the year of education. But this, they say, is "the year education goes down the tubes."

Lewisburg is five minutes away from the Virginia line, they point out. (This is not just a fact of geography, but an important fact of social and economic orientation. Interstate 64 brings numerous tourists to White Sulphur and Lewisburg, but it intensifies the natural inclination of Greenbrier Countians to think eastward to Virginia, not westward to Charleston.) "Teachers driving over the line are making $5,000 more and getting raises every year." They say it is also hard to be upbeat when public employees' insurance is $60 million behind in payments. State leaders seem to be pinning their hopes on coal, and this is not an adequate vision for West Virginia.

Indeed, in the views of these thoughtful local educational leaders, "we haven't been able to build educational vision in West Virginia. Vision is a luxury when you are forced to concentrate on meeting the terms of the 1984 court order for statewide educational equity. There's no room for creativity. It's like being in the driver's seat without a steering wheel."

Vision may also be a luxury when joblessness is the highest in the U.S. and the state's indebtedness is so deep some people are talking about bankruptcy.

But these four seem confident about Greenbrier County itself. Their schools make a respectable showing, "Students in this county go to Harvard and Yale." They feel that Greenbrier is in pretty good shape. "It's the state of West Virginia that overshadows the good things about this area." I wonder to myself whether some folks here would just as soon be annexed back into Virginia.

We are curious about life in the west end of the county and therefore invite ourselves to lunch at the Rupert Schools, where Karen Cadle is Principal. This is the last of our stops on the trip.

How can I report this visit? What can I say? I became emotional about what I saw, heard, and felt. Rainelle and Rupert might well be adjoined to southwestern West Virginia. They suffer from the same kind of coal unemployment and general economic depression as Mingo, Logan, Wyoming, and the others. Rupert looks a little shabby after historic Lewisburg, and its school buildings look a little shabby, too, in all honesty. But there is no shabbiness in the heart of Karen Cadle. Cadle is the school administrator you dream about. She cares so deeply for these kids it shows in every act and word. She is dedicated to turning around a dispirited staff and a lethargic group of pupils, many of whom are drop-out prone. It is easy to see what a difference she has made in less than one year.

We listen to her talk with three junior-high girls who have been on a trip to Washington earlier this year. The girls are obviously still excited about the trip and the things they saw and did. Cadle confesses her feeling was not exactly excitement; she didn't sleep for the duration of the trip. But she was determined to see the trip a success and to be a part of it. It was the first school trip anywhere, ever from Rupert Schools.

In less than one year she has put together a team of more than thirty parent volunteers to help work in the school. Parents who had taken their kids out and sent them to private Christian schools are bringing them back to Rupert Schools. Why? The answer is Karen Cadle.

I ask Cadle why she chose to come back (she grew up in nearby Rainelle) when, with her reputation for success she could have had any of a number of "better" assignments. Her answer: the challenge of improving a difficult situation in the place where you grew up.

Maybe Cadle sees herself in some of her pupils. On the way out of the lunch room, I glance back to see Cadle lean over and brush back the hair of a little girl whose face is down in her arms. Are you all right? The girl looks up, not in fear of the Principal, but in appreciation of a friendly touch.

That's love. That's education. That's in Rupert. And that's in West Virginia.

Country roads, take me home.

Despatch from Tennessee

This last despatch is a report of conditions in Hancock County, Tennessee. It provides a starkly realistic view of efforts to develop a local economy whose resources were severely limited—efforts of heroic proportions that failed to produce the desired consequences. Some, perhaps most, of the local participants who had given so much of their time and effort wrote off the operation as another failure. "Among these people," John reported, "there is understandable discouragement, and perhaps a few have given up. They've tried running with the big dogs and now they've headed for the porch." John's reaction was less despondent. Not that he was unrealistically optimistic, for that was not his nature. But from a broader perspective, he was able to see that the community had learned from the experience, not the least of their lessons being that they could work together. There were still good people hard at work making the best of things and looking toward better days—people with ingenuity, intelligence, enterprise, and leadership abilities. "People who share common visions. People who are willing to rise above personal animosities, willing to risk, willing to get up and get off the porch and start running again because they realize the future is at stake."

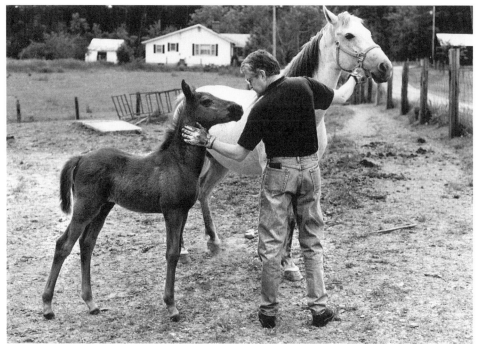

After moving to Berea, John finally had the opportunity to own his first horse. He is with his mare Star and her foal Redbud at the farm of Ken and Carolyn Davis in Berea, 1993.

IF YOU CAN'T RUN WITH THE BIG DOGS, GO LIE ON THE PORCH
JULY, 1988

We parked next to the county courthouse and immediately noticed smoke rolling from under the car. Engine fire? Boiling radiator? Panic?

Not to worry. Only overheated brake pads, brought on by the hurried drive down Newman's Ridge. Be warned, should you ever have cause to go to Sneedville from the Virginia side: take your time. The surveyor of this road followed a snake down from the top of this steep ridge. Or was chased by one.

So don't hurry. The County Magistrates (once known as Squires) may not begin their meeting on time anyway, as they did not on this occasion. We were there on time, however, with smoking brakes and rattly knees, to observe the session and to explain my presence for the next two days. Most of the Magistrates and the other county officials and those, who had business to bring before the meeting or who came as spectators were still standing with their heads together in the hallways downstairs or smoking outside the building or conferring with unstudied casualness in the courtroom on the second floor.

The session convened just as a group of men was headed out the door for another smoke. It became clear to Randy Osborne, Lynn Murphree and me that the proceedings of this meeting of the county authorities were not going to become clear to us. One presumes, in retrospect, that the items to come before the group had already been discussed and decided upon, perhaps in a working session, and that we were present to witness only the *pro forma* public actions. Having become something of a professional meeting-watcher over the years, I take pride in the ability to see the flow of group dynamics, follow power-plays, figure out who the actors are, and determine both the overt and covert rules of the game. But here I was buffaloed. The Magistrates knew what was happening, there's no doubt, but it was one of those *private* public meetings, and you'd have to ask one of those gentlemen to explain it to you, if he were willing.

Well, they did allow me to make my little speech about wanting to spend some time in places like this county, getting away from the campus to meet people and learn what was on their minds and how Berea could continue to best serve, and so on, and at least they knew we were there. If they were impressed, they managed to conceal the fact.

We left the meeting at the break and strolled around the square and around a few other blocks of downtown Sneedville to enjoy the evening and get the feel of the town. It is a small place; it doesn't take long to walk it, and even less time to cruise it, as we realized when the same Mustang rolled past us for the third time. We stopped and talked to police chief Bud Seales, who was preparing to retire for the night, and then T.J. Harrison walked over and we had a good talk with T.J. about what's happening in Sneedville and in the county. We got the feeling T.J. knows. He's the modest-seeming, understated owner of two hardware stores in town. He's a former teacher and school superintendent. His younger brother owns and runs Mike's, next to which we were standing and other than which there is no eating establishment in Sneedville. People later said T.J. was extremely influential, had a little money, was big in politics, a sort of generational thing that went back a ways and looked like it might head on in the future with the next T.J., T.J.'s son, Thomas Jefferson IV (except that T.J. says there was a mistake and he's only T.J. II, which would make T.J. IV actually T.J. III).

During our stay we met with dozens of people: County Magistrate and bulldozer operator Carl McMurry; Jane Winstead, sex-equity program director for the school system; Mike Antrican, school superintendent; Wayne Dean, County Clerk; Dora Bowlin, Election Clerk; Nancy Ramsey, energetic high school teacher; Charles W. Turner, retired businessman and civic leader *extraordinaire*; the principal, guidance counselor and students at the high school; Kyle Green, farmer and force for community progress; Raymond Morris, Berea College graduate and County Extension Agent; Ed Smith of the Soil Conservation Service; two retired householders from Florida who have moved to the green, beckoning coves of Snake Hollow; and many more. And at night we enjoyed the hospitality of Lynn and Pat Murphree, whose home happens to straddle the line between Lee County, Virginia, and Hancock County, Tennessee, and from which vantage point, one can watch the stately procession of morning fog up Mulberry Valley. (Thanks, Pat. You fed us from a groaning board as though we were hardworking farmers, when in fact we are accustomed to more meager academic diets.)

Sneedville, population 700, is the county seat of one of the most lightly populated counties in Appalachia (6,800 and slowly declining). The convoluted texture of the area, folded by ridges and valleys like a rumpled banker, makes Hancock a place of relatively unspoiled beauty and difficult travel. It is not on the way to anything most people are headed for. Jobs are not plentiful. Two furniture plants, the attraction of which to Sneedville is a source of some local pride, offer low-wage employment to four or five hundred employees from this and two adjacent Virginia counties. Signs of individual, corporate, or public wealth are few. In 1985 Hancock County ranked 95th out of 95 counties in Tennessee in per capita income. (It also had the lowest tax capacity.) Many people leave the county, or they commute to work across the sharp ridges to Morristown, an economic growth center for this part of East Tennessee.

There is a quiet, pastoral aspect to most of the outlying hollows. And Sneedville itself appears to be a sleepy mountain village, a pleasant anachronism beyond the reach of the interstates, like a somewhat worn and lived-in, real-life Mayberry. It is, first and foremost, *home*, and in fact the Hancock sojourners in Morristown refer to this place as "over home." They retreat to it whenever possible.

With no difficulty you can find Bill McMurry's barbershop (Bill's wife, Judy, also operates her beauty shop here) where the wisdom and gossip of the town are collected daily as in small towns years ago, and here you will find good humor and fellowship with old friends like the gentleman who wears the cap with the message, "If You Can't Run with the Big Dogs, Go Lie on the Porch."

But around the quiet, surface contentment, there curls a fog of anxiety. Among those who think about the future are some who think it possible Hancock County will someday disappear, sundered into pieces with its segments reattached to more prosperous and stable surrounding Tennessee counties.

In a layer beneath the anxiety one might expect to find hopelessness, and indeed there is disappointment bordering on despair. We met many people who had given their best over many years— to community development, to highway improvement, to economic growth, to beautification, to recreation, to education, and to the nurturing of civic capital. Among these people there is understandable discouragement, and perhaps a few have given up. They've tried running with the big dogs and now they've headed for the porch.

The saddest event in this visit, or in any of my visits to the mountain heartlands so far, occurred during an interview with an older man whose walls were covered with testimonials to his lifelong efforts to mobilize civic involvement and to bring improvements to his county: photographs with federal and state dignitaries, photographs of groundbreakings and ribboncuttings, membership and recognition certificates from clubs and organizations devoted to community advancement, some of which he himself founded years ago and which no longer exist. Because of age, he is unable today to play such an active role as a mover and shaker and as a link to sources of influence in Nashville and Washington. I asked him who would succeed him and maintain his spirit of progressive dynamism. He was quiet for a few moments. I realized he was weeping. He apologized for not being able to answer. But his tears were an eloquent response.

There were others, too, who seemed to feel that the best that could be done was hold on and pray for deliverance. I suppose most do as people elsewhere do: put one foot in front of the other, keep going, and don't ask too much. Some seemed tired of trying and said it was time for younger people to take over.

Part of the discouragement derived from the closing of the outdoor drama, "Walk Toward the Sunset," which in the minds of many citizens had held such great promise for the development of tourism. The events surrounding the production of this play constitute one of the most important happenings in the recent history of Hancock County. With funds from the Appalachian Regional Commission and in collaboration with faculty from Carson-Newman College in Jefferson City, Tennessee, hundreds of volunteers built an outdoor theater, took unpaid roles in the drama, gave time to its management, and even prepared the refreshments for sale at intermission. Community spirit blazed like a new star. The play opened in 1969.

But the audience gradually diminished, forcing the play to close after seven years, and the theater, used only once a year for a horse show, is slowly returning to nature. We walked into a small, dank structure which had once been the box office, and took for a souvenir a muddy, disintegrating poster advertising this drama on which the sun had set some years before.

The play, by the way, written by Kermit Hunter, dramatizes the unknown history of an allegedly triracial people known as Melungeons, most of whom, to the extent they are still identifiable,

His Holiness the Dalai Lama presents a kata to John on his
arrival in Berea for a visit of several days in 1994.
(Photo by David Stephenson)

live in Hancock County. Many books and articles (and this play) have been written about Melungeons over the past 100 years or so, most of them speculating about their origins, some about their folklore, some about how whole categories of people can be created who in fact may have no clear, identifying characteristics and no known common origin. A few years ago, it was an identity few would claim for fear of discrimination and ostracism. There aren't so many closet Melungeons today, largely as a result of the outdoor drama. People like Scott Collins, the Clerk and Master of Hancock County, now appear proud to call themselves Melungeons, pleased that their presence has helped put Newman's Ridge and Hancock County on the map. The play was in this sense an unintended success.

It was successful in another way as well: here was an undeniable, bright counterexample to the belief that Appalachian people cannot cooperate in a sustained effort to accomplish major tasks. Seldom does one encounter such an enviable case of wholesale volunteerism in the name of community and economic betterment. And it worked: the play itself worked, the people came together to make it work, and for a time people came across the ridges on those snaky roads to see what God had wrought in Sneedville.

It must have been terribly disappointing when the drama outlived its audience, and I think it may be hard for some people to look back with pride rather than a sense of failure. Having worked in an outdoor drama that closed (Williamsburg's "The Common Glory," one of the first) and now working at a college whose own outdoor drama ceased, I know of the pitfalls of such enterprises, and it is hard for me to call "Walk to the Sunset" a failure. I hope that an increasing number of those who, like Dora Bowlin, made it happen, will look back with a sense of wonder that it was possible and look ahead with confidence that if this crazy venture worked, it was because so many people volunteered so selflessly, and that some other collective escapade on behalf of the common good might be possible again. (Indeed, there is an annual October festival which is, according to Dora Bowlin, an outgrowth of the community co-operation that made the drama come to life.)

Lest the impression be left that despair emerges supreme, I hasten to say that despite setbacks and disappointment, there is no universal atmosphere of hopelessness. Despite the closing of the drama, the fall festival which succeeded it brings people together from far and near, and the same kind of volunteer cooperation makes it happen. Despite the demise of three male civic organizations, the two women's clubs in Sneedville and Hancock County are reported to be vital forces in stimulating civic capital. Despite the high dropout rate (69% according to Jane Winstead), the high rate of illiteracy, and the low educational ranking of Hancock County in the state, there is a progressive force in the county that knows what needs to be done and would like to work toward improvements. And despite the political factionalism ascribed to the operation of the County government and its schools, there are good people hard at work making the best of things and looking toward better days. There are people with ingenuity, intelligence, enterprise, and leadership abilities. People who share common visions. People who are willing to rise above personal animosities, willing to risk, willing to get up and get off the porch and start running again because they realize the future is at stake.

We met these people, and, thanks to Berea's Brushy Fork Institute, a new program designed to develop grassroots leadership in Appalachia, we know them even better now. Six of these new friends were able to come to Berea in September of this year for an opening leadership workshop sponsored by the institute. They built shared visions, learned about their hidden strengths as leaders, as a team set goals for themselves toward which to work back home, began to analyze resources and obstacles, and made plans for helping lead their county toward a better future. The results, in rebuilt hopes, new partnerships, collective goal setting, and sustained motivation, are gratifying, indeed.

I become more convinced with each foray into the mountains that, despite the migration of thousands of talented people from the hills in each generation, thousands more who remain at home are ready to step forward and take their places as bearers of the community. There is a constant renewal of intelligence and aspiration. The leaders of tomorrow come forth like springs from the innards of mountains, like new blood from these living hills. They are the hope of the future. I am of the belief that they need our respect, encouragement, and friendship more than they need our charity. These are commodities with which Berea has always been generous, and there is no reason to believe that the supply is yet exhausted.

PART 7

Special Messages to the Pres from Arthur

Among John's lesser known and more whimsical writings was a series of columns published in the college's weekly student paper *The Pinnacle*. The column, entitled "Special Message to the Pres," was purportedly written by a mouse named Arthur and left on John's personal computer in the president's office. They most likely owe their form and inspiration to the widely read and reprinted "archy and mehitabel" stories of Don Marquis, writer and New York newspaper columnist of the 1920s and 1930s.

Like Marquis's protagonist Archy the cockroach, John's Arthur was a free verse poet who typed his messages in lower case because he could not hold down the computer's shift and letter keys at the same time. John did not create for Arthur a counterpart to Mehitabel the cat, but his Arthur did grumble about a grouchy dog and lamented his unrequited love of a campus squirrel named Sybill.

Finally, and not the least of their similarities, the creators of both Archy and Arthur enjoyed writing verse, which probably offered them a welcome respite from the demands of their workaday world. The four "special messages to the pres" reproduced here were published in early 1988 and offer good examples of John's series.

vita brevis

(Arthur Mouse, a literary rodent who claims to be reincarnated
and whose gentleness and frustration sometimes show up in
lines left on the MacIntosh in the President's Office, has spent
the summer recovering from an accident reported in an April
issue of *The Pinnacle*. Judging from this message, he is now able
to hobble around on the keyboard.)

what a way to start the year mr pres
being busted up by a mousetrap is not my idea of a joke
and only now do i feel i may recover

the only good that comes from being sick and disabled is
that you learn who your friends are and learn that
life is short and art is long

therefore i say do not eat drink and be merry
for tomorrow you may really die but
without anything to show for it
rather you should
spend your days writing poetry

even if its not any good
it will last longer than the brittle bones and rotting cells
that are the life of your body

so thats why i give it everything i have
banging my bruised carcass around on your keyboard
as though it may be my last chance to leave a scribble and a thought
because you can ever tell but what
it might be

on a lighter note buster the dog has been spending some time with
one of your cats who must have gotten too old to
care with whom he associates
anyway he says nosey the cat is pretty nice for a cat
and i should get acquainted with him if i can find some time
when he is not too busy begging caresses from the girls at er*

or maybe i can stow away in your so-called briefcase some
night and get safely across the street for a visit
meanwhile tell him I would not make good eating because
living over here where nobody ever remembers to leave anything
     for nourishment
has left me a very skinny mouse indeed
with nothing to eat but my own words

your friend arthur
[*Elizabeth Rogers Hall, a women's dormitory—Ed.]

apostles of the living light

(Arthur is back. It appears he has become maudlin about trees.)

great trees outspreading and upright
apostles of the living light
wendell berrys lines are sure
will our apostles here endure
great trees outspreading and upright

i have been thinking of trees mr pres
and i sadden each time i look back
and recall the thick green canopy
and the vigilant spires now so thin

the quadrangle looks so forlorn
like a smile with too few happy teeth
and theres no one to blame but the wind
and the rain and the shade lying too close to earth

the shade in our yard grows too small
as the canopy tatters and shreds
the enemy is no one but time
and nature both mothers and kills

where are the leaping greenly spirits of spring
and what will come of us when the tall sentinels of winter
crash to toothpicks
and can watch our passing no more
sad is my watch from your window
when an oaken methuselah dies
its stiff corpse so strangely laid
in unseeing and final repose

plant a thousand new seedlings today
that will tower us all in days hence
these sprigs in the group trampled down
will be soaring and watching again
give us summer green overhead
give us wintry bones against the sky
give us autumn sun glinting through gold
give us the comfort of the watched

your friend arthur

i think its that time of the year again mr pres

(This is the latest of a number of messages left overnight on the
MacIntosh in the Presidents Office. Neither *The Pinnacle* nor the
President claims any responsibility for the contents or point of
view of this alleged mouse.)

i think its that time of the year again mr pres
that time of year thou mayest in me behold
when yellow leaves or few or none do hang
upon the limbs which shake against the winters cold
bare ruined choirs where late the sweet birds sang

the sweet birds aint been singing lately though
on the bare ruined treelimbs
outside ritas window
mr pres it looks like a fight for survival for that second storey
knothole nest in the maple tree

its time for those dumb birds to go south anyway
says sybill the squirrel
who has a tendency to justify whatever she wants
on the basis of some one elses needs

sybill wants that hole in the tree
like nobodys business
and feels a bit of privilege is due
since her mother was the model for
a famous painting of the berea squirrel
parenthesis she is rather attractive I think close parenthesis

arthur she says through the window
you cant possibly understand how important it is to get these acorns
put away and to find a place to hibernate
before its too late

she looks a little possessed to me
but maybe thats squirrels for you

come to think of it
i see that same look in students eyes this time of year dont you

I guess mr pres we all feel the need to get
our acorns gathered and find our places
before it is too late

i hope sybill wins out over the birds
even if she is a little egotistical
shes out on a limb this time

by the way you dont leave soft drink cans
in your trash anymore
does this mean anything in particular

your friend arthur

as the days of winter lengthen mr pres

(Here's the latest leaving from Arthur. Seems the sap is rising
early this year.)

as the days of winter lengthen mr pres
i spend more time at the window
after you and melissa and rita and randy and dallen and julia
have left for the day

then i can concentrate on
the object of my affection

it could hardly be said that she walks in beauty
its more of a scamper really
or maybe a scurry
but I think she is beautiful

and she can fly
without wings
that nimble footed light legged creature can
sail soar swoop dive glide
like nobodys business

i watch her early in the mornings
and my heart takes fire
i watch her in the eventide
and i drown in the flames of the setting sun

we talk sometimes and we are friends
at least i am a friend to her
what she is to me mere words cannot contain
my longing becomes so heavy i feel pulled into the earth

she does not know these things
nor should she
i am just a mouse and she is
everything
your students think they suffer loves pangs
as no one ever before or since
but tell them to pity a poet mouse
in love with a squirrel

i see her twitchy little nose edging around
the hole in the tree where she lives
outside ritas window
she doesnt even know I am here

speak to me sibylline sybill

but no
she would be more interested if i were a walnut

and i must fasten my affection elsewhere

maybe ernest would trade domiciles
and i could meet some of those interesting
ark people he tells me about

meanwhile to those who suffer unrequited love
please know you suffer not alone

your friend arthur

*After his retirement from Berea College, John was invited to teach a
semester at Harvard University. He stands on the shore of
Walden Pond just two months before his untimely death in 1994.
(photo by Jane Stephenson)*

PART 8

Children's Stories

Like many fathers, John told bedtime stories to his children. Unlike most fathers who make up and tell such stories, John wrote his down—at least some of them—and had them printed in booklet form as Christmas gifts to his children and grandchildren in 1992. The booklet was entitled *The Persnickety Papers: Little Tales for Little Persnickety People.* Featured in the stories were members of the Persnickety family who, not by coincidence, consisted of the father Henry, the mother Sybill, and three children: Mary Ann, Josephine Louise, and Murgatroyd. There was also the family dog Bucephalus. The most frequent occupant of the doghouse, though, was the well-meaning but inept Henry, who in most of the stories ended up in trouble. Was there an empathetic relationship? Perhaps, but as the author frequently concluded, "That's another story."

Mary Ann Persnickety Is up a Tree

Mary Ann Persnickety was a little girl about four years old. She lived with her mother Sybill (which is pronounced with equal emphasis on both syllables), her father Henry (who slept a lot), her sister Josephine Louise, her baby brother Murgatroyd, and the family dog Bucephalus.

Mary Ann lived in a house in a big city, but many times she and the rest of the family would visit her Grandmother Arbutus, who lived in a very small village in the mountains. Her grandmother was very kind, baking pies and cookies for everyone, and she never said an unkind word about anyone else. She always had a smile for Mary Ann, Josephine Louise, Sybill, Murgatroyd, and even Bucephalus. And Henry.

The children and their parents and the dog usually smiled back, but one evening Mary Ann, who had had a most unpleasant day and hadn't taken her afternoon nap and was sulled up like a possum, said something to her poor old hardworking well-meaning Grandmother Arbutus that really upset the dear lady.

I forget exactly what was said, but the sweet old grandmother hobbled back into the kitchen wiping her eyes.

Henry, who had been asleep while the children watched television and played with dolls, heard what was said and saw Grandmother Arbutus walking away sadly. He thought Mary Ann should learn a lesson about treating people nicely, especially one's grandmother, and so he took Mary Ann outside and thought about what to do.

Well, what he finally did was put Mary Ann Persnickety up in the fork of a tree in the nearby woods and left her there. He told her she was mean to her grandmother and that she needed to become fit for human company or else live in a tree with the animals.

"Mary Ann Persnickety," he said, using her whole name, which always meant she was in trouble, "you have hurt Grandmother Arbutus' feelings very badly. You must learn to be considerate of other people. You just stay up in this tree for a while and think about that. I'll come back for you in a little bit." Then he went back inside and fell asleep again without meaning to (he used to fall asleep almost anywhere, anytime).

Mary Ann thought this was kind of fun for a while, sort of like camping out. But when it began to get darker after twilight it wasn't much fun at all. She heard noises that were scary. It was getting cold. And there wasn't anybody to talk to.

She was up in the tree all by herself.

Little tears started rolling down her cheeks. Pretty soon they became big tears. She began to sob.

About that time a woodcutter from the nearby village was walking in the woods near Grandmother Arbutus' house. He was looking for a tree to cut down for firewood for the night.

Soon he came to a tree that looked like the right size, and he sat down under the tree to sharpen his axe so he could cut it down. While he was sharpening his axe, he thought he could hear a funny noise. It sounded like a little girl crying.

He stood up and looked up at the tree. It *was* a little girl crying.

She stopped her crying long enough to say, "Mister, please don't chop down my tree."

"Little girl," he said, "what are you doing up in this tree? Here, let me get you down."

So Mary Ann didn't have to spend the night up in the tree after all. She told the woodcutter that she was being punished for being mean to her grandmother and that she would never be that way again, and the woodcutter took her back to Grandmother Arbutus' house and everyone was glad to see her, and Mary Ann Persnickety was always nice to her grandmother and everyone else after that.

They all sat down in Grandmother Arbutus' kitchen and had a nice cup of hot chocolate and a piece of cherry pie, and Grandmother Arbutus said, "Bless her poor little heart."

Of course, Henry got in trouble with Sybill because he fell asleep and forgot Mary Ann was up in the tree. But that's another story.

Mary Ann and the Kite

One spring Sunday afternoon when Mary Ann Persnickety was very small, she got to fly a kite—but not in the way most people do. It happened like this . . . .

It was quiet around the house. Josephine Louise was playing with her dolls, teaching them how to dance. Murgatroyd was gooing in his crib. Sybill was reading the newspaper. Henry was dozing on the sofa, dreaming of horses and living in the country.

Mary Ann looked out the window. It was very windy. She had an idea.

She went to the sofa and woke Henry. She had seen kites for sale in the drug store where she and Henry went to get the Sunday paper after church. This would be a great day to fly a kite.

When he became fully awake, Henry thought it might be fun, too. So off to the store he and Mary Ann went, and soon they came back with the biggest, most colorful kite in the whole city. They put the pieces together on the living room floor, wound up the extra-strong string on a stick, and went outside.

Wouldn't you know it? The wind had died down to nothing.

Henry tired of running up and down the street trying to create enough wind to get the kite up in the air, despite Mary Ann's encouragement. Soon he sat down to catch his breath, and Mary Ann sat down with him. Pretty soon after that he leaned back on his elbow to get a better look at the clouds, and then he lay on his back to get an even better view. Then the sun came out from behind a cloud, and it was so bright that he closed his eyes. That was when he fell asleep.

Well, about the time Henry fell asleep, the wind came up again and this time it was very, very strong. Mary Ann poked Henry to wake him, but he just kept sleeping. She thought, "Maybe I can get it to fly without bothering Daddy."

So, she ran up the street with the kite, and sure enough, up it went. The wind was so strong and the kite was so big that when it bobbed up and down, Mary Ann bobbed up and down, too. Then suddenly, a great gust of wind came along and sent the kite way up into the sky, and sure enough, Mary Ann went with it, hanging onto the kite string very close to the kite.

Boy, was this fun! She could see the whole neighborhood. Then she could see the whole southern edge of the city, then the entire city, and then the countryside around it.

That was when she wondered how she was going to get down from the sky. She held the string more tightly still and tried to yell at Henry, who was just a speck and who was still asleep on the ground near their house.

Thank goodness, the stick with the kite string wound round it had stayed with Henry, and when the string unwound fully it jerked the stick lying under Henry, and it woke him up. He looked around, but he didn't see Mary Ann or the kite. He wondered where they had gotten to. Then he noticed the stick and the string.

He followed the string, up into the sky with his eyes, and there, far away, he saw what looked like a kite with a little girl hanging from it. What in the world!

He grabbed the stick and jumped up and began winding the kite string as fast as he could, which was pretty fast (Henry was very agile when he wasn't asleep). Very slowly the kite came back down to earth. Henry could see that there *was* a little girl hanging from the kite, and not just any little girl, but Mary Ann. Mary Ann could see Henry well now. He wasn't just a speck. She could see that he was pulling her back to the safety of earth. She was pretty happy about that.

When Henry pulled her all the way to the ground they hugged each other, and Mary Ann said, "That was fun! When can we do that again?" As they went back into the house, Henry mumbled something noncommittal (that's the word for when parents won't say yes or no).

Henry hoped nobody had seen what happened, but Sybill with the eyes in the back of her head saw it, and Henry was in the dog-house for several days after the kite-flying episode. But that's another story.

Josephine Louise Finds Bucephalus

Josephine Louise was about four years old when this happened. Mary Ann was six, and Murgatroyd was one—still just a baby.

The Persnickety family had outgrown their little house in the city where they lived, and so they had to move to a bigger house. Everybody was excited about this except the dog, Bucephalus. She could tell something was going on, but she couldn't figure out what it was. She wagged her tail and smiled even more than usual. She flounced her furry little pantaloons around when she trotted down the hallway, trying to remind people that she was around and needed somebody to play with her.

Usually her tail fluttered like a flag, and she held it high in the air. But now she dragged it behind her, and when she wagged it, it looked like she was trying to sweep the floor.

Poor doggy! Everyone in the family was too busy to pay attention to her. They were thinking about the new house and about themselves.

Finally the day came to move to the new house. Everyone was excited and running around carrying things to pack in boxes so the movers could take them out to the big truck.

The movers were big men with strong arms, and they carried out furniture, rolled-up rugs, the washing machine, and boxes of clothes. Pictures from the wall went into the truck, and so did boxes of dishes, not to mention Josephine Louise's box of dancing dolls.

Finally, everything was in the truck, and the big men climbed in and left to find the new house. Very soon the Persnicketys climbed in their car and drove to the new house, too.

By the time it was dark outside, the Persnicketys had unpacked enough furniture and boxes to fix places for everyone to sleep. They ate sandwiches for supper and filled the dog dishes with water and food for little Bucephalus.

"By the way," said Sybill, "I haven't seen Bucephalus recently. Has anyone else?" Now if Sybill with the eyes the back of her head hasn't seen something, it isn't there to be seen.

Sure enough, no one had seen the little dog since the move. In fact, no one could remember Bucephalus in the car on the way to the new house. Mary Ann looked down at her plate, feeling sorry for the lost doggy. Josephine Louise had a puzzled look on her face. Murgatroyd tried to imitate Josephine Louise. Henry looked sleepy.

"I know where she is," said Josephine Louise. "We must have left her back at our old house."

"That must be the answer," said Sybill. "Henry, you and Josephine Louise must go back and see if that is where Bucephalus is." She had a hand on her hip, which always meant "Don't argue, just do it."

So they did. They drove back to the old house and searched and searched everywhere, inside and outside, upstairs and downstairs. No dog. Where could she be?

Sadly, they drove back to the new house, and everyone got ready for bed. Josephine Louise washed her face and brushed her teeth and put on her nightgown. She still wore a puzzled look on her face. She was trying to figure out where Bucephalus could be. When everyone was in bed, she got up and quietly walked through the house thinking to herself, "If I were a little brown doggy, were would I be?"

Pretty soon she walked into the living room. It was dark, and she had to be careful not to bump into all the boxes and rolled-up rugs lying around waiting to be unpacked the next day.

Just then she thought she heard a noise. She stopped and listened carefully. There it was again! It sounded like a squeal or a whine or—or a crying sound! That's what it was! It was a little dog-crying sound. Where was it coming from?

She walked around to all of the boxes and put her ear against the side of each one, listening for the sound. No luck. She could still hear the crying sound in the room, but it wasn't coming from any of the boxes.

Josephine Louise was tired and discouraged, but she didn't want to give up. She lay down on the floor and rested her head against one of the rolled-up rugs. Suddenly she sat up again. The noise was inside the rug!

Josephine Louise ran to wake up Henry and Sybill and Mary Ann and Murgatroyd. "She's here, she's here!" she shouted.

"What? Who? Where?" said Henry sleepily.

"Come on, Daddy, get her out," said Josephine Louise. So everyone gathered in the living room, and Henry untied the ends of the rug and everyone helped to unroll it, and just at the very end little Bucephalus rolled out.

She was the happiest dog in the whole city. She waved her tail like a flag. She had a big grin on her face. And she licked everyone in the face to say, "Thank you."

Josephine Louise was the heroine of the day. She had found their little doggy. She was just happy to see Bucephalus again.

Sybill turned to ask Henry why he hadn't thought of looking for the dog in the rug. It was obvious, she said, that Bucephalus had crawled into the rug after it was rolled up, in order to get out of the way of the big men and the family running back and forth, and she had been accidentally tied up in it.

But Henry had gone back to sleep on the rug already. He was in the doghouse again and didn't even know it. But that's another story.

Murgatroyd and the Pony

I believe Murgatroyd was about six years old when this story took place. It seems that he had wanted a horse or a pony ever since he was three, when he saw them for the first time running around the fields of the horse farms that were located near the city.

He had asked his Daddy and Mother many times if they wouldn't get him a pony, and their answers were always the same: We just don't have the money right now, and besides there's no place to keep a pony. (Doesn't that sound like just what a mother and father would say?) He could understand not having enough money, but he was just certain he could keep a pony in the garage, and if not there then in the back yard.

Murgatroyd was very disappointed, but the idea of having his very own pony never left his head for a minute.

Now, little Murgatroyd was a very lucky boy. He was always finding money that people had dropped on the sidewalk, or finding other things that people had left behind or didn't want. He even found money lying in the street in London, England, when the family went on a trip there.

When he learned how to write his name, he entered all kinds of contests and drawings. It seemed like he always won. He even won a garden hose at a grand opening of a new hardware store.

One Saturday when Murgatroyd went with Henry to the farm store to get some fertilizer and grass seed, he happened to notice a sign on the wall that said, "Win a Pony! Register Here!" And so while Henry was busy paying for his seed and fertilizer, Murgatroyd quickly wrote his name and address and telephone number on a slip of paper and put it in the box.

He thought to himself, "I'm finally going to get my pony. I'm just *sure* I will win."

Well, the drawing for the pony was two weeks away, and every day, Murgatroyd walked around in a daze, thinking about his pony and how much fun they would have. Maybe when they got to be good friends he could even ride the pony to school, and when school was over, just think, he could walk out and there his pony would be, tied to a tree, waiting for him and whinnying when he saw Murgatroyd coming.

At night his dreams were filled with scenes of Murgatroyd riding his pony up hill and down dale, Murgatroyd showing his pony to his friends, Murgatroyd feeding his pony, Murgatroyd hugging his pony, brushing his pony, and singing to his pony.

Finally the day of the big drawing came. It was on a Saturday, and Murgatroyd hadn't slept a wink the night before. He just knew he would get a telephone call from the farm store at any time now, and learn that he had won the pony. The time passed very slowly while he waited. He waited all morning. In the early afternoon he called one of his friends and asked him to call him right back so he could make sure the telephone was working. As the afternoon wore on he began to think there must be some mistake. Maybe he wrote down the wrong number. Maybe the store didn't open today for some reason.

Or maybe they were waiting until the last minute to surprise him. But no, night came, closing time for the store passed, and there was no telephone call.

Poor little Murgatroyd. He was so unhappy he was just about to cry. He was so pouty that Sybill said to him, "Murgatroyd, your bottom lip is stuck out so far a bug could sit on it." None of the family knew why he was so blue, because he hadn't told them about registering for the pony at the farm store.

Then Sybill tried to make him feel better. She prepared some cookies and milk for him, helped him get into his pajamas, and read his favorite stories to him as he went off to sleep. (Henry used to read to him some, but he would often fall asleep in the middle of the story, a habit which Murgatroyd found most unsatisfying.)

The next morning the poor little tyke was still down in the dumps. He climbed into his chair at the breakfast table and just stared at his corn flakes. He was one sad little kid. He was just sure he would win that pony, and he just couldn't get over not winning.

Henry said, "Why don't you go look in the back yard and see what you can see."

Dragging his feet, Murgatroyd did as his father asked. He looked out the window into the back yard, and what do you think he saw?

It was a pony! A little black pony standing in the middle of the yard with a big blue bow around its neck along with a sign that said, "Hello, Murgatroyd. My name is Midnight."

"Oh, Boy!" said Murgatroyd as he ran back to the table. "It's a p-p-p-pony! Is it mine?"

"Yes, it's yours," said Henry and Sybill together, "as long as you will let Mary Ann and Josephine Louise enjoy him, too."

The whole family went out into the back yard and petted the pony. It seems that Henry and Sybill had been trying to think of a way to afford a pony and to find a place to keep one. Grandmother Forsythia heard about the idea and wanted to help, too. So, among them all, the grown-ups had found a way to buy the pony and they found a nearby farm where he could stay. And everything worked out just fine.

Except that Sybill said to Henry, "Poor Midnight looks hungry. Where did you put his feed?" And Henry realized that he had forgotten to buy horsefeed for the little pony, and all the horsefeed stores were closed on Sunday. Henry was in trouble again. But that's another story.

Mary Ann and the Acorn Tree

One Sunday afternoon when Mary Ann Persnickety was a little girl she decided to play in the back yard, where Henry was sleeping under a tree. She set up a little table and chairs, put a small tablecloth on it, placed tiny cups and saucers around, and sat her favorite dolls in the chairs. Then she went back inside to mix up some Kool-Aid "tea."

Soon she came back outside with a little teapot and filled all the tiny cups. She spoke to each of her dollies, and they talked among each other about the weather, about their favorite dresses, and about the funny man asleep under the tree close by.

After awhile Mary Ann grew tired of playing tea-time with her dolls, and so she looked around for something else to do. Well, it happened that there was an oak tree in that back yard, and Mary Ann began to notice all the acorns that had fallen to the ground. She collected up quite a few of them and placed them in a pile. Then she started wondering what to do with them.

"I wonder if I could grow a tree if I put one of them in the ground," she said to herself. She knew from her books that oak trees grew from acorns. And she knew that all plants grow if you put them in the ground and give them water and sunlight. So she went to work in a corner of the yard, digging a little hole, placing an acorn it, putting soil back on it and patting it down. Then she watered the little mound with the "tea" left in the little teapot. And she sat down to watch.

Nothing happened that day, except that Henry woke up and saw Mary Ann sitting, staring at the ground, and asked what she was doing.

"Waiting for a tree," she said.

"A tree? What tree?" he asked.

Mary Ann explained what she was doing, and Henry was very excited for her. He explained that it would be several days before the tree began to peek above the ground. He was proud to know all about trees, and I'm afraid he bored poor Mary Ann telling her all he knew, until she yawned and went back to her dolls.

But she came back to the acorn place the next day, and the next, and the next, until finally one day she could see a tiny little stem and leaf pushing up from the earth. She was so excited! But she didn't tell anybody, and kept it a secret all to herself.

She watched it grow and gave it water from time to time until it began to look like a little tiny tree, about four inches tall. She wondered how long it would take to be a big tree like its mother tree.

Then a terrible thing happened. Henry was poking about in the back yard one afternoon when Mary Ann was in school, when he discovered her little tree. He was pleased to find it, happy for Mary Ann. And he wanted to help his little girl grow her tree. He thought he knew all about trees, you see. And he thought of a way to protect Mary Ann's little tree from bugs and other dangers.

"Why not put a little greenhouse around it?" he thought to himself. "Greenhouses are good for plants."

So he went in the house and brought out a big glass jar and placed it over the little sprout, thinking he was doing a good thing but, do you know what happened? The sun shone very bright and hot, and the little tree inside the jar became so hot that it wilted and died in a very short time. It was cooked by the sun just like spinach cooks in a pot on the stove, except that you can't eat little oak trees.

Poor Mary Ann. When she came home from school that day, she ran to see about her little tree. When she saw what had happened, her face fell. It was so sad to see the poor little thing wilted and lying on the ground. She knew it would never become a tree now.

She went to tell her father, and they both came outside to see what had happened. Henry could see right away he had done the wrong thing, and he told Mary Ann it was all his fault, and he was so sorry.

What could he do to make up for it? He thought and thought about it. Finally, after almost twenty years, he gave Mary Ann a nearly grown-up tree to make up for his mistake. She was glad to have the new tree, but the truth is that nothing could ever replace the memory of her own little acorn tree that would never be.

It's a sad story, in a way, but it teaches fathers never to think they know more than they do. Sometimes little girls are a whole lot smarter. Little boys, too.

At a luncheon in the President's Home during his 1994 visit, the Dalai Lama poses with the Stephenson family. L-R: David, Rebecca, Jane, the Dalai Lama, and John.

PART 9
Poems

It is in reading John's poetry, I believe, that one feels the greatest impact of his premature death. Perhaps it is his poetry that tells us most why his death was premature. Not because of his 57 years, although in our time this is an age no longer considered elderly. Nor his unachieved goals which, while falling short of his aspirations, were far outnumbered by significant accomplishments. Rather it was the unfulfilled potential to inspire us with his intense perception of life. He had something to say about life—and impending death—and what he had to say was meaningful and moving. Our loss is in the muting of his voice while he still had so much to tell us.

Basically there are two themes intertwined in the poems that are reproduced here: love of nature and the confrontation of death. John's love of nature was a lifelong affair, a relationship that he saw threatened by the encroachment of urban ways. The unwelcome intrusion of cultural and ecological interlopers is a familiar topic of John's writings—one found, for instance, in his observations of Shiloh, where newcomers were invading and altering a rural community. The theme reappears in his poetry, as seen in the poems "As Country as Stovewood," in which life in town is described as "An obligation, a frantic necessity," and in "We Understand Nature Now through Urban Metaphors." In the latter, John laments that:

> Dead decibels from the city
> Have become the measure of nature's life-noises.

Likewise evincing the nature theme is "December Rain," in which dejected trees ask for salvation from human improvements:

> Give us rain, God.
> Drown us in holy water
> Scurry, you humans, get inside, go back to town
> And leave us be.

Less directly, the poem "I Meet the Dalai Lama in a Dream" is also concerned with the invasion of urban culture. As was often the case in John's writings, Appalachia was the victim of the intrusion. His meeting with the Dalai Lama was not merely the subject of a dream, for John had been his real life host in Berea. In that role he had served as the spiritual leader's guide to the Appalachian region. No doubt John felt some anxiety that the purveyors of regional stereotypes would prevail in what he saw as the "competition for truth about a region and its people." The question posed in the final line of the poem invites speculation but remains unanswered.

Several poems that follow have death as their common theme. They were evoked by a diagnosis in 1989 that John was suffering from leukemia. It is a disease that develops in a variety of forms, many of which are characterized by a high mortality rate. It would take an individual of extraordinary impassivity not to respond to the realization that death could be imminent. John was not such a person, and while he could and did discuss his condition with considerable detachment, in his poems he was able to voice his innermost feelings. As it turned out, leukemia was not the immediate cause of his death, but may have weakened his immune system so that he was unable to resist a lethal virus a few years later.

John wrote poetry because he loved it, but it also provided a hope of posthumous remembrance, if not immortality, denied open expression by his genuine humility. This desire is perhaps most evident in the message *"vita brevis"* left for "the pres" by John's alter ego, the office mouse Arthur. (See page 314.)

the only good that comes from being sick and disabled is
that you learn who your friends are and learn that
life is short and art is long

therefore I say do not eat drink and be merry
for tomorrow you may really die but
without anything to show for it
rather you should
spend your days writing poetry

even if it is not any good it will last longer
than the brittle bones and rotting cells
that are the life of your body

The selected poems are presented here in the order in which they were written except for the poem "Anglin Fork," which was read at the dedication of the John B. Stephenson Memorial Forest on October 13, 1996. Located near Berea, the forest contains Anglin Falls, a beautiful natural site to which generations of Berea College students have hiked. For John, a frequent visitor, it provided a source of inspiration and spiritual recuperation. And it is where "Anglin Fork" was written.

Fearful that the pristine domain would fall victim to encroaching logging operations, John supported an effort to organize the Friends of Anglin Falls. The organization had as its goal the purchase of the area to serve as a nature preserve owned and maintained by Berea College. This goal achieved, the designation of the area as the John B. Stephenson Memorial Forest was fitting recognition of his dedication to the preservation not only of Anglin Falls but of Appalachia and, indeed, all places of natural beauty. It was a dedication that extended beyond place to include the people who shared his love for such places. It was a dedication expressed in his deeds as well as in his writings—a dedication that truly made him a man to remember.

Treetops

> Ranks of undressed soldiers
> Surrendered and still as skeletons against the sky
> The silhouettes of January trees only seem to
> Whisper death in the still air.
>
> The quiet yearning for light
> The gathering of forces for life
> Cannot be told in these solemn days
> When cold calm rules the hills.
>
> In my doleful sleep I wander
> Through gaunt shadows
> Readying for the day of renewal
> The day my life begins.
>
> 1-27-92

The Nature of Complaint

The small irritations of crows in our neighboring trees
Raise questions about the nature of complaint.
I have a plenty to eat and am sheltered from rain and snow.
Clothing I have in too much abundance.
Whatever I have coveted I have won—and more besides.

My neighbors, the crows, act as though cheated, the
    grouches,
Though they seem to me fat, sleek, shiny with crow oil.
Without need, they are nonetheless heavy with wanting.

3-10-93

As Country as Stovewood

Woodsmoke has settled into the bones of the house
Stinging the senses when we enter.
It can be forgotten, but it cannot be ignored.
It is a fresh surprise, an ancient memory,
A return to an unremembered cave
Where we have always lived.

Life in town is a sojourn,
An obligation, a frantic necessity.
Sky and tree and hill are removed,
Light dimmed, by brick walls,
Birdcalls smothered by street noise.
There is nothing to smell.
The future is all; now is never.

Now lives here in the country,
Where the stars still breathe at night,
Where trees, not people, compete naturally,
Where hawks can shriek, crows grumble
And be heard;
Where our jaded senses
Are startled to awakening
When we open the door.

4-3-93

I Dreamed I Rode a Wild Grey Horse

I dreamed I rode a wild grey horse,
Fleeting shadow galloping uphill in a white lather.
Aspiration, hope and fear pulsing with iron hoofbeats.

We flew against death
Green spring grass sped beneath us
Clouds of mortality rushed overhead
Life liquefied in a momentary blur
As we turned to light
And vanished.

4-4-93

When a Horse Steps on Your Foot

What do you think of God when a horse steps on your foot?
Should I be grateful for signs of my own stupidity,
As if I needed any?
It's never the horse's fault, I remind myself.
I put my foot in harm's way.
It's what I get, dumb me.
As for God, I don't think of Him at times like these,
Any more than He probably thinks of me.
I hope.

4-4-93

Speak My Name

Speak my name
Only then may I live

Toward the silent gray sky,
Illumined pearly nothingness,
The leafless bones of trees strain
In search of light.
I lie facing heaven,
Empty, ready to die,
To live again
When you utter my name.

Give me pain, break my body,
Give me sacrifice, break my will.
Take what is me and give only your breath:
Breathe my name,
Then will I live.

4-4-93

Going Back

Easter. Spring. Death and Life.
A time not to look back.
And yet the dream last night was so vivid
It took me back.
I had to go back.
There were others in the car,
And I suppose I wanted to show them what it had been like,
      so I drove out U.S. 250 west from Staunton.
Instead of stopping at our house,
I pulled into the steep drive up to the house of our neighbor,
      Mr. Boyd G. Heatwole, and labored uphill.
I did not stop, sensing that by now Mr. Heatwole
      must surely be dead.
And so back down we went, very carefully
      so as not to lose control on the incline.
Then I drove across the flat yardspace below our former property;
      the place where we played croquet,
      the landing for our furiously fast wagon-rides
         downhill through the trees,
      the rough lawn shaded by a huge oak
         in whose welcome branches I nestled
         in the afternoons when school was out.
This flat space next to the road, below the trees, was the place
      I wanted to go back to.
It was a magic place,
      made special by the presence of occasional arrowheads
         which I collected and subsequently lost
         but which are nonetheless immediately available
            to me in memory.

Hour after hour, day after day,
      I would methodically comb the place,
         rewarded almost daily with a precious find.
Through those stone points I knew my native American forbears
      and felt kin to them.
I was ten, eleven, twelve years old.
I was in love with a piece of ground.
I am still attached to that place,
      despite my later finding that my good friend and neighbor
        had purposely seeded the ground daily
          with his own collection of arrowheads.
In my dream I drove over this ground,
      intending to explain to my passengers its significance,
But I could not find the right words.
I could go back, in a way, but I could take no one with me.
Spring is the time to understand that the dead must die
And that we live for now, for birth, for the living.
We do not forget—and should not—but going back is not possible.
We only take what we recall of the past into the future.

4-11-93

We Understand Nature Now through Urban Metaphors

There is competition for the ear
Out here
On Anglin Fork.

A screech owl
Attends to his own voice
Late in the season,
But I hear it uselessly
Not being an owl.

Water falls on the drip rock
Half-drowning owl sounds—
But now the radio requests my ear, and
There is no resistance.

The appetite of my civilized, degenerate ear is for fast food,
And I surrender to the sound of hot grease,
Knowing no owl would vote
"Yes!" to these kinds of airwaves.

The sounds of the woods, when it comes to it,
Lose in the contest for the overfed ear,
In the way that postcard picture art
Will win over raw reality every time.

("It's as pretty as a picture!"
"Isn't nature just a symphony of sound!")
Dead decibels from the city
Have become the measure of nature's life-noises.

9-26-93

October

This is the month of arthritic trees
This is the season of stiff limbs:
Breezes bring rustles, not sighs.
Now leaves break before they bend.

Trees will soon shed to nakedness;
The skeletal truth is promised.
But for now the bones are yet barely covered,
Creaky, resistant arms of autumn
Eased by lubricious hope.

10-18-93

December Rain

Herr Kallos, my German professor, used to recite
"Es regnet, es regnet, es regnet, seine laut.
Und wo es hat geregnet. . . ."
It starts raining all over again.

Our trees know no German
But they know the truth about rain.
It's not of Hanseatic quality or quantity,
But Kentucky rain has its way.

It can make creeks boil,
Uncurl Saturday's parlor-fried hair,
Make dogs long for August,
And hint of the promise of insulation, isolation,

Protection from city life.
Our trees often moan in the night:
"Save us; go away.
We've a sufficiency of your improvement.

"Give us rain, God.
Drown us in holy water.
Scurry, you humans, get inside, go back to town
And leave us be."

12-7-93

Waiting

waiting
time passes
I am a watch
tick
tick
long life?
oh
tick
ticktick
exclamation point
tick
comma
more
waiting
tick
meaning?
period

1-24-94

I Meet the Dalai Lama in a Dream

I accompanied the Dalai Lama on a tour of Appalachia.
I understood my role as chief of party,
Head interpreter.
But others whispered, intruded, murmured,
Projected onto him their ill-informed notions.
He was attentive, as usual, taking it all in.
Of course he had his own thoughts, and
I now wonder what they were.
But it seemed I was constantly on guard,
Countering assertions about violence, abject poverty, hopelessness.
There were more of them than of me.
Occasionally we became separated, and I became near-panicked,
Trying to find my way back to him.
They, whoever they were, would win this contest, I feared,
This competition for truth about a region and its people.
It was desperately important for him to see more (and less) than
Media-spawned images.
He was dressed casually in light jacket and khakis,
Solemn and smiling at the same time, silent, eager to learn.
The Dalai Lama shucked, as never before, off his maroon and yellow
robe:
A divine tourist.
Yes, he would say in response to my "This is true, but. . . ."
I know he knew there was both more and less,
He did not need me in the least to increase his wisdom.
Yet I felt fear and failure, and
I awoke anxious and wet with sweat.
Where are you now?
Why is it so important to know what you think of this place?

3-4-94

Anglin Fork

Night flows here like a slow creek among dark rocks.
The moon is more shadow than light in these thick woods,
Penciling narrow beams on trunk and boulder.
The ear is filled with sounds of water seeking its level;
The uphill source is as unending
as sky, the destination
A vast, waiting sea.

Human purpose seems a small eddy in this timeless flow.
The night will come and go whether or not it is watched;
The moon will write its name on the hillside forever.
Water will descend until the law of gravity is repealed,
Until we return to earth and sea,
And give up mere humanity.

3-6-93

John enjoyed many reflective moments at Treetops,
the family cabin 1/2 mile from Anglin Falls.
(Photo by David Stephenson)

John at Berea College homecoming
(Photo by Berea College Public Relations)

A Bibliography of
John B. Stephenson

A Bibliography of
John B. Stephenson

Books

Shiloh: A Mountain Community. Lexington: University of Kentucky Press, 1968.

And David S. Walls, editors. *Appalachia in the Sixties: Decade of Reawakening*. Lexington: University Press of Kentucky, 1972.

Ford: A Village in the West Highlands of Scotland. Lexington: University Press of Kentucky; Edinburgh: Paul Harris, Ltd., 1984.

A Scottish Diary. Photographs by J. David Stephenson. San Francisco: Custom and Limited Editions, 1990.

Book Chapters

"Is Everyone Going Modern? A Critique and a Suggestion for Measuring Modernism." In *A Reader for Research Methods*, edited by Lawrence Rosen and Robert West, 142-55. New York: Random House, 1973. Reprint of article of same title originally published in *American Journal of Sociology* 74 (November 1968).

And Robert F. Sexton. "Institutionalizing Experiential Learning in a State University." In *Implementing Field Experience Education*, edited by John Duley, 55-65. New Directions for Higher Education, vol. 2, no. 2 (Summer 1974). San Francisco: Jossey-Bass, 1974.

And Robert F. Sexton. "Experiential Education and Revitalization of the Liberal Arts." In *The Philosophy of the Curriculum: The Need for General Education*, edited by Sidney Hook, Paul Kurtz, and Miro Todoravich, 177-96. Buffalo, N.Y.: Prometheus Books, 1975.

"The Lasting Impact of Reform: The Development of Human Resources in the South." In *Improving Undergraduate Education in the South*, edited by William R. O'Connell, Jr. Atlanta, Ga.: Southern Regional Education Board, 1975.

"Eskimos, Scots, and Appalachians: Some Thoughts on Energy, Ethnicity and Organization." In *Perspectives on the American South: An Annual Review of Society, Politics, and Culture*, vol. 1, edited by Merle Black and John Shelton Reed. New York: Gordon and Breach Science Publishers, 1981.

"I Remember It Well." In *Images of a University: Presenting the University of Kentucky to the New Student*, edited by Raymond F. Betts, 15-17. Lexington: University of Kentucky, Office of the Dean of Undergraduate Students, 1977.

"There's a Place Somewhere." In *Sense of Place in Appalachia*, edited by S. Mont Whitson, 165-81. Morehead, Ky.: Morehead State University, 1988.

"The Soul of the College: A Requiem or a Manifesto for Independent Higher Education." In *Issues in Kentucky Higher Education: Essays by Kentucky Educators*, edited by A. D. Albright, 19-23. Lexington, Ky.: The Prichard Committee for Academic Excellence, 1993.

"Place for Sale: Repopulation and Change in an Appalachian and a Highland Scottish Community." In *Perspectives on the American South: An Annual Review of Society, Politics, and Culture*, vol. 3, edited by Charles Wilson and James Cobb. New York: Gordon and Breach Science Publishers, 1985. Reprinted in *Appalachia in an International Context: Cross-National Comparisons of Developing Regions*, edited by Phillip J. Obermiller and William W. Philliber, 29-44. Westport, Conn.: Praeger Publishers, 1994).

Journal Articles

And Richard A. Lamanna. "Religious Prejudice and Intended Voting Behavior," *Sociological Analysis* 25 (Summer l964): 121-25.

"Is Everyone Going Modern? A Critique and a Suggestion for Measuring Modernism," *American Journal of Sociology* 74 (November l968): 265-75. Translated by Anna Maria Levi in *La Modernizzazione* (Rome) 19, nos. 106-108 (December 1972): 125-40.

"Commentary and Debate." *American Journal of Sociology* 75 (July l969): 146-56. Alex Inkeles comments, pp. 146-51; JBS replies, pp. 151-56.

And C. Milton Coughenour. "Measures of Individual Modernity: Review and Commentary," *International Journal of Comparative Sociology* 13 (June l972): 81-98.

"Efficiency and Vocationalism—Renewed Challenges to Liberal Education," *Liberal Education* 60 (October l974): 385-99.

"Appalachia and America's Third Century: On the Eve of an Astonishing Development—Again," *Appalachian Journal* 4 (Autumn l976): 34-38.

And Griffith R. Dye. "Learning Ethics through Public Service Internships: Evaluation of an Experimental Program," *Liberal Education* 64 (October l978): 341-56.

And L. Sue Greer. "Ethnographers in their own Cultures: Two Appalachian Cases," *Human Organization* 40 (Summer l981): l23-30.

"Politics and Scholarship: Appalachian Studies Enter the l980's," *Appalachian Journal* 9 (Winter 1982): 97-l04.

"Escape to the Periphery: Commodifying Place in Rural Appalachia," *Appalachian Journal* ll (Spring l984): l87-200.

Reports

Consolidation: The Impact of a New High School on the Achievement, Aspirations and Adjustment of Students in an Appalachian County. Final Report of research conducted under U.S. Office of Education Grant No. OEG-3-70-0022(010). U.S. Department of Health, Education, and Welfare, Office of Education, National Institute of Education. Washington, D.C., October 1973.

And Michael R. Nichols. "Improving Instruction at the University of Kentucky." An activity report published by the Southern Regional Education Board's Undergraduate Education Reform Project Activity Report. [1975].

And Barbara Benson, Dennis Haggard, and Rosanne Hogan. "Changing Profiles of Entering Freshmen at the University of Kentucky [1967-74]. A report based on the American Council on Education Cooperative Institutional Survey, 1967-74." Lexington: University of Kentucky, Office of the Dean of Undergraduate Studies, Summer 1975.

Chronology

Chronology

1937   Born to Louis and Edna Stephenson in Staunton, Virginia, on September 26

1955   Enrolled at College of William & Mary, Williamsburg, Virginia

1959   Graduated from William & Mary with Bachelor of Arts degree in sociology

1959   Entered graduate school at University of North Carolina, Chapel Hill

1961   Received Master of Arts degree from University of North Carolina, Chapel Hill

1961   Accepted teaching position at Lees-McRae College in Banner Elk, North Carolina

1962   Engaged to Jane Ellen Baucom

1963   Married to Jane Ellen Baucom

1964   Entered Ph. D. program in sociology at University of North Carolina, Chapel Hill

1964   Visiting Assistant Professor, College of William and Mary

        Birth of daughter, Jennifer Ann

1966   Awarded Ph. D. degree in sociology from University of North Carolina, Chapel Hill

        Birth of daughter, Rebecca Jane

1967   Appointed assistant professor of sociology with joint appointment in the Department of Behavioral Science, University of Kentucky

1970	Birth of son, John David
	Appointed Dean of Undergraduate Studies, University of Kentucky
1973	Named Fellow in the Academic Administration Internship Program of the American Council on Education
1975	Co-founder of the Shakertown Conversations on General Education
1979	Appointed Director of the Appalachian Center, University of Kentucky
	Appointed to the Executive Council, Association for General and Liberal Studies
1980	Incorporator and first chairman of the Appalachian Studies Conference
1981	Awarded Fulbright Senior Research Scholarship for community study in Scotland
1982-83	Member of planning staff and founder of the Kentucky Governor's Scholars Program for gifted high school juniors from Kentucky
1983	Appointed Special Assistant to the Chancellor for Academic Development, University of Kentucky
1984	Named President of Berea College
1984-86	Member of the Lieutenant Governor's Commission on Kentucky Tomorrow
1986	Board of Directors, Kentucky Foundation for Literacy
	President of the Berea College Appalachian Fund
1988	Named Consultant to the Bonner Foundation, Princeton, New Jersey

1991   Appointed Member of the Advisory Board for Campus Compact's Institute on Integrating Service with Academic Study

1993   Chair of the Governor's Kentucky Appalachian Task Force

1994   Board of Directors of the Mountain Associates for Community Economic Development

Retired as President of Berea College

Appointed Visiting Professor, Graduate School of Higher Education, Harvard University

Died at Berea, Kentucky, on December 6

Notes

Notes

Notes for "Adapting to Modernity"

1. The "situational approach," which supplies a major partof the orientation in this chapter, owes its greatest debt to W.I. Thomas. Others, either independently or through Thomas' influence, have utilized a similar kind of microsocial approach, even in the study of large-scale organizations (for a recent example, see Jean H. Thrasher and Harvey L. Smith, "Interactional Contexts of Psychiatric Patients: Social Roles and Organizational Implications," *Psychiatry*, XXVII (Nov. 1964), 389-98. To my knowledge, however, there has been no explicit attempt to link up notions of the situation with the study of social change—though the linkage is implicit in the work of many writers, including Thomas, Parsons, Hughes, and many others.

2. "So long as social life runs smoothly, so long as habits are adjustive, 'situations' can scarcely be said to exist. There is nothing to define when people behave as anticipated. But when influences appear to disrupt habits, where new stimuli demand attention, when the habitual situation is altered, or when an individual or group is unprepared for an experience, then thephenomenon assumes the aspect of a 'crisis.'" Edmund H. Volkart,"Introduction," in *Social Behavior and Personality*, ed. Edmund H.Volkart (New York: Social Science Research Council, 1951), 12. See also Everett C. Hughes on "critical situations," in his "Institutions," in *Principles of Sociology*, ed. Alfred McClung Lee (New York: Barnes and Noble, 1955), 236: "But situations occur in which the expected does not happen and the unexpected does. Such situations are crises in which—to quote W. I. Thomas—'the attention is aroused and ex-

plores the situation with a view to reconstructing modes of activity.' The 'cake of custom' is broken."

3. "Following education and the development of new commitments and tastes, the economic demands of these (traditional) workers can be expected to increase," says Etzioni summarizing an article by Wilbert E. Moore. See Amatai Etzionia nd Eva Etzioni, eds., *Social Change* (New York: Basic Books, 1964), 225, 291-99, for the Moore article.

4. See Werner J. Cahnman, "Culture, Civilization, and Social Change," *The Sociological Quarterly*, III (April 1962), 93-106. He maintains that an increase in cultural complexity (which he calls civilization) marks one of the most important aspects of social change: "The processes which transform a monocultural into a multicultural system bespeak social change" (98). This point is also expressed by Parsons, Eisenstadt, Smelser, and others as "differentiation."

5. Arthur J. Vidich and Joseph Bensman, *Small Town in Mass Society* (Gloucester, Mass.: Peter Smith, 1958). The "surrender" to mass industrial society has not been as complete in Shiloh as it has in Springdale, to be sure, but the direction of movement is the same. Decisions concerning roads, electricity, telephones, schools, public health services, commercial development, and the like are scarcely affected by local sentiment and are mainly determined by county, regional, state, and federal bodies. A local antipoverty agency was just gearing up for action in 1965; what effects it will have on the area await future assessment.

6. See Herbert Blumer, "Industrialization and theTraditional Order," *Sociology and Social Research*, XLVIII (Jan.1964), 129-38, for a convincing statement of this point. He contends that within any traditional society there is likely to be appreciable variation in commitment to the past, and that one is likely to find a mixture of five types of response to industrialization: rejection, toleration of indus-

trialization as a separate disjunctive arrangement, assimilation, use of industrialization to strengthen the traditional order, disintegration of the traditional order.

7. See Berton H. Kaplan, "Social Change, Adaptive Problems, and Health in a Mountain Community" (unpublished Ph.D. dissertation, University of North Carolina, 1962), 108-11.

8. One man in the community calls men like this "go-getters": "The saying around here is we have a lot of go-getters. The men take their wives to work in the morning and in the afternoon they go get'er!"

Notes for "Is Everyone Going Modern? A Critique and a Suggestion for Measuring Modernism"

1. I am grateful to the University of Kentucky for financially assisting the project out of which this paper grew. I would also like to express my gratitude to David Lewis Smith, interviewing assistant, and Mrs. Edna Urie, research assistant. Critical readings of this paper by Leonard Jordan, Thomas R. Ford, and George A. Hillery were also very helpful.

2. For recent general discussions of these types of change, see, for example, Daniel Lerner, *The Passing of Traditional Society* (Glencoe, Ill.: Free Press, 1958); S. N. Eisenstadt, *Modernization: Protest and Change* (New York: Prentice-Hall, Inc., 1966); George M. Foster, *Traditional Cultures and the Impact of Technological Change* (New York: Harper & Row, 1962); Bert F. Hoselitz and Wilbert Moore (eds.), *Industrialization and Society* (Paris: UNESCO-Mouton, 1963); Ralph J. Braibanti and Joseph Spengler (eds.), *Tradition, Values, and Socio-Economic Development* (Durham, N.C.: Duke University Press, 1961); Myron Wiener (ed.), *Modernization: The Dynamics of Growth* (New York: Basic books, 1966).

3. The term "secularization" and others of its order are seen as more specific classes of change within the larger category of cultural change.

4. Stephen Kellert, Lawrence K. Williams, William F. Whyte, and Giorgio Alberti, "Culture Change and Stress in Rural Peru: A Preliminary Report," *Milbank Memorial Fund Quarterly*, XLV, No. 4 (October, 1967), 391-415.

5. Ibid., pp. 407-8.

6. Ibid., p. 408.

7. Ibid., p. 409.

8. Such criticisms are perhaps unduly harsh in view of the primary research interest of Kellert and his colleagues, who are more interested in the correlates of high rates of psychosomatic illness than in modernization. Still, the relevance of the particular indicators of modernism in the study has not been as fully demonstrated as one might desire.

9. David Horton Smith and Alex Inkeles, "The O-M Scale: A Comparative Socio-Psychological Measure of Individual Modernity," *Sociometry*, XXIX, No. 4 (December, 1966), 353-77. Samples are drawn from six countries: Chile, Argentina, Pakistan, India, Nigeria, and Israel.

10. Actually, the authors present a long-form scale and several shorter forms consisting of subsets of items.

11. Ibid., p. 353.

12. Ibid., pp. 354-55.

13. Ibid., p. 362. A footnote to this sentence, however, appears to contradict it: "Actually, we have not established that there is one and only one dimension underlying this item set, not that all types of items enter equally, not that the main underlying dimension is 'modernity.' But we have established at least one pervasive underlying dimension, and on prima facie grounds we can argue from the content of the items that this dimension is psychological mo-

dernity as we have conceptualized it. No other explanation, such as response set, will suffice."

14. Ibid., p. 371.

15. There is no quarrel with the authors' conceptual definition of modernity; what is not clear is how they got from this abstract definition to the specific indicators of modernity that comprise their scale. Was it through intuition, or logic, or some empirically grounded linkage? Unfortunately, we will have to wait for the book to find out. But one suspects that members of populations later assessed by means of the scale may not have been permitted to suggest what traditionism and modernity meant to them, a shortcoming (and we cannot really be sure it is one in this case) which can have the unfortunate consequence of leaving the scientist with a well-constructed measuring stick which measures we know not what.

16. A closely related problem associated with measures of modernism which assume universality is that they do not allow for the possibility that tradition-to-modern changes are totally absent from a given population. One may find that he is able to classify personality types into "traditional" and "modern," but finding differentiation in a society does not offer anything but circumstantial evidence for change. The fact of change is assumed, not demonstrated; all we are offered is a static classification of cultural and personality types made by a professional observer.

17. Lerner, op. cit., p. 46.

18. Ibid.

19. Ibid., p. 47.

20. Ibid., p. 47. Also see Eisenstadt, op. cit., p. 1.

21. Bert F. Hoselitz, "Economic Development and Change in Social Values and Thought Patterns," in George K. Zollschan and Walter Hirsch (eds.), *Explorations in Social Change* (Boston: Houghton Mifflin Co., 1964), p. 679.

22. A more complete description of the community and the changes it has undergone since 1940 may be found in my forthcoming (1968) book, *Shiloh: A Mountain Community* (Lexington, Ky.: University of Kentucky Press), especially chap. I.

23. The extent to which modernism is related to social class has never been made clear. Some have said that it is social class, while others have maintained that the two are separate dimensions. While I tend to hold the latter view, I know of no evidence which has direct bearing on the issue. This will be the subject of later study.

24. Placing an item into the "ambiguous" pile was considered an error and was scored "1." Placing of what was intended to be a modern or a traditional statement was also considered an error and was scored "2" on the assumption that it is an even less clear indicator than had it been placed in the "ambiguous" pile. Total error scores for each statement range theoretically from 0 to 14. Two of the items used had error scores of 0, ten had error scores of 1, and five had error scores of 2.

25. A fifteenth statement was inserted in the instrument at the last minute without adequate justification. Interestingly, it was one of those discarded during construction of the scale.

26. Five individuals did not give sufficient information for mobility to be measured.

[Note: Notes 27–29 referenced material deleted.—Ed.]

30. At the risk of being unduly repetitive, it will be pointed out that I make a claim, not to have studied modernization, but to have devised a way of meaningfully measuring modernism which can later be used to gauge the extent of change over time. The present study (like most such research) is not a study of change because it omits the temporal dimension.

31. If this is true, then the most "traditionalism" (or "modernism") can mean is "the belief in tradition (or modernity), whatever

that may be." We have seen that modernism means more than that to at least a few students of the subject. It seems clear that either the terms must be defined so generally as to be useless or the specific content must be left to vary from culture to culture.

Notes for "Alex Inkeles' Comments...."

1. Stephenson makes particular reference to only one of our project's publications (Smith and Inkeles 1966). He expresses himself as eager to know the logical connection between the themes we measured and our definition of modernity, but he evidently did not take the trouble to read the article we cited as presenting that connection (see Inkeles 1966).

2. Stephenson's scale includes items such as "The old ways are mostly best for me," rather like our question (CH-3) concerning the adoption of "new ways of doing things" in agriculture. In other respects as well, his questions parallel those used in our scales to measure themes in value areas, such as sex roles, religion, etc. It is of particular interest to note, therefore, that the type of item Stephenson used correlates with our summary scale of modernization no more strongly than the type he did not use. For example, the Stephenson-type item on "new ways of doing things" produced an item-to-(modernization) scale correlation averaging .273 for the six countries, while that on interest in world news yielded an average item-to-scale correlation of .294. These correlation coefficients apply to the Long Form of OM reported in table 1 in Smith and Inkeles (1966).

3. Indeed, we have used the question in Hazard, Kentucky, an Appalachian community I suspect is very similar to Shiloh. Furthermore, in our footnote 5 on page 357 of Smith and Inkeles we report that our student, William Lawrence, found in his sample of that community that the structure of attitudes in Kentucky was

basically similar to that in the six developing countries. In other words, in Kentucky too, individuals who thought the "old ways" best were also less likely to join voluntary organizations or to take an interest in world over local news. Why Stephenson chose to ignore this information is not clear.

4. The scale we derived by the criterion method correlates around .80 with the scales derived with theoretical constraints playing the decisive role. This is highly relevant to the issues discussed above, since it indicates that sociological theory can identify dimensions of individual modernity which are validated by measures derived from empirical association with objective indicators.

5. This phase of the work was under the supervision of Dr. Amar K. Singh, chairman of the Department of Psychology, Ranchi University, Bihar, India. A preliminary report is given in Singh and Inkeles (1968).

6. This was because our rule in constructing the transnational scale provided that we would use only questions asked in all countries. The transcultural measure did, of course, contain reasonable analogues of these distinctively Indian questions. This should enable us to recognize, again, that a sensitive theoretical orientation, however transcultural in conception, may be much less divorced from the concrete reality of diverse local cultures than, at first glance, it seems to be.

7. This correlation applies to the Indian sample of cultivators, industrial workers, and urban nonindustrial workers, totaling 1,300 cases. The transcultural measure used for this correlation and those given below was the OM Long Form described in Smith and Inkeles (1966).

8. Our scale of "political information," for example, was one of the highest reliablities and the strongest relations to the independent variables. It correlated .604 with that form of the summary modernization measure (OM-2) which did not itself include any information questions.

REFERENCES

Inkeles, Alex. 1966. "The Modernization of Man," in *Modernization*, edited by M. Weisner. New York: Basic Books.

Singh, A.K., and Alex Inkeles. 1968. "A Cross-cultural Measure of Modernity and Some Popular Indian Images." *Journal of General and Applied Psychology*. Vol. 1. Ranchi/Patna, India: Bihar Psychological Assoc.

Smith, David, and Alex Inkeles. 1966. "The OM Scale: A Comparative Socio-Psychological Measure of Individual Modernity," *Sociometry* 39: 353-77.

Stephenson, John. 1968. "Is Everyone Going Modern? A Critique and a Suggestion for Measuring Modernism." *American Journal of Sociology* 74: 265-75.

Notes for "The Author Replies"

1. And from that offered in the Inkeles chapter in Weiner, which I have reread carefully since receiving Inkeles's comments. "The Modernization of Man" is, the way I read it, basically a proposed definition of individual modernity. It is more elaborate than the definition presented in the Smith and Inkeles article but essentially no different from it. The elements of this definition are based on what the author feels are requirements for successful functioning of an individual in "modern" social structures. My personal feeling is that the linkage between theory and scale dimensions is weak and not explicitly stated, but perhaps I am being unduly harsh. The linkages between empirical findings and scale dimensions I also feel are weak. Although Inkeles claims that he has established the elements of modernity on the basis of the findings of others, on only a few instances does he tell who found what, let alone how. Despite such generalizations as "Many analysts of the problem pro-

pose . . ." and "Almost all serious scientific investigations of the question have shown . . .," only one reference is offered in the entire essay. Although I respect Inkeles's opinion about what constitutes modern man, it still remains just that—an opinion.

2. In this connection, Inkeles is incorrect when he says I would claim that indigenous scales would "work" where the scale of the social science outsider would not. The "nonsalient" scale may well show variations on a number of social indicators, but the scientist may still not know what the scale means to the people.

3. Also note the relatively low coefficients between scale scores and external criteria, reported in Inkeles's comments and in the original article on page 360, referred to again below.

4. A quick check reveals that the thirty-four items in Short Form 3 constitute approximately 29 percent of the items contained in the Long Form. Items contained in Short Form 3 which are also found in Short Form 1 comprise about 58 percent of the latter. Comparable figures for Short Form 2, Short Form 5, and Short Form 6 are 52 percent, 100 percent, and 71 percent, respectively.

5. I would not agree with his statement that my use of judges is inconsistent with my principle of using indigenous criteria of modernism. The judges were chosen not only because they were social scientists (not all of them were, anyway), or only because they were familiar with any abstract theory or definition of modernism, but because they were considered "experts" on the culture of the southern Appalachia region. Therefore the scale items were not exactly screened by "outsiders."

6. One of the few studies attempting to relate attitudinal to "structural" variables of modernization is Arnold Feldman and Christopher Hurn (1966).

REFERENCES

Feldman, Arnold, and Christopher Hurn. 1966. "The Experience of Modernization" *Sociometry* 19, no. 4 (December): 378-95.

Gusfield, Joseph R. 1967. "Tradition and Modernity: Misplaced Polarities in the Study of Social Change." *American Journal of Sociology* 72, no. 4 (January): 351-62.

Editor's note for Social Change in a Village of the ScottishHighlands

*"Escape to the Periphery: Commodifying Place in Rural Appalachia," *Appalachian Journal* 11 (Spring 1984): 187–200.

Notes for "Ford Tomorrow: Survival, Continuity, and Change"

1. Art Gallaher, Jr., and Harland Padfield, "Theory of the Dying Community," in Art Gallaher, Jr., and Harland Padfield, *The Dying Community* (Albuquerque: University of New Mexico, 1981), pp. 1-22.

2. In addition to several of the essays in Gallaher and Padfield, op. cit., the works of Willis Sutton, Roland Warren, Kai Erikson, Joseph Gusfield, and Howard Newby have been highly useful to my thinking. See, for example, Willis Sutton and Jiri Kolaja, "Elements of Community Action," *Social Forces*, 38 (May 1960), 325-331; Willis Sutton and Jiri Kolaja, "The Concept of Community," *Rural Sociology*, 25 (June 1960), 197-203; Roland L. Warren, "The Good Community—What Would It Be?" *Journal of the Community Development Society*, 1 (Spring 1970), 14-23; Kai Erikson, *Everything in Its Path—Destruction of Community in the Buffalo Creek Flood* (New York: Simon and Schuster, 1976), esp. the concluding chapter, pp. 246-259; Joseph R. Gusfield, *Community—A Critical Response* (New York: Harper and Row, 1975); Howard Newby, *Social Change in Rural England* (Madison: University of Wisconsin Press, 1979).

3. Art Gallaher, Jr., "Dependence on External Authority and the Decline of Community," in Gallaher and Padfield, op. cit., pp. 85-108.

4. One exception is the interesting and helpful essay by anthropologist Judith Ennew entitled "Self Image and Identity in the Hebrides" (in Anthony Jackson, ed., *Way of Life and Identity*, Social Science Research Council, North Sea Oil Occasional Paper No. 4. n.d. [circa 1980], pp. 49-62). Professor Ennew describes four relatively distinct constructs of identity: those of the State, Academia, Tourism, and Self-Image. I am concerned with the last of these sources of image and identity in this section.

5. Edward Relph, *Place and Placelessness* (London: Pion Limited, 1976), Preface.

6. Quoted in Relph, op. cit., p. 38.

7. Ibid., p. 43.

8. Ibid., pp. 58-9.

9. Ibid., p. 90.

10. HIDB, "The Highlands and Islands, A Contemporary Account" (Inverness, February 1979), p. 102.

11. James Hunter, "Taking Root: The Strangest Export Trade in Scotland," *Sunday Standard* (September 27, 1981), p. 17.

Editor's note for Comparative Changes . . .

Ford: A Village in the West Highlands of Scotland (Lexington: University Press of Kentucky; Edinburgh: Paul Harris, Ltd., 1984).

Editor's note for School Consolidation and Its Consequences

*John B. Stephenson, *Consolidation: The Impact of a New High School on the Achievement, Aspirations, and Adjustment of Students in an Appalachian County*. Final Report of Research Conducted under U.S. Office of Education Grant No. OEG-3-70-0022(0l0). U.S. Department of Health, Education, and Welfare, Office of Education, National Institute of Education. Washington, D.C., October 1973.

Notes for "Conclusions to School Consolidation and It Consequences"

1. Peter Rossi, "Social Factors in Academic Achievement: A Brief Review," in A.H. Halsey, J. Floud, and C.A. Anderson, eds., *Education, Economy, and Society*, New York: Free Press (1961), p. 271.

2. Because the design of the study was not a "before-after" model, it would be a serious mistake to infer that the general conclusion of little or no difference refers to pre- and post-consolidation comparisons.

Editor's notes for Challenges to Liberal Education

*A description of the development of the program is provided in Robert F. Sexton and John B. Stephenson, "Institutionalizing Experiential Learning in a State University," in *Implementing Field Experience Education*, ed. John Duley, New Directions in Higher Education, vol. 2, no. 2 (Summer 1974) (San Francisco, Jossey-Bass, 1974), pp. 55-65.

**"Efficiency and Vocationalism—Renewed Challenges to Liberal Education," *Liberal Education* 60 (October 1974): pp. 385-99.

Notes for "Efficiency and Vocationalism: Renewed Challenges to Liberal Education"

1. To emphasize the two factors of "efficiency and vocationalism" in this paper is not to deny that other challenges to liberal education exist. The threat of extinction or reduced vitality faces many private liberal arts colleges with severe economic prob-

lems; the loss of their voices will certainly befelt in the discussion of the value of liberal education. Another force which could be cited is the de-emphasis of the college as a place of learning, resulting from the growth of commuter campuses, the erasing of distinctions between residence and non-residence credit, and the ascendance of the certifying and crediting functions over the teaching function in higher education. But these factors, we assume, are either already understood or are in some way related to the concerns elaborated in this paper.

2. Thorstein Veblen, *The Higher Learning in America, A Memorandum on the Conduct of Universities by Business Men* (New York: Hill and Wang, 1957), p. 5. Veblen's concern echoes John Henry Cardinal Newman's complaint, made in 1852 and quoted at length here because of its relevance: "Now this is what some great men are slow to allow; they insist that Education should be confined to some particular and narrow end, and should issue in some definite work, which can be weighed and measured. They argue as if everything, as well as every person, had its price; and that where there has been a great outlay, they have a right to expect a return in kind. This they call making education and instruction 'useful,' and 'Utility' becomes their watch-word. With a fundamental principle of this nature, they very naturally go on to ask, what is there to show for the expense of a University; what is the real worth in the market of the article called 'Liberal Education,' on the supposition that it does not teach us definitely how to advance our manufactures, or to improve our lands, or to better our civil economy; or again, if it does not at once make this man a lawyer, that an engineer, and that a surgeon; or, at least if it does not lead to discoveries in chemistry, astronomy, geology, magnetism, and science of every kind." John Henry Cardinal Newman, *The Idea of a University Defined and Illustrated* (London: Longmans, Green and Co., 1910).

3. Ibid., p. 144. Veblen, incidentally, saw the trend toward increased student curricular choice as supporting growth of "practical" interests. That he saw this trend as pernicious is clear from his comment that "A decisive voice in the ordering of the affairs of the higher learning has so been given to the novices, or rather to the untutored probationers of undergraduate schools, whose entrance on a career of scholarship is yet a matter of speculative probability at the best." (Ibid., p. 143)

4. Ibid., pp. 146-7.

5. Hitchcock, op. cit., pp. 48-9.

6. Ibid., p. 47.

7. "A college or university should be judged in terms of the character, the quality, and in some respects, the quantity of the education that it produces as well as by such factors as the quality of its faculty, library, and physical plant or the size of its total budget. The challenge in higher education is to raise students to a superior standard of excellence by the time of their graduation, regardless of their competence when they enter college. With excellence as the central concern, acceptable means should be devised for evaluating achievement. Otherwise, it is nearly impossible to demonstrate that increased expenditures can produce any improvement in the quality of graduates." CED, *The Management and Financing of Colleges* (New York: CED, 1973), p. 34. The report is sensitive to both technical and non-technical problems in measuring outputs of research and service, as well as of teaching activities.

8. Ibid., p. 29.

9. Veblen, op. cit., p. 159.

10. James R. Topping and Glenn K. Miyataki, *Program Measures— Technical Report 35* (Boulder, Colo.: NCHEMS at WICHE, February 1973).

11. Ben Lawrence, George Weathersby, and Virginia W. Patterson (eds.), *Outputs of Higher Education: Their Identification, Measurement,*

and Evaluation (Boulder, Colo.: WICHE, 1970). Robert A. Huff, "Inventory of Educational Outcomes and Activities," *Technical Report 15* [Preliminary Draft], (Boulder, Colo.: WICHE, January 1971).

12. Warren W. Gulko, *Program Classification Structure* (1st ed.; Boulder, Colo.: WICHE, January 1972).

13. Topping and Miyataki, op. cit., p. 12.

14. Ibid., p. 129.

15. Huff, op. cit., p. 6.

16. "Report of the Commission on Liberal Learning," *Liberal Education*, LVII, 1 (March 1971), p. 38.

17. Sidney S. Micek and William Ray Arney, *Outcome-Oriented Planning in Higher Education: An Approach or an Impossibility* (Boulder, Colo.: NCHEMS at WICHE, June 1973), p. 13.

18. The National Commission on the Financing of Postsecondary Education, *Financing Postsecondary Education in the United States* (Washington, D.C.: U.S. Government Printing Office, December 1973).

19. Ibid., p. 53.

20. Ibid., p. 57.

21. Ibid., p. 349. "Although the Commission is aware of a variety of efforts to support and measure excellence in postsecondary education, it finds excellence difficult to evaluate and finds no adequate measures to fully assess the level of achievement of the objective of excellence." Also see pp. 168-172, where certain recent efforts to measure quality are reviewed.

22. Ibid., p. 61.

23. George W. Bonham, "The Debate Over National Standards," *Change*, VI, 2 (March 1974), p. 15.

24. "Report of the Commission on Liberal Learning," op.cit., p. 37.

25. Ibid. There is a nice irony in the fact that a desperate diagnosis of near-death is buried in a volume devoted to the theme of "Institutional Priorities and Management Objectives" containing

such no-nonsense, businesslike titles as "Beating the High Cost of Low Ratios," "Admissions: The Key to Fiscal Stability," "Cutting Instructional Costs," "Planning, Programming and Budgeting Systems," "Consortia and Fiscal Efficiency." The irony was completed with the following year's conference which was organized around the theme of "The Liberal Arts: Death or Transfiguration?" That such a conference was held at all is extremely heartening, of course.

26. John Ciardi, "An Ulcer, Gentlemen, Is an Unwritten Poem," *Canadian Business*, June 1955, reprinted in R.A. Goodwin and C.A. Nelson (eds.), *Toward the Liberally Educated Executive* (New York: New American Library Mentor Books, 1960).

27. e.e. cummings, "pity this busy monster, manunkind."

Editor's notes for "Experiential Education and the Liberal Arts"

*"Experiential Education and Revitalization of the Liberal Arts," in *The Philosophy of the Curriculum: The Need for General Education*, edited by Sidney Hook, Paul Kurtz, and Miro Todoravich (Buffalo, N.Y.: Prometheus Books, 1975), pp. 177-96.

**John B. Stephenson and Griffith R. Dye, "Learning Ethics through Public Service Internships: Evaluation of an Experimental Program," *Liberal Education* 64 (October 1978): 341-56.

Notes for "Experiential Education and Revitalization of the Liberal Arts"

1. Quoted in Alfred Whitney Griswold, *Essays on Education* (New Haven: Yale University Press, 1954), p. 150.

2. Sidney Hook, *Education and the Taming of Power* (La Salle, Ill.: Open Court, 1973), p. 30.

3. This phrase is taken from Charles Hitchcock, "The New Vocationalism," *Change*, April 1973. Also see John B. Stephenson, "Efficiency and Vocationalism—Renewed Threats to Liberal

Education," *Liberal Education*, Oct. 1974.

4. This statement was actually an attempt by Sidney Marland to use A. N. Whitehead's words to support career education. The source is an Office of Education film, *Career Education* (Maryland State Board of Education, through Olympus Research Corp., n.d.).

5. Marvin J. Feldman, "The Relevance Cap in American Education," *Conference Board Record*, June 1972.

6. Quoted on "The Reasoner Report," ABC News, March 23, 1974.

7. Bolling's comment, made in 1973, was quoted in the Louisville *Courier-Journal*, July 8, 1974.

8. Sidney Hook, *Education for Modern Man* (New York: Dial Press, 1946), especially Chapter 8.

9. Louisville *Courier-Journal*, April 17, 1974.

10. "Values in Contemporary Society," typescript of a conference held by the Rockefeller Foundation, March 10, 1974, p. 21.

11. Hitchcock, "The New Vocationalism."

12. Ideas relating to this continuum of learning are discussed in Daniel S. Arnold, "Differentiating Concepts of Experiential Learning," contained in John B. Stephenson, et al., "Experiential Education: A New Direction for an Old Concept, " ERIC Clearinghouse on Higher Education Document No. ED 086079. These papers were initially presented at the 81st annual convention of the American Psychological Association, Montreal, August 1973.

13. Here, we are not including discussion of experiential education as it relates to learning prior to enrollment in an educational institution or "prior experience."

14. "Values in Contemporary Society."

15. Hook, *Education and the Taming of Power*, p. 200.

16. Ibid.

17. Griswold, p. 7.

18. H. Bradley Sagen, "The Professions: A Neglected Model for Undergraduate Education," a paper presented at AAHE Regional

Conferences, 1972-1973.

19. Sagen, p. 2.

20. In fairness to Sagen, it should be mentioned that we have taken the liberty of reordering his treatment of competencies.

21. Sagen, p. 9.

22. Robert Nisbet also seems to support the general view that the liberal arts may be rejuvenated by joining with professional education in new ways. He has recently stated: "The prosperity of the liberal arts will be far greater if they are woven into those professional fields central to the university's history, rather than being treated as they now so commonly are as a kind of museum of interesting exhibits which one should pass through on his way to chosen interest." *Change*, Summer 1974, p.30.

23. Shelton L. Williams, "Policy Research in Undergraduate Learning," *Journal of Higher Education*, April 1974, pp. 296-304.

24. Daniel Bell, The Reforming of General Education (New York: Columbia University Press, 1966), pp. 286-287.

25. John Henry Newman, *The Idea of a University Defined and Illustrated* (London: Longmans, Green, 1910), pp. 151-152.

Editor's note for The Place of the Independent College

*A.D. Albright, ed., *Issues in Kentucky Higher Education—Essays by Kentucky Educators* (Lexington, Ky.: The Prichard Committee for Academic Excellence, 1993), pp. 19-23.